THE RAILWAY AGE IN AUSTRALIA

THE
RAILWAY
AGE IN
AUSTRALIA

ROBIN BROMBY

Lothian
BOOKS

Thomas C. Lothian Pty Ltd
132 Albert Road, South Melbourne, 3205
www.lothian.com.au

National Library of Australia
Cataloguing-in-Publication data:
Bromby, Robin, 1942– .
  The railway age in Australia.
  ISBN 0 7344 0715 7.
  1. Railroads – Australia – History. I. Title.
385.0994

Commissioning editor Cathy Smith
Cover design by Andrew Cunningham, Studio Pazzo
Text design and typesetting by Studio Pazzo
Cover image kindly supplied by Great Southern Railway
Map by John Frith, Flat Earth Mapping
Printed in China through Bookbuilders

CONTENTS

PAST AND PRESENT
RAILWAYS
OF AUSTRALIA

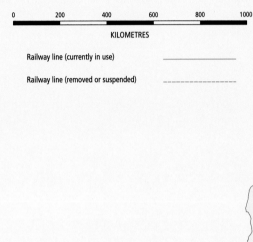

0   200   400   600   800   1000

KILOMETRES

Railway line (currently in use) _____

Railway line (removed or suspended) - - - - - - -

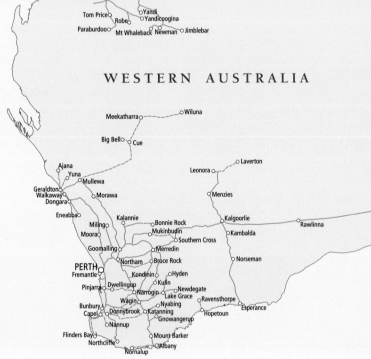

INDIAN

OCEAN

WESTERN AUSTRALIA

Port Hedland • Yarrie
Wickham
Dampier
Pannawonica
Tom Price Yandi
Robe Yandicoogina
Paraburdoo Mt Whaleback Newman Jimblebar

Meekatharra • Wiluna

Big Bell Cue

Ajana
Yuna
Geraldton Mullewa
Walkaway Morawa
Dongara
Eneabba Kalannie
Miling Bonnie Rock
Moora Mukinbudin
Goomalling Southern Cross
Northam Merredin
PERTH Bruce Rock
Fremantle Kondinin Hyden
Dwellingup Kulin
Pinjarra Narrogin Newdegate
Wagin Lake Grace
Bunbury Nyabing
Capel Donnybrook Katanning
Nannup Gnowangerup
Flinders Bay
Northcliffe Mount Barker
Nornalup Albany

Laverton
Leonora
Menzies

Kalgoorlie
Kambalda
Rawlinna

Norseman

Ravensthorpe
Hopetoun Esperance

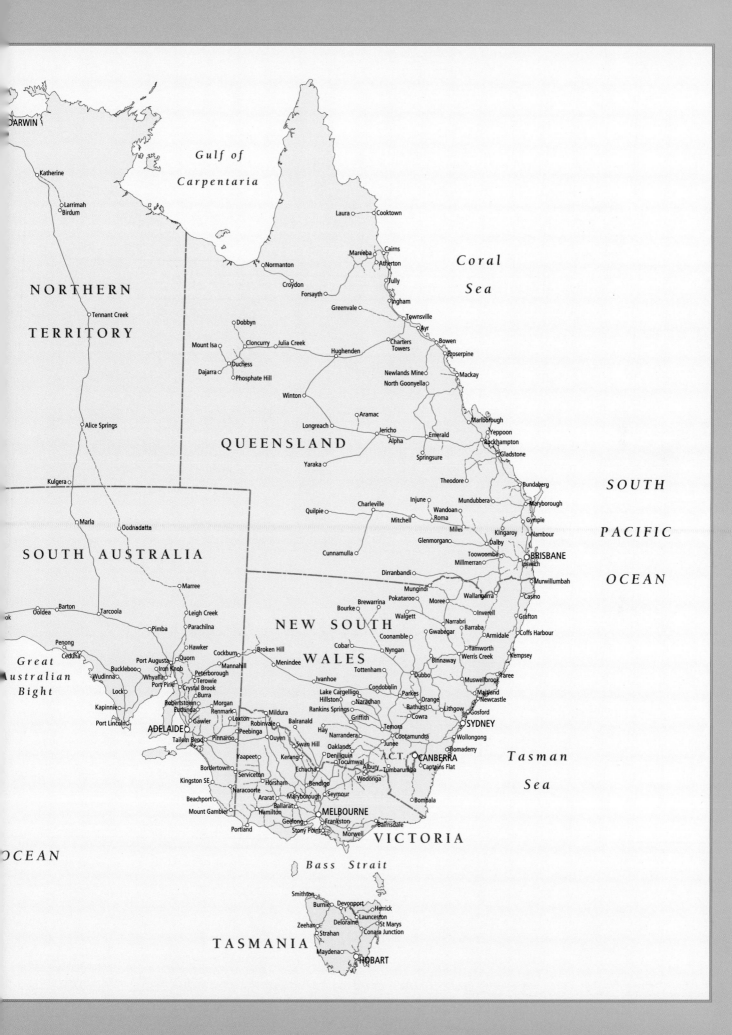

INTRODUCTION

'Railroading is only ten per cent iron; the other ninety per cent are men.'

— Legendary Victorian Railway Commissioner Harold Clapp heard
this from the President of Southern Pacific Railroad, and made it his motto

WHEN THE NEW SOUTH WALES mining town of Cobar celebrated the centenary of its connection to the railway network in 1992, a local historian recalled how the daily train departure to Sydney was the big event of the day. Around the start of the Great War, women would come to the station to farewell friends; they would be dressed in tailored suits, their hair done up in a bun, both their hair and hat kept in place by several long pins. Veils and gloves would always have been worn. Shopkeepers armed with warrants would be watching to see whether any of their debtors were skipping town; if so, they could call on the policeman who always attended the daily departure. Children returning to boarding school would be neatly dressed, complete with school ties. Commercial travellers would be boarding with their sample cases, as would businessmen needing to have meetings in Sydney. The guard's van, placed opposite the parcels office, would be in the process of being loaded, with huge steel trunks belonging to passengers being heaved aboard. Portmanteaux and Gladstone bags would be taken inside the carriages by the travellers and placed in the luggage racks. The guard's van included a travelling post office, and letters could be posted through a slot in the side of the van right up until the train departed.

Welcome to the age when the railway was part of almost every Australian's life. Even if they did not travel on trains all that often, the average Australian would have got most of the necessities of life via the railway. For those boarding our train at Cobar, the trip would be twenty hours, complete with refreshment stops at Nyngan, Wellington and Orange. But it was a good deal better than the week it would have taken to cover the same distance by horse-drawn vehicle.

The term 'railway age' can be defined in many ways. At its broadest, it could span one hundred and fifty years from the first steam-hauled journey in Melbourne on 13 September 1854 to the present day. After all, the completion of the transcontinental line to Darwin in 2003, along with the recent introduction of the Tilt Train in Queensland, demonstrate that railways are, in one sense, even now renewing themselves either as lines for suburban trains in our state capitals or for long-haul freight over vast distances on this continent.

Fifty or more years ago, many Australians would have seen trains as part of their lives: wagons left at their local country station siding either to have their loads of fertiliser collected by farmers or be stacked with wool bales bound for the sales; going down to that same small station to catch a railmotor or a slow, mixed goods and passenger train to the nearest mainline terminus, there to board an express for the big city. Or they might have worked for the railways; some centres employed hundreds, even thousands, of men and women to keep the trains rolling. And railways were a part of life in the sense that so many knew someone who worked on the railways, or had a relation employed there. Scratch a third or more generation Australian, and the chances are that their grandfather, or great-uncle, was a driver here or a stationmaster there. Chris Holley, who spent most of his working life at Werris Creek, the important junction in northern New South Wales, had a father who was an engine driver. His two brothers were also employed by the railways, one as a fitter and turner, the other a locomotive engineman's timekeeper. His daughter was a clerk at Werris Creek, his son-in-law became an engine driver and his brother-in-law was the yard controller at the huge

Enfield marshalling yards in Sydney. There are thousands of families with stories like this.

Much of that era has gone, and with it, what might be called the 'railway age'. Yet, even as late as Easter 1974, people still turned to rail in surprising numbers. Normally, the one overnight Vinelander service was sufficient for people wanting to travel from Melbourne to the Sunraysian capital, Mildura. But on Good Friday that year, such was the demand, Victorian Railways announced there would be three trains that night going north-west. It was still not enough; a fourth train was added, and between them the trains carried sixty-five cars on motorail wagons. They were scheduled to pull out of Melbourne at 8.20 pm, 9.05 pm, 9.30 pm and 10.30 pm. Even though the stationmaster at Mildura had organised to have the yard as free as possible of goods wagons, the passenger movements put great strain on the station facilities, the last train having to wait at Irymple until the preceding consists could be moved to sidings and the platform line cleared.

Another definition of the 'railway age' could see it as running from 1874 until 1920, the years that saw the greatest burst of railway construction and the completion of most of the main lines of the national network, including the long steel road across the Nullarbor. Yet even that is not entirely satisfactory as a definition. For example, in the 1950s, Victorian Railways ordered new fleets of railmotors for country lines because, even then, many rural people were without their own motorcar. In 1955, Victorian Railways had opened 838 railway stations; only 205 of those were listed as having no passenger services. It was in the 1950s, too, that Victorian Railways launched its Operation Phoenix under which £80 million was earmarked for the upgrading and modernising of its

OPPOSITE ABOVE: **Even in the outback, one dressed up for special occasions. The occasion for this 1912 scene is unknown, but it seems to have brought out many of the people of Longreach, Queensland. The train, with at least four passenger cars, is apparently ready for departure as people on the platform have their last few words with those heading off on their journeys. The men are wearing suits, ties and hats while all the women are dressed in typical pre-1914 fashion of long dresses and long-sleeved blouses and, of course, hats.** State Library of Queensland.

OPPOSITE: **Stacks of boxes in the Spencer Street goods shed at Melbourne in 1901 testify to the era when everything went by rail.** Author's collection.

system. It was under this scheme that, for example, Melbourne's blue and gold seven-car suburban sets were introduced to the travelling public of that city.

In all the states, railways were still an important part of everyday life. The line closures had not begun in earnest and country stations retained their stationmasters and porters, not to mention locomotive crews.

For our purposes, the term 'railway age' will be left rather blurry. While we try to recapture the life and times of our rail systems between the 1880s and 1960s, the narrative will stray over those boundaries from time to time. At all times, this book will try to keep in mind Harold Clapp's dictum. Much of the history of railways in Australia has been preoccupied with the iron part; too little with the man (and woman) element. You can find any number of photographs of classes of locomotives. However, pictures of yard gangs during shunting and loading, stationmasters checking their orders, firemen shovelling coal, women serving pies and cups of tea — all these are few and far between.

At its zenith in 1941, the governmental railway system throughout Australia reached a length of 44,344 route kilometres, almost three times what it had been in 1891. Railway building seems a very nineteenth century sort of thing, but these figures illustrate how much of the construction took place in the twentieth century.

But the second half of the twentieth century also witnessed a rapid shrinkage of the rail network as road transport took over the role that trains had provided in the days of unsealed country roads and horse-drawn transport. By 1987, Western Australia had closed almost a third of its rail system in terms of track kilometres, the largest single slice involving the closure of the Mullewa–Meekatharra–Wiluna route. Victoria

also closed many of its branch lines. New South Wales and Queensland maintained their systems much longer, but even those started being pared back in the 1980s and beyond. (In the case of NSW, many uneconomic lines were truncated or closed when damaged by flooding, or had maintenance neglected until there was no option but to close.)

The ideal of a golden railway age, when the railway systems boomed financially, is also misleading. In the period 1885 to 1920, branch lines, even in the fertile Darling Downs regions of Queensland, lost a total of £62,000. Many railway lines remained open long past their need. Victoria closed only 10 km of track between 1919 and 1939, and it was a Royal Commission which in 1948 brought home to Western Australia the fact that major closures were inevitable. Queensland Government Railways announced that, as at 1 July 1955, it would close five branch lines. This was, at the time, somewhat sensational news because that same department in its entire existence to that date had closed only *four* lines: Nankin–Broadmeadow, near Rockhampton (24.3 km closed on 19 August 1929), Mingela–Ravenswood, near Charters Towers (38.6 km closed on 7 November 1930), Qunaba–Pemberton, near Bundaberg (10.4 km closed on 30 May 1948) and Oona–Mt Cuthbert, near Cloncurry (9.8 km, closed in two stages in 1943 and 1949).

However, Australia today still has about 42,000 km of railways, partly due to the construction of new private railways in the iron ore province of Western Australia, the laying of dedicated coal routes in NSW and Queensland and the completion of the Alice Springs–Darwin link adding another 1,420 km. (There was also 4,150 km of narrow gauge tramways in the sugar-growing districts of

So much has disappeared in twenty years. As late as 1982, trains on the line from Bomaderry to Sydney would often stop at the dairy factory then operating at Gerringong and shunt on the short siding. *Author's collection.*

Queensland, but these are beyond the purview of this book.) The main line interstate standard gauge system amounts to about 8,000 km.

As former South Australian Railway Commissioner and railway author Ronald Fitch has explained, railway development in this country was prompted by three things: mineral discoveries, primary production and the provision of inter-capital links. Each system followed the same pattern, but at different times and speeds. Indeed, railway construction often preceded settlement and was intended to assist that settlement (which it lamentably failed to do in many places, particularly the Mallee Region that straddles South Australia and Victoria). Many of the non-trunk loads were constructed on the cheap; the resulting steep grades, light axle loads, low speeds and the need for regular track maintenance meant they were hobbled in terms of turning a profit.

A note on measurements

It is difficult, sometimes meaningless, to convert from imperial to metric. Saying that someone paid 22c for a train ticket in 1903 does not convey the reality as the straight conversion value is meaningless; 22c today buys almost nothing but, in 1903, 2s 3d (two shillings and threepence) could represent a day's work. The only meaningful conversion is that of distance and speed. So, consistently throughout, miles and feet have been converted to kilometres and metres, and miles per hour to km/h. Well, almost consistently, as it is awkward when talking about the nineteenth century to speak of New South Wales adopting the 1,485 mm gauge. In such instances, the original measurement will be given with the metric equivalent in parenthesis. Generally, the measure of the time will be used; tons in 1930, tonnes in 1990.

TO HELP THOSE READERS EDUCATED SINCE THE INTRODUCTION OF DECIMAL CURRENCY AND METRICS, THE FOLLOWING ARE THE CONVERSIONS:

£1 (one pound) = $2
The pound consisted of 12 pence per shilling, and 20 shillings a pound. So the modern equivalent of $22.75 will appear as £11. 7s 6d. The younger reader will now understand the extent to which decimal currency has made life a good deal simpler.

1 inch = 25.4 mm	1 ton = 1.01 tonnes
1 foot = 0.3 metres	1 gallon = 4.53 litres
1 yard = 0.91 metres	1 hp (horsepower) = 746 watts
1 mile = 1.609 km	

One other matter that may perplex some readers is the wheel arrangement often given for steam locomotives. For example, a 2–6–2 arrangement refers, in sequence, to the leading wheels, then the driving wheels (those actually turned by the rods driven by expelled steam) and the trailing wheels. Otherwise, jargon has been avoided where possible. Two locomotives heading a train are described as such, not in the modern and overdone term of 'lash-up'. However, some terms are unavoidable.

Consist	This means the assembly of wagons/carriages that make up a train.
Up/Down	Up trains work toward capital cities and Down trains work away from them, except in Queensland
Running light	A locomotive with no train attached.
Running on	Locomotives backing to be coupled to a train consist.
Triangle/Turntable	A triangle is just that — a three-sided rail system whereby a locomotive backs down one side of the triangle, then comes up the other side and ends up facing the opposite direction. These were often cheaper to build than turntables, which are balanced platforms on which the locomotive is pushed around to face another direction.

1

LIFE IN THE RAILWAY AGE

OF ALL THE TORMENTS suffered by the railway traveller in Australia — and there were many — none was so great as the break of gauge, where a train running on one railway gauge met another on tracks that had wider or narrower spacing between the two rails. At state borders, and within states (at places such as Kalgoorlie or Terowie), it was often impossible to complete a rail journey without passing through one of the many stations at which the track width changed from one gauge to another, the legacy of Australian colonies building their railways to their own needs without account for what was happening elsewhere. There was usually a rush from one train to the other as passengers vied to get the best seats on the waiting carriages. It was not unknown for the second train to have fewer cars than the first one, so that some passengers would be left without seats. Tempers would be short as passengers tried to get their luggage from one train to the other. It was worse at night as a change of gauge meant that passengers in sleeping cars had to get up, dress and cart their luggage across the platform in the early hours of the morning. Even Melbourne travellers who wanted sleeping compartments on the journey to Sydney found they had to sit up until 10.00 pm, at which time Victoria's plush, broad gauge Spirit of Progress reached Albury. Only then could they transfer to New South Wales rolling stock and settle down for a night's sleep. Coming the other way, the traveller would be woken up in the early hours of the morning once the train from Sydney had slid into Albury's long platform in order to make the transfer to the waiting Victorian train. Luggage would have to be closed up, the children gathered out of their beds and a porter hailed. In winter, the cold weather in the dead of the night was another thing to be borne with fortitude by rail travellers as they moved between trains. At 5.00 am on the Broken Hill Express from Cockburn and The Hill, there was the dreaded call: 'Change trains — Terowie' (for the remainder of the journey to Adelaide).

The American writer Mark Twain, writing in 1897 of his travels in Australia, told his readers what the interchange at Albury meant:

At the frontier between New South Wales and Victoria our multitude of passengers were routed out of their snug beds by lantern-light in the morning in the biting-cold of a high altitude to change cars on a road that has no break in it from Sydney to Melbourne! Think of the paralysis of intellect that gave that idea birth; imagine the boulder it emerged from on some petrified legislator's shoulders. It is a narrow-gauge road to the frontier, and a broader gauge thence to Melbourne. The two governments were the builders of the road and are the owners of it. One or two reasons are given for this curious state of things. One is, that it represents the jealousy existing between the colonies — the two most important colonies of Australasia. What the other one is, I have forgotten. But it is of no consequence. It could be but another effort to explain the inexplicable. All passengers fret at the double-gauge; all shippers of freight must of course fret at it; unnecessary expense, delay, and annoyance are imposed upon everybody concerned, and no one is benefited.

He also had plenty to say about the standard of the rolling stock. His conclusion was that the Australian colonies had spent so much on grandiose railway stations (such as the one at Maryborough, Victoria) that they had to economise on the trains themselves:

Why, that train from Maryborough will consist of eighteen freight-cars (wagons) and two passenger-kennels; cheap, poor, shabby, slovenly; no drinking water, no sanitation arrangements, every imaginable inconvenience; and slow? — oh, the gait of slow molasses; no air-brake, no springs, and they'll jolt your head off every time they start or stop . . . They spend tons of money to house you palatially while you wait fifteen minutes for a train, then degrade you to six hours' convict transportation to get the foolish outlay back.

Endurance was a quality much needed in the rail traveller. Take the trip to Brisbane from Sydney by rail before 1 May 1889, at which date the Hawkesbury River was bridged. The train pulled out of Sydney at 4.53 pm, terminating at River Wharf, Brooklyn, at 6.30 pm. The railways department then allowed one hour and fifteen minutes for the transfer across the Hawkesbury River with the steamer *General Gordon* carrying all the passengers, luggage and mail to Mullet Creek for loading onto another train. There the Northern Mail awaited, ready for a 7.45 pm departure. Next morning, passengers in the sleeping compartments were woken early and told their cars would be coming off when the train arrived at West Tamworth by 7.00 am, with the annoyed travellers having to get out of bed, pack and move to sitting cars. The train reached the border town of Wallangarra, where the New South Wales standard gauge met the Queensland narrow gauge, at 5.00 pm the following day. A connecting Queensland Government Railways narrow gauge train pulled out thirty minutes later, reaching Brisbane at 6.05 am on the third day of the journey. When, on 1 May, the Hawkesbury River bridge was brought into service, two hours and twenty-seven minutes were cut from the overall journey — although this first direct Sydney–Wallangarra train was fifty-seven minutes late arriving at its destination.

Hayden Biggs, recording his memories of early rail travel in 1938 for the railway news sheet *Bulletin*,

OPPOSITE LEFT: **The rails from Darwin reached Emungalan on 4 December 1917. Noreen Kirby, writing in 1982, recalled life at the hotel there owned by her father, Tim O'Shea. 'Dad and his brother had horse teams and carted from the railhead to outlying stations. Seen here in 1953 they carted building materials for the soldiers who were settled south of the Katherine River . . . They built a guest house in Emungalan as such a lot of the station folk came in to catch the train, which ran once a fortnight from Darwin. A lot of sick men travelled by train to Darwin, where the only doctor in the Northern Territory was located and, if they missed the train, my mother would care for them until the next train arrived. Mother would have as many as a dozen sick men to care for, suffering mainly with the fever (influenza) in 1919 and 1920.'** *Peter Dunham collection.*

OPPOSITE RIGHT: **Observation car Yarra was one of two observation cars built by Victorian Railways to be attached to the Sydney Express, which ran between Melbourne and Albury from 1908 until 1937. This express was replaced in the latter year by the Spirit of Progress, and Yarra remained unused until taken over by a preservation group in the 1960s. This was the interior in 1971, but since then the car has been further restored to its full original glory.** *John Beckhaus.*

remembered deciding to go to the Royal National Park near Sydney, the branch line having opened in March 1886. The following month he arrived at Redfern station to find that three divisions of the 10.25 am train had already departed for the newest extension to Sydney's suburban rail network. Then a rake of cattle wagons was backed into one of the platforms and the waiting passengers told to board for the Royal National Park. They proceeded to their destination at an average 16 km/h.

Fifteen years later, Glaswegian geologist J. W. Gregory and his university party set out on 31 December 1901 from Adelaide to Hergott Springs (later Marree), on what was then South Australia's Great Northern Railway to Oodnadatta. He recounted that the rails had had to be laid with the great daily variations of temperature in mind (contracting at night, expanding during the heat of the day) and this placed speed restrictions on the trains. Moreover, missing a train meant considerable delays: between Quorn and Hergott the service operated every other day; Hergott to Coward Springs once a week; and beyond to Oodnadatta only once a fortnight. Gregory reported that almost everything required to maintain the barren south-west of Queensland — from customs books to police officers — came by rail from Brisbane, via Melbourne and Adelaide and then up the Great Northern Railway. In all, it was a journey of 4,105 km.

While some of the train journeys in early Australia were certainly arduous, the alternative was normally worse. One recent account recalls the situation before Melbourne and Adelaide were fully linked by train services. In 1886, the train left Melbourne for Casterton, which took more than twelve hours overnight with no sleeping cars. Then there was a *twenty-four hour* journey by road coach to Naracoorte

in South Australia, then on to another train as far as Kingston. Thence it was a road coach again, a four-hour journey by steamer across Lakes Albert and Alexandrina to Port Milang, with the exhausted passengers ending at their destination four days after setting out.

Between 10 October 1864 (when the rail reached Echuca) and 1873 (when trains reached Wodonga for the first time), it was not uncommon for travellers to go to some length to reduce their exposure to the rigours of travel by coach between Sydney and Melbourne. This they did by taking the train to Echuca, a journey of seven hours compared to many more by the direct road route to Albury, and then travel by paddle steamer to that New South Wales town where, of course, they finally had to succumb to road coaches for their onward journeys.

But even fifty years ago, rail could still be a slow way to get anywhere. Take the obscure Kunama branch in New South Wales which ran off another branch, the Cootamundra to Tumut line. The Kunama line, 34.7 km in total, was a late addition to the system, having been opened on 17 December 1923, to handle fruit traffic from around Batlow as well as timber. By 1954, the line was served by a mixed train (that is, goods wagons with a passenger car attached), usually pulled by a 19 Class 0–6–0 locomotive. The line boasted the longest stretch of 1 in 25 gradient in the state; the track climbed 455 metres in 16 km and the steepness meant that a train could start out on the flat section with a load of 250 tons, but was allowed only 100 tons beyond Wereboldera station. The speed limit for the branch was 40 km/h, but on the steep climb up the side of the valley towards Batlow, the train was down to less than 13 km/h which, as one writer put it, 'gives ample opportunity to view the scenery'. Moreover, drivers were

required to stop the train at three specified points along the branch and check the hand brakes.

The 228 km journey in the 1950s from Port Pirie to Adelaide took 4.5 hours, resulting from twenty-three intermediate stops and, usually, a heavy load of up to fifteen carriages and five wagons containing fresh produce for the Adelaide market.

The people of Kojonup in Western Australia had the luxury of a railway line that offered alternative routes of travel to Perth. They could travel west to Donnybrook and connect with the line from Bunbury to the state capital, or they could go east to Katanning and join the express trains running from Albany. A Royal Commission appointed by the Western Australian Government in 1948 to examine the condition of the state's railway network was told that passenger traffic on country lines too often involved roundabout travel because of the routes over which the lines had been built. The then Commissioner of Railways said in evidence that this routing 'often lengthens the time of the journey to an abnormal degree'. The chief traffic manager then offered a stark example; until 1941, residents of Kojonup travelling to Perth faced a journey of either 370 km (via Donnybrook) or 415 km (via Katanning). Either way, it took eighteen hours by train. When a motor coach service began in 1941, it ran by a direct route of 256 km and took just six and a half hours — a little over a third of the time.

The comforts of train travel varied. By 1897, the inter-colonial trains between Adelaide and Melbourne were equipped with McLaren's patented foot-warmers. These contained acetate of soda and could be heated by immersion for fifteen minutes in a tank of boiling water, retaining heat for up to eight hours. They could, after that,

be shaken and would warm up again for a period.

Queensland Government Railways introduced foot-warmers in 1911 on the overnight train from Brisbane to the border crossing at Wallangarra, then eventually in other mail trains in the winter months. They were allocated on the basis of one for every three first class passengers and stayed in use until 1958.

Eventually some of the railway systems adopted heating of carriages by running steam from the locomotives through pipes into the passenger cars. By 1952, the New South Wales Government Railways had adapted fifty carriages for steam heating and twenty-eight locomotives were equipped to pump the steam to the cars behind. The steam from the locomotive's boiler passed through a reducing valve which lowered its pressure and then was pumped to pipes contained within cylinders on the carriage floors. Between 1 May and 30 September each year, the cars were heated in this manner, the passengers being able to adjust the heat in their section of the car. The Federal City Express to Canberra and the Southern Highlands Express to Goulburn, along with some of the overnight mail trains running to western destinations, were among those provided with this new heating system. Queensland never adopted steam heating.

Passenger services, in the pre-motorcar era, existed almost everywhere the rails went. A narrow gauge line was laid northwards of Kalgoorlie, the first section being opened in 1899 and then the rails reaching Leonora in 1903. This, along with a spur from Malcolm to Laverton that opened two years later, sustained a daily passenger train over its 259 km length to service the mining communities dotted along its path. Many long-forgotten stations — Paddington, Broad Arrow, Scotia, Comet Value,

Excursion trains were a familiar feature in the railway age. Here, such a train pulls into Albany, Western Australia, having travelled from Katanning. The double-heading is unusual in that the lead locomotive is an ex-Great Southern Railway T Class 4-4-0 while the second is a Western Australian Government Railways R Class with the same wheel arrangement. These locomotives were capable of high speeds with six-foot driving wheels. The passengers would have joined the train at Katanning in the early hours of the morning and could expect to be home well after midnight after their outing to Albany. *Noel Inglis collection.*

Yunndaga, Jessop's Well and Gwalia — burst into life every day as the lifeline from the south arrived. Ron Fitch, who spent much of his railway career in Western Australia before rising to Commissioner in South Australia, recalled that the mixed trains in the western states ambled along at an average 27 km/h. The passengers were subjected to the risk of whiplash due to the loose couplings on goods wagons assembled between the locomotive and the passenger cars. There were also long and frustrating delays at intermediate stations where the locomotive performed shunting duties as it dropped off or picked up wagons. If there were livestock vans in the consist, the smell from the animals and their droppings were clearly discernible in the carriages. (The Kalgoorlie–Leonora line was converted to standard gauge in 1973 to serve mineral trains, while the Laverton branch was closed in 1959.)

He also points out that some train names were extremely misleading. For example, the Kalgoorlie Express stopped at thirty-five stations between Northam and Kalgoorlie with an average speed of 37 km/h, while the Broken Hill Express ground to a halt at twenty-nine stopping places in all between Gawler and Broken Hill. Passengers in the sitting cars of the Kalgoorlie train, should they need a drink of water, had to walk out onto the open end platform of the car where there was a canvas water bag from which hung a small drinking vessel. This was a common practice in various parts of the Australian rail network.

But there was also plenty of style and comfort. Douglas MacGregor remembers travelling from his home at Cunnamulla, Queensland, to Brisbane in the days before the air-conditioned Westlander offered more modern train services. The consist of wooden carriages on the old train offered the traveller a choice between first and second class sleepers, and a dining car was attached to the train as far as Mitchell, where it was stabled until being attached to the returning service from Brisbane. Passengers sat down to three-course meals, complete with silver service, and could also take morning and afternoon tea in the car. The task for the staff aboard the dining car was not easy; there was no refrigeration so ice blocks were taken aboard to help keep the food fresh in the searing summer heat. The cook, apart from having to stoke the wood stove, had to contend with an often uneven track. To make sure the soup would not spill, it had to be heated in a large cup placed inside an even larger saucepan. Two waitresses ferried the courses to the tables. Beer had to be consumed at those stations that were equipped with bars; there was no means of keeping ale cold on the train. After this dining car was taken off at Mitchell, there were plenty of opportunities for passengers to buy food and drinks when the train stopped at subsequent stations down the line. Those refreshment stops were located at Mitchell itself, Miles, Chinchilla, Dalby, Toowoomba and Helidon.

Queensland introduced parlour cars on the Sydney Mail to Wallangarra, and first class passengers could pay an additional five shillings (50c) to use this car. In 1923, three new cars were ordered that were furnished with eighteen swivel leather arm chairs, and a small kitchen. When the coastal route via Kyogle was opened in 1930, offering a more direct and all-standard gauge run between Sydney and Brisbane, the trains to Wallangarra lost their importance, and the parlour cars were transferred to the mail trains running between Brisbane and northern coastal destinations. A third series of parlour cars was built for the Sunshine Express. All parlour cars were

withdrawn in 1942 because of the shortage of rolling stock in the wartime, and all but one were converted to hospital cars.

For those who travelled by train in the heyday of rail, there was nothing quite like it — an atmosphere that died with the move to buses and aeroplanes. L. F. Holmes, writing in 1965 of his childhood memories of Sydney Terminal, recalled the:

> . . . rush and bustle, the smell of newsprint and fruit, people streaming in all directions, luggage trolleys and loudspeakers adding to the din and the sheer youthful wonder of standing beside a hot, steaming 38 class, just arrived from Albury, a dead pigeon lying below the smokebox as mute testimony to its speed.

The most luxurious form of rail transport was reserved for vice-regal appointees, commissioners and ministers, with special cars usually being provided. The representatives of the monarch were usually treated to the highest level of comfort. In New South Wales, the Governor-General was allotted Car GG. It had an open platform at the end, the aprons being decorated with intricately patterned brass work. Inside, there were three bedrooms, the main one having a double bed, a dining room with six chairs, and an observation room, along with a shower recess and attendant's cabin. An electric fan for the hot weather and a radiator for use in winter were provided, along with a radio and water heater.

On the next rung down in the hierarchy was the New South Wales State Governor's carriage, Car SG. It was slightly less ornate than the Governor-General's, and its dining table seated only four. But it, too, had three bedrooms and an observation room. The Premier's carriage, PAM-11, could sleep eight — the Premier in a bedroom, the others in standard two-berth compartments, allowing up to four ministers and two attendants to travel together. Bob Heffron (whose term concluded in 1964) was the last head of the state government to travel by special car.

The New South Wales Commissioner had a three-car set, AAH 7, AAH 8, AAH 9 — the latter being for the Commissioner himself. It had four bedrooms, an office and a sitting room. AAH 8 was the officers' car, containing ten berths, a bathroom and dining space for twelve, while AAH 7 had half its space allotted as a kitchen, the remainder being an attendants' dining room, a shower recess and the guard's compartment. All three cars were equipped with curtains, blinds and carpets and the wood panels on the interior were kept highly polished. These cars were all kept at Eveleigh Carriage Works in Sydney when not in use. The main carriage was the Commissioner's private and exclusive space; none other than his immediate staff was allowed to travel in the car.

As late as 1939, South Australian Railways decided to build a new vice-regal car costing nearly £19,000. Such was the care taken that welds were hand-filed rather than allowing a more coarse finish from a mechanical grinder. It was also the first South Australian car to be fitted with air-conditioning. Two bedrooms were provided for the vice-regal couple complete with fully appointed bathroom, and there were also compartments for the ladies-in-waiting and the Governor's aide. There was, of course, a dining room at one end and an observation lounge at the other, meaning that the latter end of the car was designed to be at the tail of the consist when in use (as it was on

several occasions when attached to the Overland express to Melbourne for the Melbourne Cup). This carriage is now to be seen at the National Railway Museum in Adelaide.

Even in the post–World War II era, rail travel was hardly smooth and comfortable for many Australians. Noel Inglis, whose father was a relief driver in the early 1950s at Lake Grace in Western Australia, would get home from Albany, first, by railcar to Wagin and then on the branch train known to the locals as 'the Wheatbelt Flyer'. After that train was withdrawn, about 1952, the transfer at Wagin was to a Western Australian Government Railways passenger–freight bus which ran between Perth and Hopetoun, which Noel believes was then the longest scheduled bus run in Australia. The bus travelled mostly on gravel roads, and there was no toilet on board.

Being a member of a railway family, Noel had the option of leaving Albany on the night express to Perth, getting off at Wagin close to midnight and, if the express had run to time, he would be able to catch a freight working, ride in the guard's van, and arrive at Lake Grace around breakfast time. If, however, the express had been delayed, it would mean five hours sleeping on a bench in the Wagin waiting room (where a coal fire was kept lit during the winter nights) and catching the morning goods to Lake Grace. This train had a guard's van with passenger compartment.

However, the railways did try to respond to the growing competition from road transport. In 1929, New South Wales tightened many of its longer distance timetables to reduce travelling times. One such service was between Newcastle and Sydney. In 1929, the Pacific Highway between the two had been completed and the

railways felt they had to offer a faster run to compete. On 11 June of that year, seven-car trains behind locomotive 3307 made the distance in two and three quarter hours, including stops at Strathfield and Hornsby. From 11 November, three expresses a day ran in each direction timetabled to take 2 hr 43 min. Then, in 1934, locomotive 3614 was the first to get the Newcastle Limited over the distance in two and a half hours. New South Wales also introduced new trains to cater for the growing leisure travel. In 1938, it unveiled the Kosciusko Express which on Fridays departed Sydney at 10.55 pm and was timed to reach Cooma at 8.00 am.

Ahead of the introduction of the prestige train, Spirit of Progress, on 23 November 1937, Victorian Railways also put its mind to reducing train times. As discussed later, buffet cars were added to branch line trains to eliminate time wasted at refreshment stops. On 23 September 1937, it was announced that the Sydney Limited would, on six days a week, run non-stop between Melbourne and Albury, making it the longest continuous passenger run in Australia over the 306 km distance. It was scheduled to leave Melbourne at 6.30 pm, arriving at the New South Wales border changeover at 10.30 pm. Only on Sundays were intermediate stops — Seymour, Benalla, Wangaratta and Wodonga — included in the timetables. Victorian Railways also introduced a new express train running to Numurkah on the line which led to Tocumwal in New South Wales. The daily passenger train to Dimboola had all stops as far as Ballarat eliminated and the onward connection to Serviceton (at the South Australian border) was on some days run by a railmotor rather than a mixed steam train. The saving in time on the eastbound journey was four hours and twenty minutes.

LEFT: **Not a weed in sight and everything looking very new at Coffs Harbour where the rails arrived in 1915.** *Coffs Harbour Historical Society and Museum.*

RIGHT: **In the days before a motorcar sat in every driveway, outings were usually by rail. Staff of Broken Hill Proprietary (probably from Newcastle) detrain at Blackalls Park for the annual works picnic.** *Lake Macquarie City Library.*

A busy day in Binnaway

Trains brought life — often only for the duration of the train's stay — to many towns around Australia. An account by L.A. Clark in the rail magazine *Bulletin* of a journey between Dubbo and Werris Creek in New South Wales illustrated how the small town of Binnaway, located 453 km from Sydney by rail with a population then of fewer than eight hundred people, became a place of noise and bustle three days a week. The town was on the route of trains travelling east to west, others coming up the Wallerawang to Merrygoen line (via Mudgee) and it was the junction for the 145 km branch northwards to Coonabarabran and Gwabegar.

All passengers travelling between Dubbo and Werris Creek had to change trains at Binnaway because the lines from the respective towns came together outside Binnaway and then ran into the station in parallel. The station had a refreshment room, ample sidings (which were needed, as we will see), a turntable and locomotive roundhouse. Passenger trains were at this time normally hauled by either 12 Class or 30T Class locomotives. On one of the three days when the station was at its busiest, the action would begin at 10.54 am when the train arrived from Werris Creek; passengers disembarked, the van was unloaded at the platform and the van and carriages were then shunted into one of the sidings while the locomotive went to be serviced for its next trip. At 12.18 pm the train from Sydney via Mudgee arrived; its passengers disembarked, that van was unloaded and then the carriages were shunted off to another siding. By this time, the platform was covered with luggage as the passengers waited for connections to their various onward destinations. At 12.42 pm, the diesel train pulled in from

Dubbo; more luggage was deposited on the platform. Finally, at 1.06 pm, a second diesel train arrived, this time from Gwabegar. It came in on the loop to pass the diesel set already sitting at the platform, then reversed back into the platform so it now had a clear run for its onward trip. Even more luggage was unloaded. This meant that, apart from any travellers whose destination was Binnaway itself, four train loads of passengers were milling about, some having been there for more than two hours. To add to the business on the sidings, a goods train usually turned up during this three-hour rush period.

However, the dispersal began at 1.25 pm when one diesel train departed for Dubbo, and then five minutes later the other accelerated away from the platform bound for Gwabegar. Following their departure, one of the train consists — having been reassembled — reversed into the platform, loaded its passengers and departed for Werris Creek at 1.55 pm. At 2.05 pm, silence again returned to Binnaway after the last set of carriages slid out bound for Sydney via Merrygoen and Mudgee.

In any town of size, the railway station was a scene of activity for much of the day. In Queensland fifty years ago, Townsville station could see up to twenty passenger departures a day, from the 6.20 am workers' train to the Oolbun meatworks to the last suburban working to Stuart late in the evening. At 6.25 am, the Sunshine Express for Cairns pulled out after a short stop on its way from Brisbane. Two afternoons a week it was the turn of the Inlander setting off for Mount Isa. In between were passenger trains and railmotors heading to Ingham, Proserpine, Cloncurry, Home Hill or Charters Towers as well as the suburban services to Stuart. To cope with all this traffic, and yard shunting, Townsville station had a

The station is unidentified, the date unknown, but it could have been the scene at one of scores of New South Wales stations as a handful of passengers alight from a railmotor. *Author's collection.*

large roster of steam locomotives, including the PB15, B15, BB18¼, C16 and C17 classes.

Even smaller stations could see a good deal of activity. Take Gilmore, an unattended station on the Tumut branch in New South Wales. This branch left the main line at Cootamundra and then at Gilmore a second branch, the Kunama line, veered off. While there was not much sign of life at Gilmore for much of the time, even fifty years ago (there was not even a village around the station), there were a few weekly occasions when things got busy. On Saturdays, three trains stopped there in the space of forty minutes. At 9.50 am, the Batlow Mixed arrived from Cootamundra, did whatever shunting was required, then ran on to the Kunama branch and waited. At 10.06 am, the diesel train from Tumut ran on to the loop and came to a halt on one side of the island platform. This was soon followed by the passenger train coming in the other direction from Cootamundra bound for Tumut and sliding into the main platform. These two trains then pulled out for Cootamundra and Tumut respectively, after which the Batlow Mixed reversed back into the station to pick up any passengers, mail or parcels before heading off to Batlow itself about 10.30 am.

Then there were what was known as 'flag stations', the small shelters which dotted lines all over the country at which train timetables allowed stops only if there was a passenger waiting or wanting to get off. The intending passenger waved a flag installed there to stop the train. At the small Western Australian station of Tenindewa, 15 km from Mullewa on the line to Geraldton, there was a variation on the flag stop: a green lantern was left on a hook at the shelter and was lit by anyone wanting a train to stop. If the approaching locomotive intended to stop, it would give two short blasts on its whistle; but the driver of a goods-only train would deliver the bad news to the waiting passenger that he would not be stopping by one long, one short blast. At Wahpunyah in South Australia, a South Australian Railways weekly notice recorded in 1914 that a flag and lamp had been provided so that intending passengers could signal enginemen to stop their trains.

Trains were still a vital part of country life even fifty years ago, as was amply demonstrated by the royal tour of Queen Elizabeth and the Duke of Edinburgh in 1954. New South Wales Government Railways organised two hundred and eighty-six special trains to transport people to see the royal couple. When they were in Newcastle on 9 February, sixteen special trains ran from Wyee to cater for those wanting to see the spectacle, while another forty specials came in from the west and north (from Maitland, Cessnock, Kempsey, Armidale and Moree). Seven specials ran to Casino the following day when the Queen visited. When Dubbo was the host city, seven specials came from the west including Parkes, the Warren branch, Nyngan and Bourke; another five ran from Orange and Wellington; three steam-hauled trains and eight diesel trains came down from Binnaway and beyond, and another three steam-hauled trains were allocated to the Coonamble branch. Thirty-three specials headed into Wollongong when the visitors were there. Bathurst, Lithgow and Wagga Wagga also saw frantic railway activity when they were the centre of royal attention. It was a triumph of planning by railway officials as they juggled their train sets: one set of carriages travelled about 4,500 km by the time it returned to the sidings at Clyde on 18 February, having been at Newcastle, Orange, Dubbo, Bathurst, Parkes, Temora, Stockinbingal, Wagga Wagga, Goulburn,

FOLLOWING SPREAD: **In 1927, the Duke and Duchess of York (later George VI and Queen Elizabeth) visited Australia, and much of their itinerary involved train travel. Here, the well-groomed pair of C32 Class 4-6-0 locomotives pose with the royal carriages before the journey from Sydney to Wallangarra, on the border between Queensland and New South Wales. Like Sir Henry Parkes and many thousands of other travellers before them, the Duke and Duchess would have alighted from their comfortable standard gauge train on Wallangarra platform and traipsed into a Queensland narrow gauge consist waiting to take them to Brisbane.** *Noel Inglis collection.*

Canberra as well as taking a military party back to South Brisbane after the Canberra phase of the tour.

All the way by rail

Fifty years ago, it was possible for a traveller in Australia to make a continuous rail journey of more than 7,400 km — from Wiluna in the Western Australian goldfields to Mount Isa in Queensland. It required nine changes of train along the way, first at Mullewa, then Perth. At Kalgoorlie there was another change, this time because the Western Australian narrow gauge met the standard gauge of the transcontinental line. At Port Augusta, that line met the South Australian narrow gauge system, so trains had to be changed again and then again at Broken Hill, where the New South Wales standard gauge began.

At Sydney, it was a matter of transferring from the western line express to the train travelling north to the Queensland border (you could travel through to Brisbane on a standard gauge line from 1930, but the more intrepid rail user could take the inland rail route) where, at Wallangarra, the standard gauge met Queensland's narrow gauge. Our by now weary traveller could rest for a few hours until Brisbane was reached where he or she had to transfer to yet another train, this one running north to Townsville; thence to another for the final leg inland to Mount Isa.

While running trains was the prime objective of the various state railway departments, each employed vast numbers of staff at the hundreds of manned stations spread around the country.

But it was the termini in the various state capitals that were the epicentre of railway bustle, and some remain so

today in spite of decades of depredation of long-distance railway services. Holiday times were always busy at the big city stations. Holidays usually began with the departure of all the boarding school pupils for their homes. The stalls in the main concourses would have been well stocked with pies and comics; but behaviour on the train would have been maintained. In New South Wales, it was common practice to have the schoolchildren in their own carriage so that the guard could keep a close eye on what went on there. And, for those travelling in Queensland who wanted to freshen up after a long and sooty trip, it was possible to have a bath at Brisbane, Rockhampton or Townsville stations; at Mackay and Cairns, shower rooms were available.

Victoria's Railway Commissioner Harold Clapp did much to help bewildered long-distance passengers by introducing the 'Man in Grey' — a person who stood on the main concourse and whose job was to answer all the questions posed by people trying to find the right platform and train. Between 1933 and 1942, Spencer Street station in Melbourne boasted a room where mothers could change their babies and heat baby food.

In 1916, South Australian Railways (SAR) decided that passengers suffering from either cancer or tuberculosis could ask a stationmaster to reserve a compartment for them although, in the same year, SAR employees were told not to provide physical assistance to those with infectious diseases. By 1922, licensed luggage porters were provided at Adelaide station and ordinary uniformed porters were no longer required to help passengers with their luggage. Two years later, SAR provided luggage delivery to the better inner city hotels and clubs.

OPPOSITE ABOVE: **Charleville railway station in 1928.** *Author's collection.*

OPPOSITE RIGHT: **A branch line train at Warren, New South Wales.** *Author's collection.*

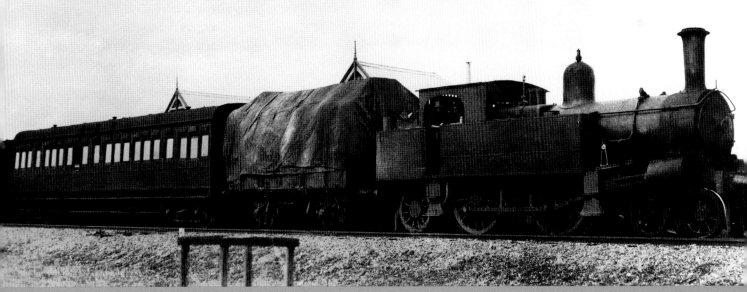

Refreshing the traveller

Dining cars did run on some of the more important expresses but, for the average rail traveller, there were the ubiquitous refreshment rooms at all the main stations around Australia. In many instances, private operators ran these by way of a concession; eventually, the government railway departments took control. They had to be well-organised, the meals and snacks all prepared in advance. As the first traveller rushed in the door off the platform to the dining rooms, the staff would be ladling soup into bowls. At the snack counters, rows of cups would be lined up ready for tea or coffee as scores or more people surged toward the staff.

Many refreshment rooms provided set table meals (we would, perhaps, call them 'sit-down meals'). In South Australia in 1912, there were such dining rooms at Adelaide itself and also at Brinkworth, Murray Bridge, Port Wakefield, Riverton and Terowie. The operators of these rooms were required by SAR to provide linen napkins when they served soup, hot roasts (alternatively chops, sausages or cold meats), vegetables, bread, butter and cheese, marmalade and tea or coffee. Counter refreshments were available at secondary stations such as Kapunda or Peterborough (soup, pork chops, fresh milk, tea and potatoes being some of the items on the menu). The next grade down was the availability of sandwiches, buns, soup, tea or coffee, local white wine and beer, and Havana cigars at, among other places, Balaklava, Mount Barker and Naracoorte. Outer stations (Keith and Leigh Creek, for example) provided fruit stalls. Gradually, SAR took over management of the refreshment rooms. There were gradual closures as services ended or food became available on board trains. However, in 1917, with the completion of the line between Port Augusta and Kalgoorlie, SAR converted the goods shed at Eurelia into a refreshment room for passengers making the long transcontinental journey. From 1929, SAR required a deposit on each piece of crockery taken outside their refreshment rooms.

South Australian Railways did allow some private concessions: the Nestlé and Anglo-Swiss Condensed Milk Company was charged one pound a year for each chocolate dispensing machine it located on platforms around the state from 1915, with the railways cancelling the arrangement ten years later.

When the magnificent refreshment rooms opened in late 1884 at the important northern NSW junction of Werris Creek, it seated between forty and fifty people at dinner. The rooms were entered from the main platform by large double doors, inside of which an impressive cedar staircase provided access to bedrooms on the upper floor. The dining room itself had a large cedar counter along one side. For the staff, there was a scullery, pantries and a cellar as well as the main kitchen.

Junee, on the main rail line south from Sydney, had refreshment rooms that were just as grand. The main dining hall's ceiling was lined with kauri panels; the main counter was more than twelve metres in length and its top made of marble. A wide, polished cedar staircase led to a private dining room and bedrooms on the upper level. The refreshment rooms were extended in 1891 to cope with increasing rail traffic in the Riverina and, in 1918, the private contractors were dropped and all the staff became railway employees; many of them were live-in staff as the rooms were operated for many hours a day. However by the 1950s, as more and more passengers switched to road

OPPOSITE ABOVE: **As soon as the train arrived at a refreshment station, there was an excited rush of famished passengers. The** Victorian Railways Magazine **of May 1926 described the scene: 'The vanguard usually comprises a handful of alert seasoned travellers who have given their orders by the time the main body begins to stream in. Old and young, sturdy and frail, tall and short, plump and thin, all sorts, sizes, shapes and conditions of humanity jostle towards the counter, each and every one's sole concern clearly being to wrap his or herself around a satisfying amount of refreshment with the least possible delay.' The staff at Shepparton would have seen this every day, but were able to withstand the tide of humanity from behind the solid wood counter.** State Library of NSW.

OPPOSITE: **Refreshment rooms had to take on extra staff during World War II to cope with the vast numbers of troops on the move. At Seymour, the refreshment staff swelled to fifty. At Moss Vale, New South Wales, this scene was taken during an early morning halt by a troop transport with some 500 soldiers being fed within an hour. The date was 12 June 1944.** Australian War Memorial, AWM 066882.

or air transport, vending machines were installed on the platforms. The glory days of the Junee refreshment rooms ended in the 1960s when dining and buffet cars were attached to trains.

The railway refreshment rooms at Coffs Harbour laid claim to having the best food on the NSW north coast. The fish was cooked in a locally devised batter; it was usually leather jacket but special occasions could see snapper or pearl perch being served. The dining room could seat one hundred and seventy, and there was also a counter servery for snacks and drinks. During the years of World War II, more than one hundred people were employed at the rooms to cover all the shifts which would cater for trains carrying up to three hundred men; as many as forty young women could be employed on a single shift to handle all the preparation and serving of sandwiches. Some three hundred meat pies were baked each morning. The first train each day was the Brisbane Express making its way south to Sydney, whose passengers could expect a traditional cooked breakfast at Coffs Harbour. This train was followed throughout the day by five more passenger workings.

The Depression of the 1930s apparently took its toll even on railway refreshment rooms. Staff were exhorted to use them wherever possible throughout the South Australian system, and then in 1934, the price of luncheon or dinner in country refreshment rooms was reduced from two and sixpence (twenty-five cents) to two shillings (twenty cents). Soon after, the refreshment rooms started to close, a process that was to continue for several decades: Burra shut in 1936, Euralia the following year, and Terowie in 1939. Gladstone and Alawoona fell victims in 1967, Murray Bridge as late as 1973.

The 1937 timetable for Western Australian Government Railways (WAGR) reported that set meals could be obtained from the refreshment rooms located at Perth, Beverley, Wagin, Mount Barker, Fremantle, Pinjarra, Caron, Mullewa and Yalgoo. The timetable for daily passenger services each way on the Albany line was such during some of the inter-war years that No. 7 and No. 8 arrived at Wagin at the same time. The refreshment stall was located on the island platform, and its staff rushed to meet the needs of two trainloads of passengers simultaneously.

Noel Inglis recalls that the heavy, thick china at Wagin was marked 'RRS' for Railway Refreshment Service with a blue and red crest with the initials 'WAGR'. In the 1950s, Perth had a large dining room, and Fremantle a much smaller one (although still allowing sit-down meal service). The Number One platform at Perth and Midland stations had food kiosks to serve passengers. Mr Inglis further recalls that Childows Well and Spencers Brook on the line through the Darling Ranges also had counters serving food and drinks, and in more remote places, there were once similar counters — at Northampton, north of Geraldton, and at Young's Siding on the Albany to Nornalup line.

The WAGR had a refreshment factory at Welshpool, on the suburban line to Armadale, which produced various types of cakes and the famous railway pies. These were carried in refrigerated vans attached to passenger trains for delivery to the various refreshment rooms along the way. For those travelling from Perth to Kalgoorlie, for example, there were stalls located at Northam, Cunderdin, Merredin and Southern Cross stations, with main meals available in the dining cars attached to the trains. In

D3 676 has arrived at Tocumwal with the passenger train from Melbourne. Just after the photo was taken, DS 644 would drop its goods working and couple at the other end of the passenger train for the return journey. *Des Jowett.*

addition, the trains pulled to a stop at the almost deserted sidings at Bullabulling and Karalee where the passengers made a mad scramble for the small pubs at either place to slake their thirsts.

Mavis Shaw was the cook at the Mullewa station on the line inland from Geraldton to Meekatharra and Wiluna for a period after World War II. The refreshment rooms were run by the manager and his wife; there was one full-time employee and another three who worked part-time on train days. Mrs Shaw would make the pies and pastries the day before trains were coming, either on their way to Meekatharra or returning. On train days themselves, she prepared three-course meals and waited on tables. The guards would telephone from the preceding station and alert the manager to the number of meals required when the train arrived. At night-time, she cooked for the single men employed on the railway who were based at Mullewa. There was also a tea bar, which served the pies along with sandwiches, tea and coffee, and a liquor bar (which also was known to provide an unofficial take-home supply service to the locals).

Dolores Bone went to work at the newsagency at Mullewa in 1946 when she was fourteen years old. (Mrs Bone's father was posted to Mullewa as a guard and, when he retired eleven years later, had reached the rank of night stationmaster.) As part of her duties, she would go to the station two days a week and open up the news stall on the platform that had a lift-up flap. From this stall, she sold newspapers, magazines, pouch tobacco, cigarettes and cigarette papers to travellers going up the Meekatharra line.

All refreshment rooms on Western Australian country lines were closed by 1961, the year that the Kalgoorlie Express, Mullewa Express, Albany Progress and Albany Weekender were equipped with buffet cars. These served sandwiches, pies, cakes, baked beans, tinned spaghetti, braised steak and onions, and sometimes, eggs on toast. After 1970, when the buffet cars were licensed, passengers could buy cans of the more popular Western Australian beers, some wines, and spirits in miniature bottles. (Before 1970, you had to smuggle liquor on board if you wanted to have a drink en route.)

The Westland Express, which was the narrow gauge link between Kalgoorlie and Perth until standardisation, allowed the Trans-Australian to work through to the Western Australian capital, and then depart Perth with a dining car attached. This would be uncoupled at Cunderdin after the passengers had eaten their evening meal, and then attached to the express coming the other way from Kalgoorlie in time for breakfast to be served. Meanwhile, the east-bound train, having left one dining car at Cunderdin, would pick up another at Southern Cross in time for breakfast on that run into Kalgoorlie, the staff there having served dinner the previous evening for the westbound passengers.

Troop movements in World War II presented a new challenge for many refreshment rooms as they catered for long trains with many hungry and thirsty servicemen and women. At Grafton City, New South Wales, the refreshment rooms were extended into a new structure to handle the hundreds of people who disgorged from every passing troop train. Officers used the existing room at the platform, while other ranks were herded into the new shed built at ground level behind the platform.

An important refreshment room on the Queensland Railways system was at the border station of Wallangarra.

Travellers arrived in the morning on the expresses from Sydney and other parts of New South Wales, and many ordered the substantial breakfast available at Wallangarra. The earliest refreshment rooms in Queensland were located at Ipswich, Grandchester and Helidon. In 1916, Queensland Government Railways (QGR), under a newly elected state Labor government, took control of all the privately run refreshment rooms. Twenty-eight larger ones were run by QGR staff, but fourteen smaller establishments were leased to private operators. The state's first buffet car appeared in 1912 on the Emerald–Longreach run and, with the new air-conditioned train sets that were built in the 1950s for the long-distance services, QGR adopted dining cars for all these services.

Around 1900, the traveller on Victorian Railways was well provided for by way of refreshments. Thirteen stations had set table meal service. These ranged from Spencer Street in Melbourne to the border crossing at Serviceton. The refreshment rooms had opened at Serviceton on the border with South Australia in 1889, and passengers had time to take a relatively leisurely meal while locomotives from one colonial system were being uncoupled and replaced with those of the other. A menu dating from its first years showed the passengers could choose from soup, fish, hot joints (beef, lamb, mutton or pork), with vegetables (potatoes, parsnips, carrots and beans). Bread, butter, cheese and marmalade were provided, washed down by South Australian wine, or tea or coffee. The price was two shillings and sixpence (twenty-five cents). Other set table rooms were located at Ararat, Ballarat, Benalla, Bendigo, Geelong, Horsham, Kyneton, Maryborough, Seymour, Stawell and Warragul. Another twenty-one stations provided counter

refreshments, but even at these stations there was a robust choice of fare: Irish stew, sausages, Victorian ale or claret by the half-pint, tea at threepence a cup, and ham sandwiches at sixpence. A 'Havannah' cigar set one back another sixpence. In the 1920s, more than five hundred young women were employed throughout the Victorian refreshments service.

However, there was one significant drawback to refreshment rooms: they meant that trains had to wait seven minutes or more while all the passengers were served. In 1934, Victorian Railways decided to introduce buffet cars on country lines to eliminate these time-consuming stops. Car AE 34 (named *Taggerty*) was rebuilt to include a buffet counter with seating for eighteen passengers. The car was attached on trains working the Bendigo and Albury lines out of Melbourne. In 1938 and 1939, four all-steel cars were built at the Newport workshops to be used on the Albury Express, the Bairnsdale Express and the Bendigo line trains. Initially, these buffet cars were also on trains working to Warrnambool and Horsham but they were withdrawn due to wartime economies and not reinstated. Each car had between three and five waitresses under the charge of a supervisor, along with a cook and a cook's assistant, and offered meals, light refreshments and cigarettes.

The Clapp era in Victoria — the years when Harold Clapp was Commissioner of Railways — saw an unusual development on the platforms of some stations in that system: stalls selling fresh, healthy food such as vegetables, raisins, fruit juice and cheese. Clapp had posters erected extolling the virtues of eating fruit and then supplied the stalls where travellers could follow up on that advice. But it was not just intended to improve the

The sheets from the sleeping cars as well as the pillowcases and napkins all needed to be washed and pressed after each rail journey. That was the task of the railway laundry such as this one in Victoria. *Photographer Viv Mehes, by permission of the National Library of Australia.*

health of Victorians as Clapp also wanted to help farmers sell their produce at a time when rural incomes were shrinking. From 1926, for the price of four pence (the equivalent of four cents), you could buy a glass of juice squeezed while you waited. Victorian Railways also owned a poultry farm to provide eggs and chicken meat for the refreshment rooms and dining cars.

Sleeping the trip away

As lines pushed out to the farther reaches of New South Wales, it was increasingly necessary to run overnight trains mainly to fulfil the needs of the postal service. In October 1877, the first Pullman car was placed in service on the Southern Mail run between Sydney and Murrumburrah. It was fitted out in the style familiar to anyone who has seen American movies of a certain period (notably *Some Like it Hot*): a centre aisle with two-berth compartments on either side, the occupants having a long hanging curtain to afford them some privacy. In 1880, the New South Wales system bought a second sleeping car from Gilbert Bush & Company fitted out in the same design. The department then ordered six further sleeping cars from the local firm of Hudson Brothers (later Clyde Engineering).

Queensland Government Railways ordered four sleeping cars in 1888 from the Queensland Railway Carriage, Wagon and Tramcar Company of Nundah. These had a smoking room for men at one end, a ladies' sitting room at the other, and the berths in the middle of the car. At one stage, the charge for the upper berth in these cars was lower than for the bottom bed. The year 1896 saw the first second class car and, from the start, Queenslanders who opted for these cars knew to bring their bed clothes

with them; sheets and blankets were provided only in first class sleepers — a practice that lasted for more than a century. The second class cars slept twenty-four people, compared to fourteen in first. Pullman cars, with their longitudinal bunks and curtains rather than compartments, came on the Queensland scene from 1912. QGR had ninety-four sleeping cars in service by the late 1930s to serve the many long-distance trains. In the 1950s, sleeping cars were also assigned to trains on some branch lines, notably to Kingaroy, Monto, Springsure and Clermont. Sometimes, mixed trains also had sleepers attached on the North Coast line and on runs to places such as Dirranbandi, Charleville, Longreach and Mount Isa.

Meanwhile, in 1887, South Australian Railways brought into service the Mann 'Boudoir' sleeping cars built in the United States. These had ten two-berth compartments with a side corridor, and four of the cars were employed on the Melbourne–Adelaide expresses. Between 1906 and 1923, Victorian Railways built its own sleeping cars for the Adelaide service at the Newport workshops. Nine compartments held two berths each in these cars, along with wash basins and a small area for hanging clothes.

But it was not just the main interstate services which acquired sleeping cars. In 1909, they were put on trains to Mount Gambier (and withdrawn in 1932 as a Great Depression economy measure). In 1916, several sleeping cars were added to the fleet of narrow gauge rolling stock including the cars *Alberga*, *Coonalto* and *Nilpena* which were assigned to the Broken Hill line. From 30 August 1923, a sleeping car ran each fortnight between Quorn and Marree on the Central Australia line.

Cramped but comfortable. The interior of New South Wales sleeping car XAM 1887 photographed in April 1978. *John Beckhaus.*

Victoria had only a few intrastate services with sleeping cars, as few routes were of sufficient distance to require overnight accommodation. Before 1900, these cars were placed on trains to Portland. It was possible to book a sleeper within Victoria as far as Serviceton on the interstate train, but only if there were berths left over after interstate passengers had made their bookings on the joint stock cars running between Melbourne and Adelaide. The Mildura line was the only one to have a dedicated sleeping car service that lasted several decades. Apart from joint stock cars to serve on South Australian lines as well as Victorian, the first Victorian Railways sleepers came into service in 1890. The *Perseverance* and *Enterprise* were twelve-wheel carriages built at the Newport workshops for use on the trains to Portland. When that idea proved not to be a success, the carriages were converted to an inspector's car and the No. 1 state car for the Governor-General respectively. Three more cars were built at Newport from 1903, numbered 01, 02, and 03; the latter two were named *Avon* and *Mildura* respectively. *Avon* ended its days as a staff car on the 'Better Farming Train' and was scrapped in 1930. Other sleeping cars were built in 1923 and 1928. Sleeping cars operated by Victorian Railways offered only first class accommodation; there were no second class sleeping cars.

After World War II, New South Wales had the biggest fleet of sleeping cars in Australia due to the long journeys to the Victorian and Queensland borders, and the large number of overnight trains to various distant western destinations. The fleet included the KAM car, which had four luxury two-berth cabins and one deluxe room equipped with a conventional bed. The TAM cars were the standard sleeping car on New South Wales main line trains, being used on the expresses to Melbourne and Brisbane along with some of the more important mail trains. There were forty-nine built from 1913 and they had ten sleeping compartments, each with two bunks. The MAM cars were a slight variation on the TAM. The CAM cars were composites: they had five sleeping compartments, each with two beds and, at either end, two six-seat sitting compartments. One of these was a first class seating compartment, the other second class. Overnight mail trains to destinations around the state used a variety of other sleeping cars, including the VAM, LAM, EAM and FAM classes.

The year 1950 saw the first roomette cars on Australia's rails. These had twenty single compartments equipped with lavatories, basins, and a pull-down bed. There was a common shower room at one end of each of the roomette cars. These vehicles were first built for the Overland service between Melbourne and Adelaide, being named *Allambi*, *Tantini*, *Mururi* and *Chaloki*.

Today, the only intrastate sleepers remaining are in Queensland. If you want to experience a night in bed aboard a train, it will have to be on one of the Great Southern Railroad's long-distance services: the Overland, the Indian Pacific or the Ghan.

Off to the races

In the days before widespread ownership of cars, and fast, efficient buses, racegoers usually got to the track by train. Many race meetings were held close to existing railway lines so it was easy enough to provide a stop nearby for race trains. A platform was erected at Cluden racecourse, 6.4 km outside Townsville, in 1884. Special trains were operated on the days of meetings held by the

OPPOSITE LEFT: **Apart from the strains placed upon Australian railways during World War II by the number of men and quantity of matériel to be moved to the north, the trains also had to cope with transporting prisoners of war and enemy aliens. Here a group of Japanese internees arrives at Barmera, South Australia on 11 March 1943. They are alighting at Farmer's Siding after having travelled from Hay, New South Wales, and will be placed on army trucks for their destination, the 14th Prisoner of War and Internment Camp.** *Australian War Memorial, AWM 064888.*

OPPOSITE RIGHT: **The gap between the railheads at Alice Springs and Birdum posed a severe logistical problem during World War II given the state of the road between the north and south termini. Once Japan became a threat, Australia moved quickly to seal the road surface so that goods and troops could be moved more quickly. This scene at Larrimah in October 1942 shows men of the 147th Australian General Transport Company rolling drums of bitumen off rail trucks onto waiting lorries.** *Australian War Memorial, AWM 026970.*

Townsville Turf Club. When the Ipswich Amateur Turf Club held its meetings at Bundamba course, trains ran on to the Redbank line which had a timber-faced grass platform right beside the course located on a loop off the main line. There was no turning or watering for steam locomotives so engines had to return to Bundamba station for those operations. A set of lights was installed in 1963 where the line crossed Ipswich Road but before that a flagman had to be stationed at the crossing on race days.

Thus, there were a number of short branch lines into racecourse stations, most now closed. There have been those who averred that money spent on racecourse spur lines could have been put to better use on long-distance tracks. Racecourses that had their own railway line included:

New South Wales

Rosehill. A short line was opened in 1888 to Rosehill racecourse from a junction near Clyde in Sydney's western suburbs. It was owned by the Bank of New Zealand and trains ran to the racecourse. The course was also used for other events: in 1891, it was the venue for the 5 October Eight-Hour Day Demonstration and Sports. Thirty-one special trains ran off the government track and down the line to the racecourse. It was reported that twelve train sets (each of twelve carriages) moved 27,700 people that day. At Sydney station, platforms 6, 8, 9 and 10 were set aside for the special train departures. In 1901, the track became part of the longer suburban train branch to Carlingford when it was acquired by the government.

Warwick Farm. This line was owned by the Australian Jockey Club. Part of the electrified suburban train network,

it was open to race train operations until August 1990. There were sufficient sidings on the AJC property to accommodate eight train sets on race days. In the era when horses were transported by rail, this branch had a 200 metre-long dock platform for unloading the animals.

Broken Hill. In 1899, New South Wales Government Railways took over a private tramway running north from Broken Hill to Tarrawingee. However, because the track was laid to the narrow gauge, operations were handed over to the Silverton Tramway Company which ran narrow gauge trains from 'The Hill' to Cockburn across the border in South Australia. In 1900, a 1.8 km spur was opened to the Broken Hill racecourse and race trains ran along this until 1930.

Rutherford. On the line from Maitland to Muswellbrook in the Hunter Valley, a private line branched off the Main North line on the Newcastle side of Rutherford station, running 1.9 km to Rutherford racecourse. Trains on the line were operated by the government. There was a standard wooden passenger station as well as a horse platform at the racecourse.

Gosford. From 1916, race trains ran down the 1.7 km branch to take race crowds to this Central Coast course. The line was converted to yard working in 1970 and closed sometime in the 1980s.

Victoria

Flemington. Built by Melbourne and Essendon Railway Company in 1861, the line was acquired for Victorian Railways when the government took over the private company. Today, the line remains open to race trains.

Geelong. One of the earlier racecourse branches (opened 1878) but also one of the first casualties (closed 1909).

Ballarat. Three racecourse lines existed in the vicinity of this goldmining centre. The earliest to open was from Waubra Junction to Ballarat Racecourse (3.4 km, 1881–1970). From Lal Lal to Lal Lal Racecourse there was dedicated a 3.6 km branch (1886–1941) while a 2.5 km line ran from Bungaree to the racecourse of that name, remaining open between 1900 and 1951.

Williamstown. This could hardly be called a branch. Trains ran into this racecourse off the Altona line using a 400 metre-long spur which was open to traffic between 1887 and 1951. There was also a racecourse platform on the Altona line itself.

Burrumbeet Park. West of Ballarat, a 1.8 km line ran from the Ballarat–Ararat line to this racecourse.

SOUTH AUSTRALIA

Morphettville. The Adelaide, Glenelg and Suburban Railway Company's line passed by Morphettville racecourse, but in 1880 the competing Holdfast Bay Railway Company built a 1.1 km spur from its line to offer an alternative means of transport for the race crowds. The Adelaide, Glenelg Co. refused to allow Holdfast passengers to cross its track to get to the racecourse. It was taken over by South Australian Railways in 1899. The racecourse line, opened around 1880, was closed from 14 December 1929.

WESTERN AUSTRALIA

Western Australia had five racecourses to which rail branches ran: Belmont, Canning Park, Bunbury, Helena Vale and Coolgardie. The rail to Canning Park Racecourse in Perth was closed in May 1952 while that going to Helena Vale Racecourse, Perth, was closed on 17 April 1963.

OTHER LINES

Queensland had its racecourse branch at Ascot. Tasmania had two racecourses served by rail, Elwick at Hobart that closed in 1953, while the line to Mowbray had been lifted in 1939.

The railways at war

Unlike the 1939–45 conflict, World War I did not impose strains on the railway system of vast numbers of men and amounts of matériel needing to be moved around the country, particularly to the north. While the railways did have to move troops, it was mainly to the ports within each state, so that the break of gauge at so many places was not the problem it became after 1939. Moreover, there was no large foreign army to be transported about, unlike the situation after 1942 when huge numbers of American troops moved through and around Australia. However, there was a much greater freight task imposed on the railway system as trains relieved some of the pressure on coastal shipping. Until this time, coal was transported from New South Wales to Victoria by sea, but in 1915 coal sidings were built at Wodonga to allow coal to be transhipped from standard to Victoria's broad gauge wagon fleet.

Possibly the greatest impact of the 1914–18 war was the loss of personnel: about 4,500 men from Victorian Railways enlisted for the armed services. In Queensland, the manpower loss totalled about 2,500. Large numbers also went from other systems and, tragically, many did not come back. New South Wales Government Railways lost 1,180 employees who died in action. Construction of the Trans Australia Railway between Port Augusta and Kalgoorlie fell well behind schedule as the project was hit

In the days of steam on the Central Australia Railway, stores of water were available along the line for the refuelling of locomotives and the water tanks on the carriages. In December 1942, these troops take advantage of the railway water pipes to have a wash during a pause on their journey north. *Australian War Memorial, AWM p00296.087.*

OPPOSITE: 'Somewhere in Central Australia' is all the identifying information on this photograph. This heavy train laden with military equipment is heading north to the battlefront, presumably on the line to Alice Springs. *Australian War Memorial, AWM 014394.*

by shortages of both men and materials. The rolling stock also felt the strain as locomotives were pressed into additional duties and older engines were kept running rather than being replaced as the workshops were often diverted into war work.

The situation in 1939 was to become more dire. Australia's railways were not in the best shape to cope with the strains on transport brought about by World War II. The main frustration at a time when the Japanese were threatening to invade the northern coast of Australia was the gap in the Northern Territory between the railheads at Alice Springs and Birdum which impeded shipments northwards of men and matériel. The many breaks of gauge around the continent played their part in slowing down transport movements. On top of all this was the fact that much of the rail system was in a run-down condition due to the cost cutting during the Great Depression. Investment in new equipment, including wagons, locomotives and track, had been severely reduced in the 1930s. The war brought the entire rail network to the brink of collapse. Commonwealth Railways found that its operations from Kalgoorlie, Port Pirie and Darwin were put under extreme pressure. While the Federal Government was able to offer some help in the form of extensions to workshops and new locomotive depots, the system struggled for the duration of the conflict with a lack of sufficient motive power, rolling stock and staff. So great was the shortage of men to repair lines that civilian internees were brought on the job to form track gangs. In 1943, the average annual mileage for a Queensland Government Railways locomotive was 62,781 km; for wagons, the average was 26,086 km. However, Queensland did perform well in building rolling stock

during the war years. In the five years to June 1944, all the other Australian systems between them built just fifty-five new locomotives; Queensland managed to turn out forty-three new locomotives, fifty-four new carriages and 2,000 new wagons between 1941 and 1945.

It is worth noting that, before World War II, very little freight traffic moved over the Trans Australia Railway between Kalgoorlie and Port Augusta. Three passenger trains in each direction crossed the continent each week, but only one goods train. The Central Australia Railway to Alice Springs was able to move large numbers of cattle on a seasonal basis, but its wagon fleet was such that it did not have the capacity to move other than small volumes of general freight. The main trains on that line were the Ghan, a passenger service, and the Marree Mixed (a freight train with one or more passenger cars attached).

Meanwhile, rail travel for civilians which, until then, by Australian rather than European standards, had been a reasonably efficient and pleasant experience, became anything but: trains were overloaded due mainly to some services being cancelled. These reduced timetables not only meant discomfort but also a great deal of inconvenience. Carriages became shabbier as maintenance was reduced at a time when the cars were subject to much greater use. This — and the post-war coal shortages — soured many Australians on rail travel.

It was often worse for the troops. When vast numbers of men had to be moved to the Northern Territory after Japan became a threat, the narrow gauge lines (Central Australia Railway to Alice Springs and North Australia Railway from Darwin) were simply not equipped to cope with more than two or three trains a week. Most of the soldiers and airmen posted to the north had to endure

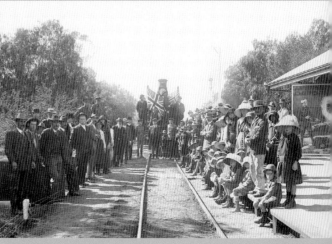

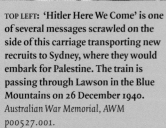

TOP LEFT: 'Hitler Here We Come' is one of several messages scrawled on the side of this carriage transporting new recruits to Sydney, where they would embark for Palestine. The train is passing through Lawson in the Blue Mountains on 26 December 1940. *Australian War Memorial, AWM p00527.001.*

ABOVE LEFT: No first class sleepers, observation or dining cars for these men of the HQ 2 Water Transport Group travelling from Melbourne to North Queensland on 11 December 1944. *Australian War Memorial, AWM 084973.*

TOP RIGHT: In World War I, there were the 'Coo-ee' marches and there were the recruiting trains. One of the latter is pictured at Wallumbilla, Queensland, about 1916, posing with the townsfolk. *Australian War Memorial, AWMh02211.*

ABOVE RIGHT: A group of eight visiting RAAF recruiters taken with 'Poppa' Harry Corones, owner of Charleville's leading hotel in 1942, in front of their recruiting carriage. *George Balsillie collection.*

OPPOSITE: The rolling stock on the isolated North Australia Railway simply was not up to the job of handling the war traffic from 1942. Servicemen soon found this out when they travelled in converted cattle trucks (and named the trains 'The Spirit of Protest'). The official photographer managed to get them to smile as they leaned out of these wagons at Larrimah but the troops may not have been so co-operative by the time they reached Adelaide River. The departure scene was taken on 23 June 1944; the card playing was captured the next morning. *Australian War Memorial, AWM 067053 (above), AWM 067054 (below).*

long journeys, often sitting on the floors of cattle wagons with poor sanitation, little food and, sometimes, no water. Converted cattle trucks were also used on the Trans Australia Railway. Three days through the heat of the Australian interior with improvised lavatories was the style in which many Australian troops travelled between Kalgoorlie and Port Augusta.

The scale of the challenge in 1939 can be gauged from the army's submission in 1945 to the Royal Commission on Standardisation. The army recommended several key changes so that trains could flow freely across the continent without being impeded by breaks of gauge, and the physical transhipment that these breaks required. The military put forward several recommendations that would have transformed the Australian rail system: these included converting the line between Port Pirie and Broken Hill from narrow to standard gauge (that did not happen until 1969); an independent standard gauge track running parallel to the existing narrow gauge line between Kalgoorlie and Perth (by 1970, the line had been converted to dual gauge); a new standard gauge line be laid from the railhead at Bourke, New South Wales, to Mount Isa in Queensland with a spur to Townsville (a forerunner of today's inland rail corridor proposal); standardisation of the Queensland narrow gauge network (as unlikely then as now); the abolition of broad gauge in Victoria and in parts of South Australia (achieved in the latter over the past two decades, but still in the process in Victoria); and the standardisation of the lines in the Northern Territory (achieved at the end of 2003 with the completion of the line to Darwin).

But it was not just a matter of changing gauges. Each of the seven railway administrations (the state systems and Commonwealth Railways) had different locomotives and rolling stock. Track strength also varied, even within states, due to the cost-cutting that led to lightweight rails on some rural branch lines. This meant that, even when there was no break of gauge, trains often had to be remarshalled to suit a locomotive change or different track conditions. For example, the South Australian branch line to Pinnaroo on the border with Victoria had been laid with light rails. This meant that freight carried on large rail wagons had to be transferred at Murray Bridge to smaller ones with lighter axle loads before it could be transported down the branch line.

In 1938, the War Railway Council, which had been formed in 1911, asked the state railway departments to lay more crossing loops on main lines and to provide additional transhipment capacity at the border stations of Albury and Tocumwal in NSW and Wallangarra in Queensland. The council also sought infrastructure improvements, especially more telephone equipment along lines, to help speed up train movements. But little happened. The departments had little spare money at the end of the economic depression.

The council, along with the wartime Director of Railway Transportation, asked again for these improvements the following year. This time there was action, and much was achieved by mid-1940. According to the official war history, the improvements meant sixteen more trains a day could move on the Adelaide–Melbourne–Sydney corridors; the same number of extra services could move between the state capitals on the inland route through Tocumwal and Narrandera. It was also possible to move additional trains between Adelaide and Newcastle by routing them on inland NSW tracks to Werris Creek and then south into

Today, grain trains arrive at ports in the form of diesel locomotives and modern bulk wagons with automatic unloading. In 1925 at Fremantle, the harvest arrived in bags, manhandled at its station of origin and again when unloaded to a waiting vessel. *Author's collection.*

Newcastle. Improved handling at Wallangarra meant that station could process an additional twelve trains a day between the Queensland narrow gauge wagons and the standard gauge ones in NSW.

Incidentally, Tocumwal was more than just a transit point for troops and equipment where the Victorian broad gauge met the NSW standard gauge. Just outside the town was located what was claimed to be, at the time, the largest aerodrome in the Southern Hemisphere. The government strategy was to build an air base well behind any front line should Japanese forces land in northern Australia. Tocumwal was chosen as the spot for the bomber base. It took just five weeks from the eviction of local farmers to the first aircraft landing. Nearly three thousand men were brought in to build the base, named by the Americans as McIntyre Field. It could handle aircraft up to the size of Liberator bombers. After the invasion threat subsided, the base was used for aircraft maintenance. At its peak, Tocumwal's airfield was home to about five thousand Royal Australian Air Force personnel, most of whom came and went by train.

Initially, the Australian railway system managed to cope with the additional wartime traffic. When the war involved only Germany, coastal shipping could continue to move most of the coal around the country, while troops and equipment were being shipped to Britain and North Africa rather than being moved around within Australia. Nearly 5 million tons of coal went by coastal shipping in 1940. But when it was no longer safe to rely on shipping, the real strain began to show within the railway network, not helped by the fact that transporting coal from New South Wales to Western Australia involved transhipping at breaks of gauge stations at Broken Hill, Port Pirie and Kalgoorlie.

By late 1940, when there was a real fear of German maritime raiders operating near Australia, the War Cabinet was asked to approve the spending of almost five million pounds (ten million dollars). This was to pay for a new bridge over the Hawkesbury River north of Sydney, as well as duplicating the busy section in southern NSW between Junee and Cootamundra and another near Seymour in Victoria. They also initially approved the cost of a third rail between Broken Hill and Port Pirie so that standard gauge trains could operate from Sydney to Kalgoorlie. However, the last item was later dropped when ministers decided it would be cheaper to improve transhipping capacity at the break of gauge stations. There was a widely held view in 1940 that the railway system was not working to its full capacity. This relaxed attitude of authorities in Canberra meant the squandering of a wonderful opportunity to rid the system of its worst bottlenecks and ordering more rolling stock. Both would have been invaluable when the Pacific War began.

Just how badly the system had, in fact, deteriorated — partly as a result of the Great Depression — was illustrated by the state of the Victorian Railways. In the early years of the twentieth century, the normal building rate was about two hundred locomotives every five years, as well as about three hundred carriages, and anywhere between three thousand and six thousand wagons. However, in the 1933–38 period, Victorian Railways managed to acquire only one new locomotive, fourteen new carriages and fewer than one thousand three hundred new wagons. By 1938, Victoria's steam locomotives had an average age of twenty-six years, meaning that the older ones were well beyond their economic working life. Some of the wagons in use were forty-five years old and

The building of the railway line to Bourke in northern New South Wales was motivated by the desire in Sydney to cut off the river trade which saw wool and other produce go down to Victoria by boat. Eventually, road transport would snatch that traffic away from rail and lines such as this closed one by one, aided by indifference in government railway departments and, in this case, fortuitous (for the politicians) flooding which washed out the line, allowing closure earlier than planned. Byrock was once a junction on this line, with the branch to Brewarrina heading off into bleak and sparsely populated country. Alan Bartley's truck has arrived at Byrock with a load of wool destined for Sydney. *State Library of NSW.*

had never been equipped with automatic couplers.

However, the war did mean that some previously uneconomic lines suddenly became an important part of the national transport chain. The isolated Cooktown–Laura section, which had been down to carrying just 208 tons of freight in the 1933–34 financial year, was suddenly working to capacity carrying equipment to be used building a new aerodrome in the interior. The line saw daily services for the first time in decades. Similarly, the isolated Croydon–Normanton line south of the Gulf of Carpentaria in northern Queensland, became useful with goods travelling from Cairns up to the railhead at Forsayth, being taken by road to the next railhead at Croydon, and thence by rail for the 151 km trip to Normanton.

One isolated section that was put under extreme pressure was the North Australia Railway (NAR), the narrow gauge Commonwealth Railways line from Darwin south to the tiny settlement of Birdum. Its track and rolling stock were fitted to one-train-a-week operations. However, from 1942, it became a vital link in the war against Japan.

By the late 1930s, the NAR was in poor shape. Most of the locomotives were past their best, and some of the wagons had been working the line since the opening of the initial Darwin–Pine Creek section in 1889. Extra locomotives were transferred there from the narrow gauge systems in South Australia and Western Australia but, inevitably, those departments chose their older engines when having to decide which they did not need. Men were rather harder to come by, with many experienced railwaymen having entered the armed services (although drivers and firemen were reserved occupations). After the

Pacific war began, many American troops — mainly black — were posted to work on the railway. In addition, gangs of civilian aliens were sent north but they were often more trouble than help given their lack of commitment to the war effort.

The freight carried by the NAR during the war showed clearly the strain under which it was operating. Trains operated 52,000 train kilometres in 1939. By 1944, the line was coping with 1,200,000 train kilometres. This translated into one train a week and one hundred and forty respectively. By the end of the war, the NAR had fifty-seven locomotives and large numbers of wagons, all antiquated and mostly borrowed from other systems.

The Central Australian Railway (CAR), which meandered up from South Australia via Oodnadatta as far as Alice Springs, was under similar pressure. Four troop trains ran up the line each day, interspersed with goods workings. The junction with the rest of the South Australian system at Quorn, itself the meeting place of the lines from Sydney and Adelaide, was busy twenty-four hours a day in order to handle all the trains. The Stuart Highway was built between Alice Springs and Larrimah to bridge the gap between the NAR and CAR. Birdum, the actual southern terminus of the NAR, was effectively by-passed.

Goods of all descriptions

Trains once carried just about everything. Before the modern era of highways and reliable lorries, coal, wheat, milk, minerals and fresh fruit and vegetables could reach their markets only by the rail. If you lived in the country and wanted a piano, the only way to get it there was by train to the nearest station.

OPPOSITE ABOVE: **A circus train has called at Orroroo, South Australia, about 1900. The photographer was more interested in the elephants but the especially modified rail wagon can be seen behind the huge beasts.** *John Mannion collection.*

OPPOSITE: **Livestock cartage continues to this day on Queensland's rail system, but it has disappeared elsewhere. Even as late as 1983, however, animals were being carted by rail in New South Wales, as these two mismatched wagons parked near Cooma saleyards testify.** *Author's collection.*

OPPOSITE ABOVE: **Selwyn was one of the more remote terminal stations in Queensland, at the end of a short branch off the Mt Isa line. The 79 km line was opened in 1910, and this scene of farmers waiting with their wool beside the track dates from 1912. (The branch was closed in 1961.)** *Author's collection.*

OPPOSITE BELOW: **Wheat being delivered on 29 January 1904, at Pittsworth, Queensland, ready to be railed to the port.** *Author's collection.*

FOLLOWING SPREAD: **Loading wheat the hard way.** *Author's collection.*

ABOVE LEFT: **Eventually, machines started to eliminate a good deal of the back-breaking work in railway yards. This early conveyor belt speeded up grain handling at Gladstone, South Australia, in the late 1920s. The broad gauge had reached Gladstone in 1927 and, as this photograph shows, narrow gauge continued to operate on the line to Port Pirie (where this wagon load was destined) and the branch north to Wilmington.** *Author's collection.*

TOP AND ABOVE RIGHT: **In 1907, Western Australian Government Railways bought from Millars Timber Company a 44.6 km line running from the junction with its own track to Denmark, Millars having built the line for its timber trains to get to the port of Albany. These pictures show the two sides of these tramways that fed so much traffic onto government lines. Millars' Grafter is shown at Wellington Mills in 1910. This 2-6-0 had originally been X 49 of South Australian Railways. It was bought by Millars in 1896 and stayed in service until 1942. The proud custodians are the guard, R. Spruhan standing on the front of the engine, fireman Harold Hannan, driver John Fred Harbeck and, by the cab, an unnamed cleaner. In the second picture is the type of locomotive usually associated with timber mill operations — a Baldwin 0-4-0 — officially named Denmark but known as 'Coffee Pot'. It was used as a shunter at Millars' mill.** *Noel Inglis collection.*

Perishable goods were always a priority on the railway. Train 260, the Fruit Express, ran from Murwillumbah to Darling Harbour (then Sydney's main sea freight assembly point) although it took thirty-two hours in the days of steam haulage due to the stops at multiple stations along the way. Trains once also carted live rabbits, rabbit meat, tallow and fat. Queensland introduced a special fruit train that made the distance between Brisbane and Townsville in forty hours, a considerable achievement with the old steam locomotives and slow progress of other goods trains. It loaded fruit and vegetables at Stanthorpe on Monday and then Brisbane on Tuesday. It would deliver this produce to Brisbane early on Thursday and then be in Cains with the remaining load by Friday morning. Southbound, the train carted tomatoes and other produce from the north to customers in the state capital. In 1923, Queensland had a glut of pineapples. Queensland's railway system helped get rid of the fruit with stationmasters instructed to take orders in their areas and then arrange to have the produce delivered to the particular station. Fruit specials were also run from Mildura with refrigerated wagons attached.

In New South Wales, the Dorrigo branch was important to the local potato growers. The Crookwell branch carried iron ore from a small local mine. Stations from Grenfell to Greenthorpe to Tocumwal had private sidings to serve the local flour mill. Sidings were laid at Bombo and on the Barraba branch to quarries so that the railway could obtain supplies of aggregate for ballast.

Circuses were once big customers of the railways. The trains were big and the stops many as these entertainments involved large numbers of performers and animals, and their arrival in country towns was always a major event. In 1963, the Wirth's Circus Train in Victoria travelling to Mildura consisted of forty-eight vehicles and totalled 656 tons; seven carriages accommodated the circus staff while the long string of wagons included nine M vans with especially raised roofs. The circus did come to town — pretty well any town. In 1924, the Perry Bros Circus travelled through Victoria's mallee country, performing nightly at seven different towns: Pinnaroo (just across the border in South Australia), Murrayville, Underbool, Ouyen, Mildura, Merbein and Red Cliffs. Once, it even ventured up the private coal lines in the Hunter Valley of New South Wales owned by the South Maitland Railway for performances at Weston and Cessnock.

Over the years, railway administrators took advantage of the advent of more powerful locomotives to make the railway compete and pay its way. Before World War II, New South Wales Railways was experimenting to find a way to get greater loads — especially coal — over the Blue Mountains and to the ports. These tests involved running trains of between 1,000 and 1,400 tons, and a standard working became around 1,000 tons. This required three steam locomotives to surmount the 1 in 42 grades to Zig Zag signal box. After the war, coal train loads were lifted to around 1,500 tons; three locomotives pulled from the front, another pushed from the rear. At Zig Zag, the pusher and the lead banking locomotive were detached and two locomotives would haul the train to Blackheath, where the third engine was taken off before the downhill run to the coast. Those who were on that side of the Blue Mountains when one of these trains hauled its load up the grades remember the valley echoing to the sound of the locomotive exhausts and seeing huge clouds of billowing black smoke rising high into the sky above the slow moving train.

Sheep face a long and uncomfortable journey aboard four-wheel wagons in this 1920s photograph taken at an unidentified station in New South Wales. *Author's collection.*

ABOVE: In Queensland, there were strict rules on the handling of livestock but it was nevertheless an arduous experience for the poor animals. Here a B12 Class locomotive poses on the bridge over Bungil Creek in the late 1890s with its livestock wagons. *Author's collection.*

LEFT: PB 15 440 heading a cattle train ready to leave Charleville in the early 1920s. Note the early headlight. *George Balsillie collection.*

Livestock was an important part of railway business in most parts of Australia, none more so than in Queensland. Dajarra in the far north was reputed to be the busiest cattle loading station in the world; Cunnamulla and Quilpie were among other stations that had huge herds of cattle and mobs of sheep pass through the rail yards. Queensland Government Railways installed water sprays at Charleville and Flaggy Rock to help cool cattle being transported on trains and, by 1926, it was the rule that pigs had to be sprayed on trains to keep them from getting too hot in the crowded wagons. Cattle on long hauls had to be unloaded after twenty-four hours mid-journey to allow them to take water and walk about, although the introduction of diesel–electric haulage and faster transit times made this no longer a problem. Those shipping cattle received a free ticket for a drover for each three bogie wagons paid for and livestock trains were given priority second only to mail trains on the Queensland railway network.

Parcels were another big business. If you lived in Harden, on the Main South line in New South Wales, and belonged to a wine society that delivered by the case, even as late as 1960, that wine came by train and you went down to the railway station to collect it. In 1867, Queensland's rail system introduced parcel stamps, the same size as the postal variety with the head of Queen Victoria. Later the parcel stamps became much larger in size and bore the name of the station from which the parcel was consigned. Eventually, Queensland Government Railways offered a delivery-to-your-door service in Brisbane, Toowoomba, Bundaberg, Mount Morgan, Townsville and Mackay. In 1958, QGR had thirteen trucks running around Brisbane collecting

parcels for carriage by rail. Of great benefit to country people in Queensland was the system of cash-on-delivery which operated from 1905 until 1980. This meant that products could be ordered from the city and sent by rail, with the convenience of paying at the station for both the cost of the item and its transport.

When Ian Kauschke, an engine driver based at Port Pirie in the 1950s, was booked to work freights from Adelaide, he knew that it was no short job. In fact, the train would take twenty hours from the yards at Mile End. Fifteen hours of that would be spent making it as far only as Snowtown. Three crews were attached to the working, and long shunting operations took place at every station. Everything went by rail: bales of wool south, lengths of water pipe north, six foot sheets of roofing iron, and forty-four gallon drums. All were loaded and unloaded by hand. On the way south, a stop at Collinsfield usually meant filling an empty wagon with crates of eggs, all which had to be loaded by the crew. The fireman would usually go and help the guard with the loading, but the train still waited there for a long time as the eggs were carried by hand from the goods shed to the wagon. The train crews did much of the work on the night workings because even where stations had a porter, he worked the day shift. Another important freight south from Port Pirie was shipments from the lead smelter of silver and gold, produced as a by-product from the Broken Hill concentrates. Armed guards escorted these to Adelaide.

The past few decades have seen rail's freight role change dramatically. Many of the branch lines, and most of the wayside stations, have gone. As this was being written, the fate of the grain lines in New South Wales

OPPOSITE ABOVE: 'All hands to the pumps' was the cry during the second war, and women filled the gaps left by men sent off to fight. In 1944, this female railway porter pushes a trolley laden with wicker baskets and boxes off the platform at an unidentified Victorian station. *Australian War Memorial, p00784.195.*

RIGHT: A man who had to keep his wits about him at all times was the signalman. This impressive array of switching levers was to be found in the main signal box at Adelaide station. *State Library of South Australia.*

ABOVE: Gatekeepers were once a familiar sight at level and bridge crossings. Here, Mrs Arbuthnot demonstrated in 1970 how she closed off the bridge at Tocumwal when a train needed to use the bridge into Victoria. *Public Record Office.*

RIGHT: Few photographs were taken inside railway stations, so that the interiors of these hives of activity have disappeared with few recorded images. That there was a wealth of detail to be captured is shown by this photo taken at Drouin, Victoria, during World War II. The stationmaster and his staff were kept busy with paperwork and handling small lots and parcels. *By permission of the National Library of Australia.*

appeared to be sealed with the expectation that three more would be closed, with the others to follow soon thereafter. By the 1990s, other than dedicated grain and coal trains, the railways were having trouble holding traffic other than on the very long haul routes. Between Sydney and Melbourne, the trains accounted for only about one-fifth of freight. It was easier for many shippers to use door-to-door road, especially with the improvements on the Hume Highway. Deteriorating infrastructure also played its part: trains could not match times taken by trucks between Sydney and Melbourne due to steam age signalling and track alignments. Loops were often not long enough to hold the modern freight trains to allow smooth passing. An ancient bridge over the Murrumbidgee at Wagga Wagga meant that 'fast' freight services had to slow to 20 km/h because of concern about the state of the structure; and when the Menangle Bridge near Campbelltown was closed, with trains forced to go via Wollongong, even more freight was lost to road competitors.

State rivalries ensure that trains had to be stopped at borders to switch locomotives, thus adding thirty minutes or more while trucks flashed by unimpeded on the nearby highways. Certification issues meant that, should a driver try to run a train from Perth to Sydney, he would have to acquire at least ten different certificates. The truck driver needed only one driver's licence. Each state had a separate train radio system; signal indications could mean different things in New South Wales than they did under Victorian rules. Wagon types often had speed limitations that were different in one state to another.

Mail by rail

Wherever the railways went, they could carry mail much more quickly than could road coaches. As soon as the railways reached out in the countryside, they ensured that mail moved more quickly to its destination than had been the case with horse-drawn wagons and coaches. It was a natural progression to have postal staff travel on trains sorting the mail as the train hurtled through the night.

These were Travelling Post Offices (TPOs). Queensland introduced its first TPO van on 1 January 1887. Mail was loaded and unloaded at stopping stations. At minor stations, mail deliveries were made by tossing the bags out the van door onto the platform while the train kept moving. As for picking up mail, it was not long before railways used the mechanical arm which held the mail bag to be collected by a device on the mail van so that the train did not need to waste valuable time stopping.

These TPOs ran all over Queensland. By 1911, they were on trains running on the Chillagoe between Cairns and Almaden. A TPO van was attached to the Western Mail from Brisbane to Charleville until withdrawn from 16 August 1932. The van travelled locked until the train reached Toowoomba at 6.25 pm each Tuesday and Friday. Then the post office sorter took charge. Mail on the outward journey from Brisbane was picked up and dropped off at stations from Dalby through to Charleville, and then all letters and articles sorted for the trains travelling on to Cunnamulla and Quilpie. On the return journey, the van collected mail not only from Charleville but the Cunnamulla and Quilpie lines; it then loaded and unloaded mail at each subsequent stop to Dalby, dropping mail at Toowoomba and Ipswich. In the 1920s, at the small rail siding of Lurnea, a local landowner would use a red

flag to signal the mail train to stop so that he could post letters and parcels with the TPO van.

Many of the TPOs were gone by 1930. The last survivors on the Charleville, Wallangarra, Longreach and Mount Isa runs were withdrawn in 1932.

Victoria had mail going by rail from 1865 on trains running between Melbourne and Ballarat by way of Geelong. In 1873, TPO vans were placed on trains to Benalla, then the service was extended to Albury where it lasted until 1932. Bairnsdale and Ararat were among places to which the TPOs ran. Initially, the Victorian stock used the English system of having the mailbags hung on pegs down each side of the van. However from 1909, Victorian Railways adopted the American method of having frames with the bags held at all four corners, making it easier to throw mail in them. The TPOs were equipped with toilets, a hot wax pot, and there were letter slots in the side to allow people to post when the train stopped.

Working on the railway

Working on the railway was not an easy way to earn a living in the first hundred years or more of railways in Australia. The various colonial, and later state, systems, employed large armies of people needed to clean and operate steam locomotives, staff the many large and small stations which were served by passenger and goods trains, and maintain the track and bridges on which the trains ran. Those who actually built the railways often lived in extraordinary privation.

In 1886, the Queensland Government was hit by the failure of a London bank which conducted much of its business in the United Kingdom. All public works were either partially or totally halted because the administration in Brisbane found itself in financial difficulty and unable to call on its funds in Britain. Among the works suspended was railway construction. About one thousand men, many camped out between Helidon and Toowoomba with their wives and children, were left high and dry. The money and food supplies stopped. They marched to Helidon, which was then the terminus, and many arrived barefooted, their boots having worn out. They demanded of the stationmaster free transport to Ipswich where they could seek redress for their plight. The official refused, but many jumped in empty wagons on a train about to depart and eventually made their representations in Ipswich to a government minister. Food was promised but was never sent. The workers were on their own.

Actually, things were not much better in Queensland by the time of the Great Depression of the 1930s. Men were employed by Queensland Government Railways as part of the relief effort for the unemployed. Those sent out to build new lines lived in tents; their wives would have to cook the meals over an open fire; and all the inhabitants used communal lavatories and showers. Needless to say, these facilities were of the most rudimentary kind. But even for permanent employees of the Queensland railway system, life was tough. George Balsillie was employed as a fettler and pumper on the line to Charleville, and was based at a small station called Womalilla, about 16 km from Mitchell. His son recalls that the family lived in a three-roomed wooden house with an iron roof, with large gaps at the top of the walls to allow for ventilation in summer. But it was fiercely cold in winter because there was no lining to the walls, and the Balsillie household had no heater; what George did was put wood in a four-gallon

TAKING CARE

THE RAILWAYS TENDED to take care of their own. When, in the early 1950s, Reg Latemore, the ganger at Womalilla, a small station on Queensland's Western line, died of heart failure, his widow was given a job as stationmistress at Blaxland, near Dalby, which helped her support the four children. And not just their own. In the nineteenth century, a Mrs Delaney, the widow of a man killed by a Tasmanian Government Railways train, was granted a free lifetime pass to travel between Rhyndaston and Parattah and she became a familiar figure selling apples on the expresses which ran between Hobart and Launceston. She was noted for a ready wit and her sharp replies.

drum, set fire to the wood then place the drum on four bricks in the middle of the house. Lighting was by kerosene lamp. The old valve wireless, the Balsillie's only contact with the outer world apart from passengers throwing papers and magazines out of the trains to those they knew lived in isolated places (a common practice in country Queensland), was run off a six-volt battery which had to be taken into Mitchell on a regular basis for recharging. Apart from his duties looking after the railway track in his role as fettler, on Saturday mornings George would get the pump at the Womalilla Creek going (he held a steam ticket, so was allowed to work the vertical steam engine on the riverbank) and fill the huge water vat used by the steam locomotives. At other times, he would clamber down the pits into which the steam locomotives dropped their fireboxes, the top of his head barely visible to his son and wife, and shovel out of the ashes. Travel to Mitchell on Saturday afternoons was by a motorised four-wheel trolley; his wife Maggie constantly fretted that one day, George would come around a bend and meet a train head-on, but George always kept in touch with traffic staff to make sure nothing was on the line. In 1947, he was transferred further down the line to the Crows Nest branch which ran off at Toowoomba, where he helped maintain the track for the daily rail motor and the weekly mixed. George retired in 1952 at the age of sixty-seven, and saw out the rest of his life in Charleville.

The men who built the early railways adopted for themselves the English term 'navvies', even though they had no connection with digging canals. When there was no railway work, they trudged the countryside looking for other forms of temporary employment to keep body and soul together.

When the transcontinental line was built across the Nullarbor, a rich mixture of work titles was involved. Those laying ballast on the completed sections of track included cracker men and jumper men. There were camel men, ploughmen, horse drivers, teamsters, scoop drivers and labourers. The plate-laying gangs always included linkers, bolt scullers and back bolters. Tradesmen were paid on average fourteen shillings and threepence a day; those engaged on earthworks an average of eighteen shillings. They earned it. In the summer months, temperatures were seldom below a hundred degrees Fahrenheit and soared as high as 130°F. Work stopped during the middle of the day, and also during the great dust storms that blew up in the Nullarbor. In winter, by contrast, the temperature could drop below freezing point and the workers would wake to find frost on the ground outside their tents. Injuries were frequent: the most common were broken bones and crushed fingers. Weekends were filled by games of two-up; the boredom assuaged with liquor supplied by sly-groggers. For sex, there were local Aboriginal women — and not infrequent fights with their husbands.

Those engaged on pushing the rails over the mountainous and forested terrain of western Tasmania faced different but equally unpleasant conditions: it was cold most of the time and two-thirds of the time it was raining. Working twelve hours a day for miniscule wages, they battled the mud and cold.

Even after a line was built, privation and loneliness were part and parcel of the existence for those gangers and fettlers who kept the railways in good condition. Mavis Shaw, whose husband worked for Western Australian Government Railways as a track worker, remembers that,

The stationmaster's imposing residence at Katherine, Northern Territory, photographed in 1926. The construction was such as to maximise the air flow through and under the house. *Peter Dunham collection.*

FOLLOWING SPREAD:
Pick and shovel work constructing the line through the Pichi Richi Pass in 1888. Life would have been tough for these men; not just the manual toil, but the monotony of the food, the cold nights in tents and water often in short supply. *Author's collection.*

J. Taylor
Collofyre
Pichi = R

An old Morris car has been converted to allow its use on the North Australia Railway. Note the headlight mounted on the roof, the horn on the front fender and the water bag slung across the front. Rail workers seen here in 1953 are, from left, Bill Hackett, unknown and Angelo Zammit. *Peter Dunham collection.*

ABOVE: George James Balsillie, aged 55 in May 1940, and son George Robert Balsillie, posed on the quad used by the father in his railway duties at Womalilla siding. It was powered by a single cylinder J.A.P. motor, with a hand brake over the rear right-hand wheel. A tray was connected to front and back axles and a wooden tucker box completed the equipment. Water was carried in small galvanised tanks for the gang, and then poured into canvas water bags which were slung on the front to keep as cool as possible. *George Balsillie collection.*

RIGHT: The Balsillie family — George Robert (six months old), George James and Maggie — at Womalilla in May 1940 all set to go to the Mitchell Show. They are standing by the new galvanised shelter at the siding. *George Balsillie collection.*

on arriving at Wiluna, they decided to buy a house. However, after seven months, he was posted to another point on the line 80 km back toward Meekatharra. So they moved the house in sections and rebuilt it for twenty pounds. Twelve months later they were moved again; this time they sold the house. Gladys Bartow was born in 1903 and her ganger father was posted somewhere along the same line. However, no one was quite sure where the family was when Gladys came into the world. Hence her birth certificate bore, as place of birth, 'On the Geraldton–Cue railway line', a distance of 439 km.

The sheer scale of passenger transport around Australia until after World War II required the generation of hundreds of instructions and advices on the smallest details of train operations, and involved hundreds of people just on those duties. Some examples of notices that went out and which all staff of South Australian Railways were expected to read and remember include the following. In 1907, they were advised that SAR would make available card trays on long journeys for the fee of sixpence (five cents today). That same year, SAR warned staff not to allow boys to travel in smoking compartments, and that only holders of adult tickets should be admitted to these sections of carriages. Train staff were also told they would be severely punished if they countenanced anyone smoking in a non-smoking compartment. The SAR also expressed concern about the number of people still spitting (although the more genteel term 'expectorating' was employed) on station platforms. In 1914, staff on all the many stations around the South Australian network were told that the riding of horses on platforms was banned henceforth.

Allen Gordon worked for the New South Wales Government Railways from 1940 until 1982, and, in 2001,

recorded his memories for the Lithgow District Historical Society. He began as a callboy (at Dubbo), whose job it was to cycle around the town to advise drivers, firemen and shed staff of their next turn of duty. Notes were made out in duplicate; the staff member receiving the advice would retain one copy and sign the other to be returned to the roster clerk. The callboys would also run any other messages for the charge man or roster clerk and, in between times, would keep the station office clean and mop the floor.

Even when men were promoted to engine crew in the steam era, it was often no picnic. If you were based at Tailem Bend in South Australia, and pulled duty on one of the light Mallee branch lines, it was often uncomfortable work. On the branch that ran from Karoonda to Peebinga, near the Victorian border, train services were down to one a week by the 1960s (this line incidentally, was the last steam-worked broad gauge line in the state). There were no settlements along the 106 km branch, few fences and the state of the track was so poor that trains often kept below 24 km/h. In summer, it baked inside the cab, and in winter, the crew had to endure biting icy winds. Sand and dust blew into the cab, and sand often covered the track ahead of the locomotive. When the crew reached Peebinga, there was almost nothing there: no hotel, no motel, no café, no service station. Nothing but a general store, a post office and a telephone exchange open twelve hours a day. They trudged off to a bleak railway barracks to spend the night before the return journey the next day. On the way back, there might be some contact with the locals who would wait at the tiny wayside stations with perhaps a few pieces of mail, some crates of eggs, or a parcel of books to be returned to the Karoonda Institute.

Locomotive wheels were encased with tyres, but they were steel rather than rubber. But, like rubber, they wore out and were frequently replaced to allow smooth running on the steel rails. These New South Wales railway workshop staff are seen with an array of tyres that would have fitted leading, driving and trailing wheels in all their many sizes. *By permission of the National Library of Australia.*

Surprisingly, this branch lasted until 1990 — surprising because, in 1967–68, it carried only 11,300 tons of freight and generated revenue for the financial year of only $45,000. The trains took superphosphate, food and general goods for the small and sparse farming population; outwards the train hauled grain, firewood and livestock.

At the other end of the scale, the life of the stationmaster was also a rigorous one. In the 1947 South Australian Railways rules, many pages were devoted to the requirements placed on a stationmaster. These included daily inspections of the station yard, signal boxes, other buildings and grounds; daily checking of weighbridges and scales; securing all cash and tickets; daily checking of the duty list; and daily inspection of the lavatories and urinals to ensure they were clean, that any obscene writing or sketches were obliterated and, where stations had earth closets, that there was dry earth in boxes and disinfectants available. The stationmaster was responsible for the performance of any crossing keepers and to see that no staff partook of alcohol at the railway refreshment room bar. He was required to see that all luggage was loaded into brakevans, that all items were correctly labelled (with old labels removed) and any arriving luggage unclaimed to have 'lost luggage' tags affixed. The stationmaster had to ensure that there was an order book available to staff containing all orders issued by the department, as well as ensuring maintenance of the station property book, the train register book, and the appearance book that showed staff members who had booked on for the day. Clocks and watches had to be checked at midday each day with a time signal sent from Adelaide. The stationmaster was held responsible for the cleanliness of carriages on departing

trains. He had to ensure the platforms were well lit at night, that announcements of the station name were made as each passenger train arrived and, in the cases of refreshment-room stations, that clear announcements were made about the time for which the train would stand during the refreshment break. Above all, it was his responsibility to 'enforce quiet and order' at his station.

Discipline was a part of everyday life, lasting well after World War II. No train or station staff would have addressed a stationmaster, or even an assistant stationmaster, at one of the larger depots as anything other than 'Mister . . .' Even on the hottest days, caps and full uniform were stipulated. Part of Chris Holley's job in his earlier years at Werris Creek, NSW, was to clean the urinals with a black substance called Wollol. One day, unbeknown to him, the bucket had a small hole that leaked as he carried this cleaning mixture down the platform. Later that day, he was helping get one of the locomotives out of the shed for the Glen Innes Mail when he pulled the points under the engine, derailing it. For that offence, he was formally spoken to; for leaving drips, he was fined five pounds for defacing the platform.

But he says there was also great teamwork in the railways. When he rose to the status of guard, Holley knew that he had to work closely with the driver and fireman. A good guard would not mind climbing into the tender and shovelling coal forward to help the fireman. Conversely, a driver would often let his fireman get off the engine at wayside stations to work the points during shunting, making the guard's life a good deal easier. Remember that, in the steam era, it was possible for a crew to spend several hours shunting at one station if it was a large yard and wagons had to be placed on several different roads.

CHEAP AT THE PRICE

THE ADVANCE OF the railway into Australia's regions was aimed at providing cheap, safe and fast transport for country people and their produce. But it also brought benefits to these regions by making possible visits to regional centres of all types of entertainers. Once the rail reached Albury on the NSW–Victorian border, for example, Sydney musicians began travelling to the town to give philharmonic concerts. However, rail was still not a cheap way to travel in its early era. When the first revenue train departed from Ballarat for Melbourne on 10 April 1862, it carried only four passengers — not surprising considering that the fare was 26 shillings, almost half the then average income of three pounds (60 shillings).

As a career railway employee, you had to be prepared to take what was offered. Once Jack McGregor reached the rank of stationmaster with New South Wales Government Railways, he would serve at Deepwater, Demondrille, Bourke and Ashfield — all very different locations.

He did just over forty-three years in the railways, from 6 December 1923 until March 1967, and was the son of a stationmaster and the grandson of an engine driver. Jack's first appointment, Deepwater, where he was posted in 1947, was a peaceful little town in New England. Like other towns at the time, most of the people did not own cars so the railway was their link with the outside world. The station was manned twenty-four hours a day.

Demondrille was his second stationmaster appointment and he served there from 1950 to 1954. It was a junction station on the Main South line where the branch to Young and Blayney veered off. Its importance was even more significant, as it was the only station in the state, apart from Lithgow, to have the coal refuelling bunkers on the main line (they were usually on sidings) and just about every through train stopped there to take on coal. There were two signal boxes, the main one being the North Box which controlled the junction points. There was not much to Demondrille other than the railway, and most of the rail workers lived in the nearby towns of Harden and Murrumburrah and cycled up the steep grade to work each day; even the station's shunting locomotive was based in Harden and returned there each evening. The McGregor family, however, lived on the spot in the stationmaster's house, a substantial brick residence perched on the top of the railway cutting. For his sons John and Don, it was an ideal place for young boys — the signal boxes, the coal bunkers and the railway dam all provided plenty of after-

school interest. Don remembers the smoke and the grime from the old 57 and 58 class locomotives; when the house shook as a train went by, the soot fell out of the house's roof area meaning that Mrs McGregor had to keep the living room furniture covered except when visitors arrived. Even though Demondrille was a not a busy station in terms of goods and passenger traffic (few passenger trains stopped there apart from taking on coal), the station-master had plenty with which to concern himself. There were the staff pay sheets, the shunting, and the coal bunkers (the coal had to be separated into grades for different locomotive types).

Bourke was quite a different experience, as Don recalls it. It was the end of the line, complete with a grand railway station. The Through West Mail arrived from Sydney three days a week with just two cars attached, one first and one second-class carriage. On other days, this service was operated by a two-car diesel train from Dubbo. It was a long trip from Sydney: a traveller left Sydney Terminal at 8.30 pm on the Western Mail, changed trains at Dubbo the next morning — if it was one of the diesel train days — and then reached Bourke at 5.30 pm, twenty-one hours in all. Bourke was a busy station with traffic from a gypsum mine and huge quantities of wool going out on the rail. Cattle came in for slaughter at the Tancred Bros abattoir, then the chilled product went out to Sydney in meat vans. Jack McGregor's constant problem was staff: locals worked at the station wool dump but were prone to take off after putting together a reasonable sum of money; many of the staff recruited from Sydney found they could not stick the life in such an isolated place.

Ashfield, a station in Sydney's inner west, was not to Mr McGregor's taste. At the age of fifty-one, he found the

Removing a tyre from a C38 Class locomotive wheel-set at the Cardiff railway workshops in New South Wales. *Lake Macquarie City Library.*

constant noise of passing and stopping suburban electrics was just too much. There was a small goods yard there at the time, but Ashfield had none of the atmosphere of the type of station he liked: those with an experienced staff, where there were porters, drivers and guards all sharing the common bonds that existed in the railways of his youth. At this time, his son remembers him being dispirited by the poor quality of staff being recruited for the suburban stations; he thought, in many cases, they were usually people who could not find a job elsewhere although there were fortunately some notable exceptions. Thousands of strangers passed over his platforms every day; there were few he knew.

It was quite a different life, though, on the quiet branch lines. The Warburton branch, located on the outskirts of Melbourne, ran to Lilydale and was closed in 1965. Shortly after, J. Seletto remembered his time in 1952 as a crew member of D3 633, the locomotive based at Warburton. It was an easy life with two crews for one locomotive and a handful of services to Lilydale to connect with suburban trains. The day shift signed on at 6.00 am and, after preparing the engine and placing it on the train, they would have about twenty minutes before departure. Time for breakfast. Cocoa was made with water out of the injector and toast and sausages were cooked in the firebox. At 7.10 am, they were off for the 39 km run to Lilydale. On arrival there, a fifteen-minute break meant time for a cup of tea and sandwiches before the leisurely run back to Warburton.

Building and mending

The railway workshops were, in many ways, the very heart of the railway systems. They not only kept the locomotives, wagons and carriages running, but sometimes they built those very same vehicles. The two most important were Eveleigh in Sydney and Newport at North Melbourne, the latter opening in 1888. Workshops at Jolimont, Ballarat and Bendigo were all brought into operation in 1917.

The Eveleigh railway workshops in Sydney were built between 1880 and 1886, and lasted more than a century (until 1989). They incorporated huge running sheds where all the main line steam locomotives operating out of Sydney were serviced, along with the small local train and shunting engines, and replaced the first government railway workshops near what is today the Devonshire Street passenger subway by Sydney Central station. They achieved pre-eminence from 1889, once the completion of the bridge over the Hawkesbury River enabled rolling stock to be taken to Sydney for service; as a result, the Newcastle workshops declined in importance. In 1939, the representative of the Australian Railway Union wrote this description of the Eveleigh works:

Row upon row of drab smoked-grimed buildings, housing a throbbing energy which pulses forth to the accompaniment of the thump, thump, thump of giant presses torturing white-hot steel into servitude. That is Eveleigh workshops, the heart of the state's transport system. There is a steady drone of high-powered machinery, drilling, boring and turning in every possible fashion; the clatter of overhead cranes, hurrying and scurrying, fetching and carrying, and the staccato noise of the boilermakers' rattler. Somehow this all resolved into a unity of sound. Disturbed only by an occasional burst of excessive violence from any one part. Seemingly submerged in this medley is the human element — 2,600 individuals, the strongest of them but

Another scene no longer available to the railway traveller. This is the concourse at Adelaide station in 1976. *John Beckhaus.*

puny weaklings besides the machines they control. Yet they make all possible. Without them the roaring giant would be a whispering ghost.

In 1971, there were still 1,648 people on the payroll at Eveleigh. Other notable workshops were those at Ipswich and Townsville in Queensland; Islington near Adelaide, Midland (both the government and Midland company had their plants there), and Launceston in Tasmania. Queensland had to have more than one workshop system simply because for many decades it operated isolated sections based on the ports at Brisbane, Rockhampton and Townsville. The first railway workshops were opened in Ipswich in 1865, and began building wagons and other rolling stock right from their inception. The shops soon had to move to a bigger site and, over the years, evolved into a large industrial complex with about fifty separate buildings. It had its own powerhouse and sawmill. During the steam era, Ipswich turned out more than two hundred new steam locomotives. Victoria built satellite workshops in various locations, notably at Ballarat and Bendigo. South Australia had a large workshop complex at Peterborough.

While New South Wales had a policy of importing locomotives up until federation, Victoria decided it would manufacture as many as it could (although this began at the Williamstown plant which preceded Newport) or buy locally. South Australia also played a role in locomotive building. William Thow, who went on to be chief mechanical engineer with New South Wales Government Railways, designed the R class 4–6–0 machine during his time in Adelaide, which formed the basis of the New South Wales P class. E. E. Lucy, who followed Thow as the chief mechanical engineer in Sydney, was a noted designer: he was responsible for the NN class first built in 1914.

Railway workshops played an important role during the two world wars with their equipment and manpower being harnessed to make weaponry. Indeed, this work took priority over the normal rolling stock work. In Victoria, Newport workshops were a vital part of the war effort in both conflicts. Between 1914 and 1918, the works manufactured high explosive and shrapnel shells; in the second war, Newport built 1,364 fuselages for Beaufort fighter bombers and the hulls for eight ocean-going tug boats.

The private sector played as important a part in the development of rolling stock. The Phoenix Foundry at Ballarat was founded in 1855 and was producing locomotives for Victorian Railways from 1873. In all, the foundry produced 351 railway engines. The first was Victorian Railways' No. 83, a 0–6–0, and among the classes produced were the Q, with their elegant green painted domes, the K and U. While largely adapted from Beyer Peacock designed in Britain, Phoenix did not import any prototypes and did all the design work in Ballarat. Initially, it transported the locomotives from its works to the railway line nearby on flat-bed road vehicles, but in 1883 a line was laid to the foundry, along two streets and crossing the tramlines. New engines would be hauled out of the works to a turntable in the middle of the road, and steamed down the street. Phoenix did its test runs on Saturdays between Ballarat and Lal Lal. From 1905, the government's Newport workshops took over all locomotive construction and by 1906 Phoenix was out of business.

Victoria Foundry, also in Ballarat, built Victorian Railways' first locomotive and about 200 in all, although some of these were for other Australian colonies.

In Queensland, there was Walkers Limited. The company built its first locomotive in 1873, a vertical boiler 0–4–0, 3 ft 3 in gauge engine for a tramway near Gympie. In 1896, the company successfully tendered to build thirty locomotives for Queensland Government Railways, all B15 class 4–6–0 goods engines (to be numbered 299–328). The company also received an order from the Chillagoe Railway and Mining Company for B15 engines in 1898. By the outbreak of World War I, Walkers were turning out a locomotive a week for QGR. Walkers successfully made the switch into diesel and diesel–electric locomotive building in the 1950s.

Clyde Engineering (formerly Hudson Brothers) was one of the mainstays of rolling stock construction in New South Wales. With a plant and sidings in the Sydney suburb of Clyde, it began making rolling stock in 1898. A highlight of its history was the agreement with General Electric in 1949 — the first done with a company outside the United States — to make the American company's locomotives under licence. It thereafter became an exporter to Asia, New Zealand and the Pacific. In October 1970, Clyde Engineering had on its order books eighteen diesel–electric locomotives for Commonwealth Railways, six X Class for Victorian Railways, and one diesel–hydraulic engine for a Queensland sugar mill.

ABOVE: A somewhat derelict North Box at Demondrille, New South Wales in 2003 with the gable of what was the stationmaster's residence seen in the distance. Rod McGregor, sitting on the steps, was born at Demondrille while his father Jack was in charge there. *Don McGregor.*

LEFT: Wagin is no longer an island platform where passenger trains steam in from either direction, the passengers tumbling out of the carriages for tea, beer and sandwiches. This recent photograph shows how one set of tracks has been lifted. *Don Copley.*

FOLLOWING SPREAD: Wheat loading, 21st century style. This shows a typical harvest scene in Western Australia with state-of-the-art technology both on and off the rails. *Co-operative Bulk Handling.*

ABOVE: Narrow gauge only today, a railcar excursion has reached the border town of Wallangarra on 24 January 2004. The cars are 2034 and 2036. *Brian Webber.*

RIGHT: The trains don't stop here any more. The now deserted Serviceton station once housed large numbers of staff from both South Australian Railways and Victorian Railways — at separate ends — in the days when locomotives and crews changed at the border. Here, a special with army vehicles powers through this grand station in 1995. *Jennifer Norton.*

WHAT EVERY GOOD DRIVER AND FIREMAN NEEDED

Nothing was easy work in the early decades of the railways in the era before cranes, it was a daily task to carry coal by hand to locomotives. These railwaymen at Petersburg (later Peterborough) are fuelling a Y Class tender in the 1890s using wicker baskets. *John Mannion collection.*

Steam locomotives in New South Wales were typically equipped with the following:

· one shovel
· two tins of oil for lubricating side rods, wheel boxes, pistons, valves and air pumps
· a hand lamp with white, green and red shades for signalling if needed
· a bucket
· two cans for dispensing oil
· two flare lamps
· one brush
· a bottle of kerosene
· cotton waste
· spanners
· syringe to remove water from wheel boxes
· a packet of detonators to place on the track in case of emergency to warn other trains

2

TOWNS THE RAILWAYS MADE

THE RAILWAYS MADE or dominated towns all over Australia. Penrith, now a dormitory suburb within the vast urban sprawl of Sydney and just another station on the suburban network, was once a railway town. At one count in its early days, fifty drivers and fifty-seven firemen were based there. Midland Junction, now part of Perth, was, in the early days of the colony, a separate settlement about 16 km from the colony's capital. Its prominence was due to it being an important railway junction, and for this reason, it was selected as the site for the government railway workshops. At its zenith the workshops employed more than one thousand mechanics and other workers. Another one hundred and fifty men worked at the Midland Railway Company workshops nearby. The railway reached Midland on 11 March 1884. Its initial growth was due to its being a transhipment centre between the rolling stock and the wagons and drays that serviced the settlements beyond the railhead.

Most rail towns, however, were in regional areas. They were usually created because of distance factors, often spaced out according to where locomotives and crews were changed in the days of steam. In the case of two New South Wales' rail depots, Murrurundi and Valley Heights, the location was chosen for maintaining banking locomotives; that is, the second or more steam engines placed on a train to pull or push it up a section of steep grade. Alpha in Queensland was also a place for banking locomotives to assist in the climb from Bogantungan. In this case, however, Alpha was at the top end of the grade but it was, as is explained below, the only place in the area with good supplies of water. This meant that every time the locomotives provided the banking muscle on the 12.9 km grind up the steep grade, those same banking engines would be required to run light the 72 km from their depot at Alpha to pick up the train at Bogantungan.

Around the drivers, firemen and guards would cluster all the administrators — sometimes up to district traffic managers and their equivalents in other branches of the railways. Often gangs of fettlers would also be based there, as well as along the tracks where they would maintain their 40 km or so of track. Where there were locomotive depots, so there were cleaners, shunters and shed hands. In some

53

rail towns, as many as sixty per cent of the workforce would be involved in the railways.

These towns varied from ones that existed only because of the railway — like Alpha or Werris Creek in New South Wales — and so declined once steam was replaced by diesel and neither locomotive changes nor water supplies were required any longer. Then there was the railway town that had an economic base outside the railways, but where the arrival of the trains and those employed to keep them running meant a substantial increase in their importance.

Wherever the trains stopped, activity radiated out through the town. In Harden, New South Wales, on the line south to the border and Melbourne, as well as the origin and destination of trains working the busy branch line to Blayney from 1885, the hotels were constantly full of people staying until the train for the next stage of their journey was ready to leave. The hotels employed porters around the clock; every train was met by hotel staff, ready to shepherd travellers and their luggage to their employers' hospitality. Harden is just one of many 'railway towns'. At its peak, the station had 270 people on the payroll; and, like most, there is precious little today to indicate how important it once was. The refreshment rooms closed in 1957 and the rolling stock maintenance depot in 1967.

Then there were the towns that were important rail centres, but cannot quite be classed as 'railway towns'. Port Augusta, while not a railway town in that it had an independent catalyst, was, more than any other place in South Australia, the state's railway hub. Through it passed trains bound for Western Australia across the Nullarbor or freight trains and the Ghan off to Alice Springs in the Northern Territory (and, since the beginning of 2004, to Darwin). Running southwards from Port Augusta is the standard gauge line to Whyalla; to the south-east is the standard gauge link to Adelaide; eastwards lies Broken Hill and Sydney; and to the north, runs the line to the Leigh Creek coalfields (and, once, the connection to the narrow gauge Central Australia Railway which, when conceived, was to have run all the way to Darwin). Port Augusta was assured of its significant role first, by the building of the transcontinental line to Kalgoorlie and secondly, the standardisation of the existing narrow gauge link to Broken Hill. It was also the base for the Tea and Sugar, the weekly supply train for railway staff and their families located along the Trans-Australian line.

Pinnaroo was the end of the line for South Australian Railways' intrastate haulage in this section of the Mallee country farmed for wheat and sheep, with the line continuing to the border where it joined the Victorian broad gauge track from Ouyen. Located 243 km east of Adelaide, Pinnaroo's grain loading facilities define the town's function as a service town. In the days before the railway, conditions were so harsh — long distances for supplies, trouble with dingos killing the sheep, shortage of water — that by 1889 many farms had been abandoned. It was the arrival of the railway in 1906 that ensured that crops of wheat could be taken quickly and efficiently to the markets that saw the town develop. The town's name is widely held to mean 'big men', 'great men' or 'old men' in a number of Aboriginal languages. However, the Pinnaroo line was built on the cheap with light rails, which limited both the speeds at which trains could travel and also the axle loads over the track. All freight had to be transported in the smaller N class wagons; larger wagons were unloaded at Murray Bridge and freight transferred to the N fleet. So, the railway did make

It still looks grand, but a closer inspection of Moss Vale station shows that parts of the building need restoration. *Claire Henderson.*

the area but Pinnaroo never became a 'railway town' in the sense that is used here.

Moss Vale, south of Sydney, is another that just misses out on the definition.

It certainly has the type of magnificent station building that denotes its importance on the rail network. The original structure was built in 1867, and then in 1890 a Vice-Regal waiting room was added (complete with chandelier) to serve the New South Wales Governor who had a country house in the Southern Highlands. A year later, a hotel and refreshment room were added (there is still a refreshment stall there today). All the country and interstate trains heading south from Sydney stopped at Moss Vale for refreshments, while the station was also important as a junction with the line to Unanderra via Robertson, a cross-country route to Wollongong.

Farther south, there was Goulburn. This was an important rail centre, but the railways were not the dominant economic activity. When the tracks reached Goulburn from Sydney, it flourished as an assembly point for wool, wheat and other agricultural products to be loaded aboard trains for Sydney. The government also built repair shops there.

Recalling every town in Australia that was made, to some degree, by the railway would fill this entire volume. Instead, below is a selection taken from across the continent.

NEW SOUTH WALES
Albury
Located 646 km from Sydney
When Victoria's North East Railway opened on 19 November 1873, providing a fast connection

between Melbourne and Wodonga, the fortunes of the New South Wales' border town of Albury went into decline. The new cheap form of travel meant people living in the northern border area of Victoria could conduct their business and shopping in Melbourne almost as easily as they could cross the river in Albury. The line inching south from Sydney reached Bowning in 1876, which meant that the balance of the journey to and from Albury involved taking a road coach. In total, the trip between Sydney and Albury took thirty-nine hours before the construction of the line. In October 1880 alone, the coach owner Gregory Crawford & Co. booked four hundred and twenty passengers between Albury and the railhead.

Finally, the town got its rail link with the completion of the Great Southern Railway on 3 February 1881. Albury was to become an important railway centre because it was the transfer point between the standard gauge of New South Wales and the broad gauge of Victoria (although the two systems were initially not linked, the connection across the border still requiring horse-drawn vehicles for passengers and goods for a further two years). The station was built to befit its role as the southern rampart of the New South Wales rail network, clearly intended to impress the Victorians across the border. It cost £24,000 to build.

By 1886, the Victorians acknowledged Albury as being the interchange station between the two systems. The extent of the lack of co-operation between the Victorian and New South Wales railway systems was evinced by the fact that it was not until November 1923, or forty years after the rail link was laid across the Murray River, that it became possible to have a break of journey if you had bought an interstate rail ticket. (Initially, Wodonga station

had two clocks — one for Albury time and one for Wodonga — as there was a twenty-five minute difference between the two until Eastern Standard Time was introduced.)

From the opening of its railway station, Albury was an important destination for New South Wales' prestige trains. In 1925, the train named Sydney Express began running. In May 1941, the Daylight Riverina Express was extended to Albury having previously terminated at Wagga Wagga, and became a service that supplemented the overnight Albury Mail. Then, in 1938, the Spirit of Progress began running through to Albury from Melbourne. The platform was extended and its length was such that two NSW trains could be accommodated along it. From 1949, the Riverina Express became a fully air-conditioned train.

Junee

Located 456 km by rail from Sydney

This is one of New South Wales' most important rail junctions, sitting 301 metres above sea level, as it is the town at which traffic from many of the Riverina lines converges. In the steam era, its locomotive sheds were built to handle the largest locomotives in the state's system; the building completed in 1947 was the biggest locomotive roundhouse in New South Wales. In 1863, the town was gazetted as 'Jewnee'. The rail line from Sydney was opened to traffic as far as Junee on 6 July 1878, with the line reaching a spot some 6.4 km east of the settlement named Junee Junction. The latter was renamed Junee in 1885, being proclaimed a municipality a year later. The existing station buildings were completed in 1883 after the colonial authorities decided upon Junee as the regional

operation centre because it was strategically placed as an important junction of the main south line and several of the important Riverina branches. Wagga Wagga interests had lobbied hard but unsuccessfully for their town to be the rail junction for a new line to Narrandera, thence to Jerilderie, Hay and eventually Adelaide.

Unlike other New South Wales rail towns, the tracks in Junee are not at the edge of the settlement. Instead, the railway splits the town because the settlement grew around the station. This building was quickly followed by the erection of a locomotive servicing depot, and later by a goods shed with a three-ton crane. By 1885, the coming of the railway south from Sydney had pushed the town's population from about one hundred to more than twelve hundred.

The new station, described as a railway palace, was completed in 1885 at a cost of £10,000. It was topped by a mansard roof, and the building accommodated a spacious ladies' waiting room and a general waiting room. Post office and telegraph services were also provided at the station. The main platform was covered by a veranda supported by cast iron columns. Rainwater from the roof was collected in underground tanks.

By 1891, it was decided that the existing refreshment rooms were too small. A new wing was constructed to accommodate the rooms as well as a billiard room and samples room for commercial travellers to display their wares. Another nineteen bedrooms were added to the overnight accommodation capacity. The station became even busier in the 1920s when more lines were opened to serve the Riverina region.

Dieselisation was not so great a blow for Junee as it had been for Werris Creek, a settlement that was almost

RIGHT: **It was probably Australia's least impressive terminus on a trunk line — Birdum, population 25, at the end of the track from Darwin. Here Johnny O'Sullivan and Colleen Lunn watch the birdie outside the general store, by this time under the management of M. E. Jacobsen. In the 1940s, the townsfolk took themselves and their buildings to Larrimah.** *Peter Dunham collection.*

OPPOSITE ABOVE: **Junee, railway town. In this undated early photograph, the camera has captured the size of the marshalling yards and the imposing station building.** *Junee and District Historical Society.*

OPPOSITE BELOW: **Narrandera railway yards and station, 1929. This shows a mixed train at the main platform and a bay platform for local passenger services.** *Narrandera Shire Council.*

entirely a creation of the railway. Junee, by contrast, had benefited from the rail opening up the area for farming, so that when the labour-intensive steam era ended, the town had a more diverse economy. Cunnamulla in Queensland and Mullewa in Western Australia are similar examples.

Narrandera

Located 578 km by rail from Sydney

In 1946, there were one hundred and seventy two people employed at Narrandera railway station. There were drivers and firemen for the steam locomotives stabled there or running through, thirty-two guards, track maintenance crews (four-man teams for every fifteen miles, or 24 km, of line), and all the station and freight-handling staff down to junior porters. It was an important junction providing the Riverina with rail connections to both Sydney and Melbourne. Lines radiated out in four directions: to the west, there was the branch line to Hay, 111 km away; to the north-west, the rails passed through Griffith and the Murrumbidgee Irrigation Area before joining the Broken Hill line at Roto; eastwards was Junee, an even more important railway junction on the Sydney–Melbourne main line; to the south ran the standard gauge line through Jerilderie to meet the Victorian broad gauge at Tocumwal on the border, 180 km away. (Today, much of the Hay line is mothballed, as is the Narrandera–Tocumwal section; trains on the north-west line now run only as far as Hillston, and the connection to the main west line is closed.)

In its day, Narrandera was an important freight centre. Superphosphate came up the line from Melbourne and was unloaded there. The daily Train 416, sometimes as heavy as 500 tonnes (a considerable load in steam days), transported fruit and livestock to the Darling Harbour

goods yard in Sydney. The station's importance diminished considerably with the closure of the line to Victoria via Tocumwal in 1986. In 2002, there were just eight track workers employed in the area, while the grand old 1881 station was leased as a cafe.

Werris Creek

Located 410 km by rail from Sydney

The railway reached the town in 1878 and it soon became one of the busiest railway towns in Australia with traffic passing through to north and north-east NSW. Werris Creek had extensive marshalling yards and a railway workshop. Today, the large station building remains the dominant structure in the town. The town has also been known as 'Werries Creek'.

Werris Creek township was formed when, in August 1877, about five hundred railway navvies set up an encampment there as part of William Wakeford's construction gang given the task of building the line between Murrurundi and Tamworth. In 1879, when a branch line was opened as far as Breeza and then Gunnedah, Werris Creek became a railway junction, eventually serving three lines: the northern line to Tamworth and eventually Wallangarra on the Queensland border; the north-western line to Gunnedah and Narrabri; and the western line to Dubbo via Binnaway. There was also, of course, the southern line to Newcastle and Sydney. The staff numbers soared once the Dubbo route was opened on 5 November 1923.

Even when Chris Holley joined the railways in the early 1950s, there were eight hundred people employed at Werris Creek. It was, he says, the town that never slept with trains passing through around the clock. Goods

AFTER THE RAILS ARE GONE

JUST AS WITH MINING, there can be something akin to a railway ghost town. Morgan, in South Australia, was once the second busiest port after Adelaide thanks to the railway and its location on the 'Great Bend' on the Murray River. It became an important transhipment point in the 1850s and into the 1860s. A railway from Kapunda was opened on 23 September 1878, and Morgan was then proclaimed a town (although South Australian Railways originally called the terminus 'North West Bend'). At the zenith of its importance, Morgan saw six trains a day leave on the broad gauge line to Adelaide. But inevitably the river trade disappeared as it was overtaken by the rail and road. Morgan lost its railway branch line on 2 November 1969, and today is a stop for tourists wanting to recapture the old days along the Murray.

Werris Creek in its declining days. On Saturday 8 February 1986, a 900 Class railcar set (907/854/958) stands in the new locomotive maintenance shed at Werris Creek for the last time. A few hours later the trio worked the last daylight rail service to Moree. In the adjacent road sit 44224 and 4489, which, along with other locomotives, continued to visit the depot for maintenance. *John Currey.*

traffic was still growing in the 1950s and 1960s and, by the end of the business week, there would be such an enormous backlog of freight waiting to be moved that trains would be despatched almost every half-hour on Saturdays and Sundays. About fifty locomotives were based at Werris Creek, but on these busy weekends other motive power would run light from Newcastle to cope with the wagons traffic. Often, the infrastructure could not cope with the number of trains being generated out of Werris Creek. Trains could take twelve hours to make the 122 km trip to Muswellbrook. Intermediate stations such as Quirindi or Willow Tree could be holding two or three trains at a time on their sidings waiting for the right of way on the next single track section. On one occasion, Chris Holley was a guard aboard a train that spent eight and a half hours at Willow Tree waiting for a banking engine to help it tackle the onward grade.

To cater to staff needs outside working hours there was the Railway Institute, located in Anzac Parade, which included a main hall equipped with a piano as well as a library, a newspaper reading room, a classroom for the weekly lectures held at the institute, and a billiard room. Regular weekly dances were held there, organised week about by the Catholic and Protestant churches. Such was the tradition of families working generation after generation in the railways that Mr Holley's wife worked at the Werris Creek refreshment rooms while her grandfather had been the Railway Institute's librarian. The membership fee in the 1950s was ten shillings a year.

Of the eight hundred people employed at the station before diesel locomotives took over all the motive power work, more than seventy were employed just in the first floor office area. In 1939, several additions were made to the station including new offices and telegraph room. The station saw even more than usual traffic during World War II as troop trains passed through. Also, more freight was put on rail after coastal shipping was considered in danger from Japanese forces; such was the concern about coastal raids by the Japanese that many troop trains and war freight was sent through Werris Creek and on to the break of gauge station at Wallangarra, Queensland, even though logistically it would have been simpler to run them on the standard gauge track right into Brisbane. The staff of the refreshment rooms resorted to assembling trestle tables on the platform in order to cope with the large numbers of servicemen coming on each train.

A coal mine was opened near the town in 1925 to provide fuel for the locomotives, and this mine closed in 1963 when dieselisation took hold. The first uncertainty about the future began in 1960 as more and more trains were hauled by diesel–electric locomotives. Introduction of dining cars also led to the decline of the once important refreshment rooms; they staggered on with reduced staff until closure in October 1972. The locomotive workshops closed in the early 1970s, and this sent a shock through the town — commercial development ceased as the writing was on the wall for the future. The last steam working occurred in 1973.

The station building befitted the status of this northern railway junction. It is made up of two linked buildings: the two-storeyed railway refreshment rooms built in 1884 and the administration building which went up in three stages: stage one in 1885; stage two in 1925 as a second storey to accommodate the district superintendent and his staff relocated from Murrurundi; and stage three in 1939 to provide space for the expanded train control section needed to handle all the additional train movements

HOW TO LOSE MONEY

WHILE COUNTRY PEOPLE inevitably fought the closure of their railway lines, many of these branches were a burden on the taxpayer for much, if not all, of their lives. The Tumbarumba branch in southern New South Wales was such a case. This 130 km line from Wagga Wagga to Tumbarumba was a loss-maker from the start. The first section, to Humula, cost £355,152 to build. In its first full year of operation, after being opened in 1917, the trains earned £5,754 but the section's expenses amounted to £8,143. This was not much of a return on the capital investment in an era of no competition from road transport. The final section to Tumbarumba was opened in 1921, having added another £412,405 to the construction cost. Fortunately for the taxpayers, nature intervened, washing away part of the line in 1974 and ensuring its permanent closure.

expected during the war. The station had platforms either side to serve the lines which converged in the yard. In 1880, a post office was located in the complex, with the stationmaster also being appointed postmaster. The original building on the site was constructed of kauri pine from New Zealand, and, in 1885, a new brick refreshments room was erected. The staff numbers started to climb in 1917 when Werris Creek was designated the main northern depot of the mechanical branch of the NSW Government Railways. The district superintendent was stationed there. The refreshment rooms were open around the clock and the station also had bedrooms to accommodate travellers, mainly commercial travellers.

In October 2002, State Rail launched its Australian Railway Monument at Werris Creek.

NORTHERN TERRITORY
Larrimah and Birdum

Larrimah located 500.9 km from Darwin, Birdum 509.3 km from Darwin

The two towns were just 8.4 km apart by rail and their railway lives were intertwined. While Birdum was the southern terminus of the North Australia Railway, the town to its north was regarded as the natural terminus in the latter years of the operation. Larrimah was where highway and rail met; it became the main transhipment centre during World War II and from then on, Birdum was an inconvenient backwater. However, until a new triangle was installed so that locomotives could turn at Larrimah, the engines still had to run through to Birdum to turn, de-ash and take on fuel and water. This, of course, ended with the introduction of diesel–electric traction in 1956. From 1958, Larrimah became the official terminus. So

much was Larrimah a railway town that, when the NAR closed in 1976, it meant the end of the town, just as Birdum virtually disappeared once its railway life ended. Commonwealth Railways removed its diesel generator that had provided electricity to the locals at Larrimah, and the school soon closed.

Birdum was the official southern terminus from 1929. However, from 1940 the majority of rail movements terminated at Larrimah. Most of the people moved away between 1942 and 1945, and they took most of the building materials with them. However, the Birdum Hotel was not fully relocated at Larrimah until about 1953. Until 1939, the normal practice for those travelling up from the south was to drive their cars to Birdum, then catch the train onward.

Birdum was never much of a town. There was the hotel (where people stayed while they waited for the next train), a general store, and some houses (mostly railway dwellings). A boarding house opened in 1933. When the police or a priest was needed, they came from Mataranka. The station was equipped with a turning triangle, goods shed, water tank and locomotive shed. Water was provided from Birdum Creek, about 3 km away, and pumped to the overhead vat for the steam engines and to the townspeople.

When the line reached Birdum, there still existed plans to take it on to Daly Waters and clearing work was done for rail laying — some materials were even brought south for the work. An airstrip was built upon the opening of the railway, the idea being that mail would be flown from Brisbane and then taken by train to Darwin and other centres. By 1934, Qantas was flying into Birdum with the mail, although a post office had been opened in 1932. The best estimate of population in the 1930s was that about

Now it is passed by a modern railway, but in 1980 the old Pine Creek station looks to be in a sad state just four years after the closure of the old narrow gauge line. *Northern Territory Information Service.*

twenty-five people lived there, although it is unclear whether this included the fettlers who worked on the line from Birdum.

The end began when the authorities in Canberra decided to improve the road from Birdum to Tennant Creek. The new formation would bypass Birdum and instead take road travellers directly to Larrimah. This road was sealed by 1943.

The first timetable for trains at Birdum allowed for a mixed train to depart each fortnight, leaving Darwin at 8.00 am on Wednesday and arriving at the new southern terminus at 2.17 am the next morning. Before a hotel was built, the passengers would doss down in the carriages until daylight. Eventually, the Sentinel–Cammell railcar offered a passenger service to Birdum on alternative weeks.

QUEENSLAND
Alpha

Located 1,061 km from Brisbane on the Central Line from Rockhampton to Winton

The railway from Emerald reached Alpha on 22 September 1884 and, until the following June when the section opened to Jericho, it was a busy railhead. It was the site of a large railway construction camp due to its good underground water supply, a factor that also was to determine it as an important locomotive depot for the entire steam era. In fact, during the droughts of the late 1800s, water was carted by train from Alpha to Jericho without which that town might not have survived. Eddie Hoch, who still lives in Alpha, recalls that more than twenty steam locomotives were based in the town; that so

many engines were required was due to the difficult grades over the Drummond Range between Alpha and Bogantungan. It was usual for two locomotives to be required on goods trains mounting the steep grade on that part of the line.

The railway was the main generator of employment in Alpha and, until the cattle industry developed, the railway was the main reason for the town's existence. The steam era required not just drivers and firemen, but cleaners and servicing staff for the engines. Coal had to be shovelled into locomotives, the fires dropped and boilers cleaned. In fact, the locomotive depot lasted well into the diesel era. Railways continued to be the main mode of transport until, in 1984, the Capricorn Highway was opened and the areas along the Central Line were at last serviceable by semi-trailer lorries.

Apart from all the through traffic, Alpha was also the base for locomotives operating on the Yaraka branch line, a section noted for its high volume of livestock traffic as well as general goods. A dining car crew was based at Alpha in the steam-era days before the diesel-hauled Midlander came into service (which is now called the Spirit of the Outback, running to Longreach rather than Winton). The car was attached to the train when it arrived at 6.00 am, then hauled to Longreach for the serving of breakfast. The car returned on the afternoon departure from Longreach with the staff serving a meal before the car was detached for its overnight stay at Alpha.

In 1885, records show that 6,082 passengers passed through the station, along with more than 10,000 bales of wool.

Cunnamulla

Located 971 km from Brisbane

Before the railway arrived, Cunnamulla was an important staging post for horse-drawn traffic to the vast hinterland of south-west Queensland and northern New South Wales. A brewery was established there more than a decade before the arrival of the first train. Cobb and Co. ran a pack-horse service from Cunnamulla to Bourke, NSW, and coaches to the west.

This railway station was opened to traffic on 10 October 1898. The railway line was to have continued to Thargomindah, but that was one of the many marginal railway projects never completed. Once the rail had reached Cunnamulla, the town became a focal point for the vast hinterland of south-western Queensland. Until then, the region had depended largely on the river boats that came up the Darling as far as Bourke across the border. In the first nine months of operation, 1,535 passengers bought tickets at Cunnamulla station while trains during that period hauled 1,090 tons of wool and 41,100 head of sheep out of the town.

Douglas MacGregor has lived most of his life at Cunnamulla, and much of that was spent being associated with the railway in one way or another. In 1951, he took over his father's trucking business; the lorries carried wool in from properties in that region and returned with all the equipment and supplies needed by the pastoralists. Before motorised transport became widely available, there had been eighty-three wagon teams (horses, bullocks or camels) operating in and out of Cunnamulla. Cattle and sheep were also transported in large numbers on the rail,

especially after stock sales in Cunnamulla. The 1950s, and the early 1960s, were boom years for Cunnamulla. This was the era when wool fetched 'a pound for a pound' — one pound sterling for one pound weight of wool — largely due to the stockpiling of the commodity during and after the Korean War. Based in the town were fifteen sheep dealers, twelve shearing contractors and twenty-two droving teams. However, this period also saw the erosion of the railway's predominance. First, roads were being improved, which made it feasible for freight to be sent by truck instead of train. Secondly, the ten-month strike by shearers which ended in 1956 meant that railway workers would not handle 'black' wool — that is, fleece which had been shorn by non-union labour — nor shunt wagons carrying that wool. The upshot was that the road operators were able to win, and win permanently, much of the freight which had once been consigned by train.

Mr MacGregor eventually sold the trucking business, and took a job with Queensland Railways. He worked first as a fettler maintaining the track until a vacancy came up for a porter at Cunnamulla station. In the 1950s, there were twelve people in the traffic branch of the station, along with six men in the maintenance gang, their responsibility being twenty-two miles (35.4 km) of track from Cunnamulla. In those days, there were fettlers' camps about every thirty miles on the line. In addition, two women were employed to clean the Westlander when it arrived from Brisbane, while another two looked after the sleeping quarters used by train crews. In its heyday, Cunnamulla yard was usually busy: trains arrived with dry goods, perishables, timber and stock feed (the latter

LEFT: **The arrival of the rail at Cunnamulla did nothing to harm the incomes of the local hauliers; they still kept busy bringing wool and livestock to the railhead and distributing supplies and equipment coming up from Brisbane to the local pastoralists. Here, the first load of wool to be brought to Cunnamulla by motor lorry was captured for a postcard of the day.** *Doug MacGregor collection.*

OPPOSITE: **Petrol was an important source of business for railways in the days before modern road tankers. A load has arrived at Cunnamulla.** *Doug MacGregor collection.*

particularly in times of drought). Sheep and cattle were moved through the yard, both going to the works and new stock coming in from other parts of Queensland. Wool trains would carry up to fifteen hundred bales of wool, and Doug MacGregor and his colleagues in the goods shed could load as many as one thousand bales a day into waiting wagons.

SOUTH AUSTRALIA
Cockburn

Located 433 km by rail from Adelaide via Terowie
This station came into being largely because the New South Wales Government would not allow South Australia to extend its line across the border into Broken Hill, the route to Port Pirie being the most economic for the ore from the mines in the Silver City. In 1886, New South Wales passed the *Silverton Tramway Act* to allow a company of that name to operate the 48 km between Broken Hill and the South Australian Railways terminus at Cockburn. The first train left Cockburn on 11 June 1887, and initially, the service to South Australia comprised a mixed train each day and two goods-only trains each week in each direction. Such was the growth of traffic that, by 1908, there were thirty trains moving in each direction on a daily basis. In 1915, South Australian Railways decided that all stations on the line would be staffed twenty-four hours a day to handle the increasing traffic.

Iris Williams, one of only twenty-eight people still living in Cockburn, recalls the 1950s when about 900 called the town home (at one stage, it had reached a population of 1,500). Most of the families had at least one member employed either by the government railways or the Silverton Company. Iris Williams' father was employed by the latter as a fencer, his job being to look after the fences along the line to Broken Hill, and she is proud of the fact that many of those fences are still standing. The bulk of the traffic coming through was comprised of ore shipments from Broken Hill, but the Cockburn yards were often busy with livestock shipments after cattle and sheep were brought down the Birdsville and Strzelecki tracks. SAR maintained a locomotive depot and workshops at Cockburn, while the Silverton administration, including a railmaster for that end of the line, was located just across the border at a small station called Burns. Cockburn had two railway barracks as well as houses for the married men. The local cricket team played home and away matches against a pub team from Broken Hill.

Sole contact with the outside was the Broken Hill Express which came up from Terowie on the narrow gauge. Each week, Iris Williams' mother would send a telegram to the butcher in Peterborough specifying 'One sausages, one mince, one (something else) and a whole sheep'. This consignment would arrive in the refrigerated van and be collected by the children from the station — not a job they relished given the weight of the whole sheep. For other shopping, visiting friends or attending to medical matters, the family would catch the express the short distance to Broken Hill. That meant joining the train at 4.00 am and not getting home until 9.00 pm that evening. The journey to Adelaide required considerably more endurance. The express travelled at a maximum speed of 56 km/h and for the Williams family it was an all-night journey sitting up. The railways provided foot-warmers in the winter and plenty of blankets were made

THE MOST UNDER-USED RAILWAY

IN 1927, THE VICTORIAN Government authorised the building of a line from Robinvale on the Murray River across into NSW and on for 48.5 km to a point on the map marked Lette. The land along the proposed line was sandy scrub land, capable of supporting an occasional wheat crop but only under the most propitious weather conditions. A road-rail bridge was built across the river complete with a central lifting span. Laying of rail continued until, at a distance of 22.5 km from Robinvale, work was suspended. By this time it was 1929 and the economic downturn led to severely reduced government spending. But three stations, complete with platforms and sidings, had been completed at Euston, Benanee and Koorake. The Railway Construction Branch retained control and ran the line under a 'trains as required' basis. Between 1929 and 1935, the average use of the line was *one train a year*. The line was abandoned after 1935

available. There were no refreshment stops along the way, so you packed your own food for the night — and plenty of passengers brought liquor along to help them get through the long night. Upon reaching Terowie in the early morning, it was a case of 'all out' of the narrow gauge carriages and a short walk across planks placed between the lines to the broad gauge train standing at the main platform. Half-awake passengers would drag themselves and their luggage out of the carriages and into the cold night air.

Marree

Located 709 km by rail from Adelaide;
365 km from Port Augusta

Marree was formerly called Hergott Springs, named, with one spelling error, after a German naturalist and artist, D. D. Herrgott, who found the spring which provided the local water supply. The name 'Marree', which became generally accepted from about 1918 even though formally adopted long before, came from an Aboriginal term meaning 'place of possums'.

The narrow gauge railway reached Hergott Springs in 1884 via Quorn. Its completion brought to full life the now famed Birdsville Track, with Marree being the assembly point for cattle driven from inland properties. Even after the line was extended to Oodnadatta in 1891, the Afghan camel drivers operated for many years out of Marree, distributing the supplies and goods that came up on the train to properties along the Birdsville Track or north of Marree. In 1910, it was reported that 1,500 camels were operating out of Marree. J.W. Gregory, writing at the beginning of the twentieth century, described the

township which he visited on a tour with a party of geologists from Glasgow University. His first impression of the tiny place and its surrounding countryside was one of dreary monotony and aching barrenness, the ground a wasteland of sand and pebbles. 'As we landed from the train, we found the platform redolent with Afghan, impressing on us the fact that Hergott is one of the leading caravan centres in Australia,' he wrote.

When a new standard gauge line was built from Port Augusta to serve the coal trains from Leigh Creek, it was decided to extend the gauge conversion through to Marree because of the volume of cattle needing to be moved by rail, this being completed by March 1958. Marree once again became the railhead in 1980 when the narrow gauge line to Alice Springs was closed upon the opening of the new Tarcoola–Alice Springs standard gauge line. The town staged a lively party for the last running of the old Ghan train, even though its departure signalled almost immediate decline for Marree.

Peterborough

Located 247.5 km north by rail from Adelaide

This town, 533 metres above sea level and recognised nationally as a classic railway town, was established in 1880 as Petersburg, being named in honour of Peter Doecke, one of the first agriculturalists to take up land in the district. The change of name took place in 1917 due to World War I and antipathy toward anything German. This included renaming streets such as Kaiser Wilhelm and Bismarck along with those bearing the names of early German settlers in the district. Kaiser Wilhelm became Brown Street, Herrman became Badger, Glogau was

A typical country scene — the Dirranbandi Mail at Dirranbandi in 1986 with utility vehicles collecting consignments from the brake van. *John Beckhaus.*

henceforth Bridges, while Bismarck Street was renamed after a more suitable hero, Kitchener.

Today the town is best known for the fact that it was a triple-gauge station — that is, its track work could accommodate narrow, standard and broad gauge trains. But that was for a relatively short period of its history, from 1970 until 1988. The 85 ft (26 metre) turntable and heritage-listed roundhouse still have three-gauge capability. Peterborough was an important rail centre long before 1970. It had the biggest railway workshops in South Australia outside the Islington complex in Adelaide and was the headquarters for the Peterborough division that reached to Cockburn on the New South Wales border, north to Quorn and on the western and southern rail approaches. With all the gangers, fettlers and porters strung out at various stations and camps, there were about 1,800 people employed within the division at its zenith, with about 1,000 of these located in Peterborough itself. Apart from station and workshops staff and train crews, the division employed draftsmen, carpenters, painters, plumbers and even a stonemason. The district superintendent's house had an attached schoolroom where staff were instructed in railway rules and other subjects. Train crews were accommodated overnight in barracks.

Rails reached Peterborough in January 1881 with the narrow gauge connection to Port Pirie, and then in November the lines reached up from the south providing a connection to Adelaide via Terowie. By November, the line was opened northwards to Orroroo, and extended to Quorn in 1882. However, it was the opening of the Petersburg–Cockburn narrow gauge railway that established the town's role. By a traffic agreement between South Australian Railways and the Silverton Tramway Company, ore was carried over both systems from Broken Hill without transhipment at the border. Then the expansion of the north-eastern goldfields led the South Australian Government to erect a ten-head battery and cyanide works near the railway workshops to provide local goldminers with a reliable means of extracting their gold from ore; this operated until the early 1990s.

The standard gauge would remain until 1988 when the line north to Euralia was closed. The broad gauge arrived in 1968 when the line from Terowie was converted from narrow gauge, and then the standard gauge line from Broken Hill was opened in 1970. Many argue, with some force, that it would have been cheaper to convert all the lines to standard gauge much earlier given the cost of maintaining three sets of tracks and all the rolling stock of differing wheel width. It is an interesting sidelight that when the South Australian Railways Commissioner, William Webb, ordered a new roundhouse for Peterborough in 1927, it was constructed to accommodate broad gauge locomotives although it was to be another forty-one years before such engines could travel to the town.

The town was important because it was a junction on two main routes: east–west and north–south. John Mannion, a local historian, said it was an insular place — an industrial town surrounded by a conservative farming population. For example, the four local Australian Rules teams played only among themselves, not against outside teams. The local railway institute was an important part of the town's life. It provided tennis courts, a library, and a hall along with organising an annual carnival. Webb arranged for a YMCA facility to be provided that would be attended by about two hundred boys on Saturday mornings and provided

A panoramic view of Peterborough yard in the 1930s. *Ethel Bates collection.*

TOP: Even in diesel-only days, Peterborough had a large staff. The station was a busy place for loading and transferring along with rolling stock repairs. South Australian Railways staff posed for the camera in 1976. *John Mannion collection.*

LEFT: The predominance of railwaymen in Peterborough required activities to be organised for off-duty hours. One such activity was the motorcycle club. Lance Bennear sits outside the YMCA (where many single railway workers lived) on his 1944 Triumph. *John Mannion collection.*

ABOVE: Peterborough covered in snow, 1895. This is another photograph rich in detail for those who study rolling stock. *John Mannion collection.*

CENTRE LEFT: South Australian Railways recruited staff among the post-war refugees and immigrants pouring into the country. These men were needed to fill the gaps left either by those killed overseas or those who went into other occupations after leaving the armed services. This group of German station staff at Peterborough in 1950 have clearly already cottoned on to the concept of the 'smoko'. *John Mannion collection.*

Workers at Peterborough loco depot, 1920.
John Mannion collection.

accommodation for single railway employees in its twenty-nine bedrooms. The Webb era also saw a railway housing estate built at Peterborough West between 1925 and 1927. Known as 'View Hill Estate', it was intended to provide rental accommodation for railway workers and their families. These homes are now in private ownership.

There was plenty to divert the staff during their non-working hours. The Capitol Theatre was a purpose-built cinema (not the usual country hall used to show motion pictures); four hotels provided a place to drink and also permanent accommodation for railway men; there was horseracing, tennis, a rodeo and the railway institute built a cricket oval. Car and motorcycle clubs were popular, and homing pigeons were kept by a number of railwaymen. South Australia allowed betting shops from 1934 to 1942, and again in 1946 and 1947, but these private operations seemed only to flourish in railway towns such as Peterborough, Quorn and Port Pirie, presumably because of the large male populations. Those at Peterborough and Quorn closed in 1947 but the last surviving betting shop in Port Pirie closed only in 2004.

A little-known chapter in Peterborough's railway history was the impact of post-war arrivals of European migrants from 1948. These 'Balts' from Estonia, Latvia and Lithuania had come from displaced persons camps in Europe. They were initially employed on permanent way gangs. About forty young and single Balts were selected, usually on the basis of English-speaking ability, to be trained as firemen, drivers and porters to make up for the wartime personnel losses in the Peterborough division. Other European migrants and their families also arrived in Peterborough and today the town boasts many surnames of European origin.

Churches played a big part in Peterborough's life. The Salvation Army was active with many people on low incomes and the town affected in times of recession. The Catholic Church had a large following, and its priest was known as 'the railway bishop' because he travelled over the various lines to visit other nearby towns. The Lutherans also had a substantial presence before the Great War.

While much of the freight going through Peterborough was merely in transit, there was plenty for the staff in the yard and goods shed to do. Sheep sales were held in the town and all the livestock was transported by rail, while big quantities of superphosphate also came in by train. Cereal grains arrived from Quorn, Carrieton and Orroroo to be loaded on trains headed south. Peterborough, always a busy place, was probably at its zenith in terms of railway activity in the 1930s when more than one hundred train movements in its marshalling yards were recorded on one day and the population was estimated at 6,000. The town was self-reliant in terms of electricity from 1913 until 1992 with its own power house. The state grid reached Peterborough in the latter year.

Today, the Indian Pacific will stop on request but no others trains do; the northern line to Quorn and the one south to Terowie have long disappeared. Peterborough is no longer a railway town. But it still retains a railway identity through the efforts of the local volunteer group, Steamtown.

Quorn

Located 374 km from Adelaide via Terowie
This station achieved its status when it became the narrow gauge junction of the east–west route between Perth and Sydney where it met the line from Adelaide which

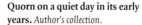
Quorn on a quiet day in its early years. *Author's collection.*

eventually reached Oodnadatta on the Central Australia Railway. The first train to Quorn ran on 15 December 1879. Later, South Australian Railways built a workshop at Quorn to service all the rolling stock which ran through the station. There were predictions that Quorn would become the most important railway station in Australia, and in 1915, South Australian Railways built a new and much grander station there in anticipation of its future role. It was not to be. The town saw its heaviest rail traffic between 1942 and 1945 when the Central Australia Railway was a vital link for troops and matériel being transported north to defend Australia from a Japanese invasion. Quorn's glory days ended in 1956 when the new standard gauge line between Port August and Marree was laid on the other side of the Flinders Ranges. Thereafter, the line to Quorn from Peterborough was reduced to branch status and was closed to traffic on 3 March 1987. The station and town lives on thanks to the Pichi Richi tourist railway that operates steam trains on the narrow gauge track as far as Stirling North.

Tailem Bend

Located on the lower Murray River, 120.5 km by rail from Adelaide

Tailem Bend got its first electricity supply due to the railway. In 1927, exactly forty years after it was proclaimed a town, Tailem Bend was hooked up to the generator at the station which had been supplied to power the workshops. In all, four hundred and seventy homes, seventy-six commercial premises, and three industrial customers were powered by the SAR generator. It was not until 1957 that the Electricity Trust of

South Australia took over the electrical supply to the town.

An account written in 1952 for *The News* shows the level of activity at the station. Unlike many other, smaller rail settlements which had disappeared when there was no longer the need to water steam locomotives, Tailem Bend survived dieselisation. The article said that the then stationmaster, C. R. Fullarton, had the busiest railway section outside Mile End (at Adelaide). Between 80,000 and 100,000 tons of goods went in or out of the station each week; practically all the rolling stock east of the River Murray was serviced there, and more than six hundred people were employed there by South Australian Railways, including fifty porters. In the nine hours after midnight on Sunday, freight trains departed for Serviceton, Naracoorte, Renmark, Loxton, Yinkannie, Pinnaroo, Peebinga and Waikerie. All returned by Tuesday evening, making those two days the busiest in Tailem Bend's working week. Thus, as much as 18,000 tons of freight was moved in fifteen hours. During this period, trains often had to wait outside the yards because there was no space on the sidings.

Terowie

Located 221 km by rail from Adelaide

Terowie became an important railway town because of its strategic location in the development of the colony's farming industry and its role as a break-of-gauge station. Terowie was the point at which the broad gauge track from Adelaide met the narrow gauge line which went north to Peterborough (called Petersburg at the time of the line's opening) and thereafter provided links to Broken Hill, Quorn, Port Augusta, Oodnadatta and Alice Springs. It

Being a break-of-gauge station (where the broad gauge line from Adelaide ended and the narrow gauge to Peterborough and Alice Springs began), the yards at Terowie were extraordinarily busy during World War II. A new south yard had to be developed to cope with all the train movements and Terowie was the place at which General Douglas MacArthur made his famous 'I Shall Return' speech. On 13 September 1944, a signalman of the 12th Division passes his guitar to a friend on the train at Terowie in what looks like a carefully posed photograph. The troops were travelling to Sydney after a period at the Terowie Transhipment Centre.
Australian War Memorial, AWM 080355.

was at Terowie that goods and passengers travelling between Adelaide and the north of the state were transferred between broad and narrow gauge trains (and, in the early days, could use the refreshment rooms which had first, second and third class dining rooms — a distinction that did not survive long). The Broken Hill Express was one of the important early trains operating from Terowie. In fact, all rail traffic between the southern part of South Australia and the rest of the nation was transhipped at Terowie. The yards at the station extended over a length of 3 km, and South Australian Railways built workshops there. Because of the labour-intensive nature of transhipment between the gauges, Terowie's station yard could at any time have had a workforce numbering in the hundreds. Its dependence on the railways grew in the twentieth century as other local sources of employment — the flour mill and sawmill, for example — closed. The yard had a two-track engine shed; one each for broad and narrow gauge locomotives. There was a broad gauge turning triangle and a narrow gauge turntable.

The rail arrived in Terowie in 1880. Trains were sent carrying wool to Port Adelaide and grain to Port Pirie — and returned laden with supplies for the pastoralists and farmers. The mineral riches of Broken Hill passed through Terowie on their way to Port Pirie. During the 1940s and 1950, the yards were busy with coal traffic from the newly developed Leigh Creek fields; the coal was transferred from narrow gauge to broad gauge wagons to be taken on to Adelaide. This work required the use of a coal tippler, which involved turning the narrow gauge wagons on their sides so that the coal would fall down a chute into the broad gauge wagons. The coal traffic reached its peak in 1953–54 when 445,500 tons went through the yards. Seven locomotives were kept busy on yard shunting duties (three Rx Class and one S Class on the broad gauge, and two T Class and one Yx Class narrow gauge).

During World War II, the break of gauge at Terowie made it an important military transfer point. There was an army camp complete with gaol. This is the place at which Douglas MacArthur made his famous 'I shall return' promise to retake the Philippines. There is a plaque at the railway station commemorating that event. Large numbers of troops and their equipment were transhipped here, and the Australian Army stationed a Railhead Operations Platoon at Terowie consisting of an officer, a sergeant and thirty other ranks. In 1944, 595.52 million tons of freight and equipment were manhandled between the gauges. A new south yard was developed during the war. It was dubbed 'Bongoola' after the rival town to Snakes Gully in the radio serial of the time, *Dad and Dave*.

The first blow to Terowie was the opening of the new standard gauge between Port Augusta and Marree on 27 July 1957, on to which the coal traffic was diverted. Then the conversion of the line between Terowie and Peterborough to broad gauge in 1969 ended the station's important role in South Australian transport.

Terowie became no more than another rural stop for passenger trains and freight trains no longer needed to stop there to transfer their loads. The remaining staff members, numbering about seventy, were transferred to Peterborough. Terowie stopped being a railway town altogether when the line passing through was closed on 26 July 1988.

LOCO IN HOBART

Tasmanian Government Railways had primitive safe working arrangements at its main Hobart station for many years. There was no signalling or interlocking until 1912 when a signal box was finally installed at Hobart Junction at the outer end of the yards. Before that, locomotives operated within the Hobart yard on a staff and ticket system (which was normally used only on sections of open line to ensure no more than one train was on a section at any time).

VICTORIA
Ararat

Located 211 km by rail from Melbourne
The railway arrived in Ararat (from Ballarat) on 6 April 1875. Even before the first train rolled into the town, Ararat's importance as a rail centre was assured by the decision made in Melbourne for the tracks to go beyond the town to Hamilton and a line to Stawell (then known as Pleasant Creek). Ararat was to see its first Intercolonial Express on 19 January 1887, following the completion of the Victorian line to Serviceton, thus completing the connection with the South Australian system. Then it became the junction for the lines to Portland and north-east to Maryborough and several grain branches.

By the late 1920s, Ararat was to have the largest country locomotive depot on the Victorian Railways system, with up to twenty-eight engines stabled there. There were twenty-four engine roads in the shed, and another six outside. The depot was equipped with an electric-powered turntable 27.4 m in diameter. The large locomotive roster was due both to the volume of traffic going through Ararat and also because an additional, or banking, locomotive was needed to push or haul heavy freight trains up the Great Dividing Range. For example, the A2 locomotive had a single load capacity departing down from Ararat of 385 tons, but with a pusher running to the stop board on the Great Dividing Range the load could be 545 tons. The grade between Great Western and Stawell determined the pusher load out of Ararat.

At its busiest, Ararat employed about six hundred people at the railway, including a district superintendent and district engineer; now, no railway staff members are stationed there. Because it was a railway junction, all trains once stopped there. Alan Butt, who spent thirty-four years working for Victorian Railways, saw the Ararat rail operation from almost every level: from joining as a lad porter, moving to number taker (recording wagon numbers as they came through the yard), to shunter and leading shunter, guard, yard foreman and, finally, to senior train controller before he left in 1988.

From dusk to dawn five days a week, Ararat yard was busy. Phosphate came up from Portland, barley went to Joe White Malting at Ballarat and wheat for export through to Geelong, plus all the myriad of items that were in the mid-twentieth century carried by four-wheeler rail wagons. Ararat also serviced the nearby Navarre branch line. As many as thirty trains a day could go through Ararat, with more during the harvest. Two pilot locomotives worked the yard at night, one during the day.

In the days of steam, the Overland changed engines in Ararat in both directions. When diesel power hauled this express, the 1965 working timetable shows the running time of the second division of the Overland from Ararat to Dimboola was 108 minutes. But Alan Butt recalls being guard on the Overland one night when it covered the ninety-four miles from Ararat to Dimboola in ninety-four minutes, including intermediate stops at Stawell, Murtoa and Horsham. That meant an average speed of 70 mp/h, or 112.5 km/h.

By contrast, today the Overland pauses only briefly and the local pickup goods train also halts at Ararat. The decline of Ararat is evidenced by the reduction of the number of roads in the yard from sixteen to three.

Echuca

Located 258 km from Melbourne
This town grew with the spread of pastoralism and was the site of a punt service across the Murray River, followed

by the construction of a toll bridge. With the arrival of the railway in 1864, Echuca became a transport hub. Boats brought wool and other produce along the river system for loading at Echuca on trains for the journey to Melbourne. So big an impact did the railway have, that the wharf on the river was eventually extended to 1,200 metres in length to accommodate all the boats wanting to load and unload there. These vessels had come from the New South Wales river system. The river fleet was able to navigate as far north as Bourke, or along the Murray into South Australia. Victorian Railways employed at least forty men at busy times to unload these cargoes and transfer them to rail wagons, covering the cost with a small stevedoring fee. At any time, there might be several thousand bales of wool waiting to be unloaded, along with skins and hides (and fruit from Mildura until that town was connected to the railway system in 1903).

In 2000, the Echuca Port Authority moved to reconnect the wharf with the railway station, the 1.5 km track having been lifted in 1968 (and the spur to Mildura wharf was closed five years later). The cost was put at $300,000, with a similar sum having been spent on restoring Echuca's historic locomotive sheds. Re-laying the missing track was to allow tourist trains travelling to Echuca to carry their passengers to wharf-side and waiting paddle steamers, rather than tourists having to board buses for the section between rail and river.

Maryborough

Located 184 km from Melbourne
This was never a 'railway town' in our sense — it owed its foundation to gold mining — but is included here because of its railway station. It was far grander than a town of Maryborough's size deserved, but it made the town famous.

While this mid-Victoria city fulfilled economic functions beyond the railway, there is no doubt that the station dominated Maryborough, which is why Mark Twain wrote in 1897 that Maryborough was a railway station with a town attached. It is believed that the design was first created with Spencer Street in mind. Of the grand station (which survives mainly as a tourist centre) he wrote:

> You can put the whole population of Maryborough into it, and give them a sofa apiece, and have room for more. You haven't fifteen stations in America that are as big, and you probably haven't five that are as half as fine. Why, it's perfectly elegant. And the clock! Everyone will show you the clock. There isn't a station in Europe that's got such a clock.

In fact, the station did not have a clock in the tower. The mayor had asked Twain to publicise the railway station so that Victorian Railways would add the all-important clock. Even so, they had to wait until 1914.

Trains first reached Maryborough in early 1875. By that time, a station had been built that seemed good enough for the average country town: a stationmaster's residence, waiting room, offices and refreshment rooms. But not for Maryborough, whose populace felt they deserved something a little more imposing, according to station historian Daryl McLeish. They got their way, and work began on the replacement structure in 1890, the plans calling for it to be built of red brick and containing twenty-five rooms. Its structure included an ornate clock tower, Flemish gables, portico, oak wall panels and a longer than average platform. Its interior furnishings included marble dressing tables in the ladies' rest rooms. All mantelpieces in the public rooms were also fashioned from marble.

MINE, AND MINE ALONE

IF YOU WERE IMPORTANT enough, in an earlier age you could have your own railway platform. Several influential people who lived in the Blue Mountains out of Sydney were recipients of this special treatment. Near Lapstone, John Lucas, a member of the Legislative Assembly, could walk down to Lucasville, his own concrete platform on the rail line until it closed along with the Zig Zag. Eager's Platform was provided on the same line for Sir Geoffrey Eager which later became a public station called The Valley and then Valley Heights. Numantia was a platform opened for Sir James Martin. It was eventually opened to the public until 1891, and thereafter was for the exclusive use of the Martin and Cliff families until closed in 1897. A platform called Breakfast Point was opened near the Lapstone Hotel for the use by a Mr Want until 1892.

Special bricks were transported from Bendigo, and the foundations made from bluestone slabs. The veranda over the platform cost almost as much as Maryborough's first station. As McLeish describes it, those arriving at the station walked up a flight of bluestone steps, through decorated iron gates and into a heavily timbered booking hall (complete with decorative timbered ceilings).

Ouyen

Located 472 km from Melbourne
By itself, Ouyen would have been destined to be just another country station when it was opened on 1 January 1903 as part of the line north to Mildura and the Murray River. That was not to be once the branch line opened as far as Murrayville, 109 km away, and then the border in 1915 (thus linking with the South Australian broad gauge line to Pinnaroo). Ouyen was the base for the railway's efforts to open up the Mallee country, with work on the branch starting in 1909. With the opening of the new route, Ouyen had its status raised: the platform at the station was extended, and a goods shed and locomotive depot opened. By 1914, a new wooden station was in place, the platform had been extended further and lit by gas lighting. Two more sidings were added to the railway yard.

During the 1921 wheat harvest, there could be as many as four loaded trains in the yard at any one time: 9,000 bags came down the branch from Murrayville each day alone. Apart from the many wheat trains, there were two daily passenger services, trains carrying general goods and perishables and trains hauling water from the Murray. Bruce McLean, in his history of the Mildura line, writes that as many as 200 wagons could be in the yard at any time, and fifteen trains could go through in twenty-four

hours. Under the stationmaster were the chief and the porters, the shed manager and assistants, eight guards, a yard porter, two platform operators, a locomotive controller, a works master, goods foreman, carpenters and labourers. Eighteen tents were erected at the edge of the station yard to provide homes for twenty-two staff at the railway. A rest home was later built at Ouyen, with twenty-one bedrooms and a dining room seating thirty-six, to accommodate the extra staff brought in to handle the wheat harvest traffic. Even by 1960, there were about 100 railway staff attached to Ouyen, including a locomotive shed staff of nineteen men and a way and works gang responsible for maintaining 450 km of track.

A refreshments room was added to the station in 1923, and in 1929, Ouyen also got a booth to serve fruit juice. By the mid-1950s, the refreshment rooms had closed and tea and coffee was dispensed to passengers from urns, usually consumed with mallee dust swirling around the platform.

Ouyen's modern role evolved from 1987, when two huge grain silos were built at the yards. By 1992, many of the staff were made redundant; only three men were kept on to handle freight work.

The station was notable for having Victoria's only country hostel, which had accommodation for forty people. It was operated by the married couple responsible for the refreshment rooms and kiosk.

Serviceton

Located 463 km from Melbourne
The small settlement of Serviceton, with its grand station, is located close to the border between South Australia and Victoria, although it lies within Victoria (it was also named after the Victorian Premier in office at the time of the

ABOVE RIGHT: **This is what you got in 1890s for £66,000: Maryborough station.** *Daryl McLeish collection.*

RIGHT: **Ouyen station in 1925. At the platform, the AEC railmotor has just arrived from Murrayville while a goods train sits in No. 3 road.** *John Thompson collection.*

FOLLOWING SPREAD: **The clothing suggests the 1950s, but the rolling stock dates from an earlier era. A lot of power in the form of A2 990 and a very short train of very old cars passes across Seymour Street, Maryborough.** *Daryl McLeish collection.*

station's construction, Sir James Service). It was built on the initiative of the two colony governments to act as a junction between the South Australia and Victorian railway systems and the town came into being on 1 January 1887 with the station being completed two years later.

The station area was located on a piece of land about 3.6 km-wide known as the 'Disputed Territory'. The dispute concerned the border between the two colonies arising from uncertainties in surveying when Victoria was still part of New South Wales (it became a separate colony in 1850). It was not until the High Court of Australia delivered judgment in May 1911 that the disputed land belonged to Victoria that the matter was settled. The stationmaster was therefore a Victorian appointment, but his deputy came from the South Australian system.

The South Australian Government had been anxious to tap into Victorian trade and decided to extend its narrow gauge railway from Bordertown to the border itself. A siding was established there in 1885 to receive wheat for transport on South Australian Railways (SAR). That same year, railway officials from South Australia and Victoria agreed that this would become the route of the main intercolonial line and the interchange station would be midway on the disputed zone — in effect, about a mile (1.6 km) within Victoria. The SAR narrow gauge line would be continued on the extra distance to the station yard, and remained in service until 1898.

In 1887, the two colonies were linked by broad gauge line, with the official opening taking place on 19 January. The station cost £4,449.9s.0d, the locomotive sheds another £4,911.19s.5d. In the centre of the large brick station structure were the refreshment rooms, kitchen, pantry, scullery and cellars. The platform was originally

seventy-six metres long and was later extended to two hundred and seventy four metres. All costs were shared between Victoria and South Australia, with each railway service employing its own stationmaster and staff. Customs duty pre-1901 had to be paid on all goods taken. The rooms at the western end of the station were administered by SAR and contained a separate booking and parcels office. This area of the station was treated first as being in a separate colony, and later state. Victorian Railways had its own booking and parcels office at the other end. An interior connection was always kept locked with spikes inserted above it. While those travelling between Melbourne and Adelaide could buy a ticket to cover the entire trip, anyone joining the train at an intermediate station could purchase a ticket only to the border; they then had to buy another at Serviceton for the remainder of the journey in the other colony.

When trains arrived at the border, crews and locomotives were changed so that there was no intercolonial working of motive power (and South Australian porters were instructed to remove all SAR towels from compartments upon arrival at Serviceton). A turntable was installed to turn the locomotives for the return run on their home colonial rails. Railway staff were accommodated at each end of the station which straddled the border. Houses for the respective colonial staff were also built on either side of the border.

Serviceton closed to railway business on 3 March 1986 and today is maintained by volunteers. The locomotive sheds had been dismantled in 1952 with the introduction of the diesel–electric locomotives; the refreshments rooms closed when buffet cars were introduced on the interstate trains.

The building is now leased by the West Wimmera Shire and run by the Serviceton Railway Station Management

Beverley was the terminus for the southern line from Perth until the government bought the Great Southern Land and Railway Company to Albany. This is a typical British-style station with an upstairs residence for the stationmaster and his family. Other similar stations existed at Claremont, York and Walkaway (the last being the point at which government and Midland Railway tracks met). This photo dates from c. 1910. *Noel Inglis collection.*

Committee. A catering operation for meals and functions began in 1991.

Seymour

Located 98 km by rail from Melbourne

Seymour claimed the title of Victoria's first railway town, although it was not planned as such. The main intermediate station, with attendant workshops and other staff, on the main line to Wodonga was intended to be at Benalla. The line from Melbourne was opened at Seymour on 28 August 1872. While Geelong thrived because it was a seaport, and Ballarat and Bendigo flourished on the back of gold, Seymour owed its rise to the railway. Only a few cottages were dotted around the banks of the Goulburn River before the rail arrived, but the tracks were laid several miles away to avoid flood-prone country. Immediately, the population started to settle around the station which was opened in the form of a temporary wooden structure sitting on a raised earth platform. Only later was a more substantial brick station erected. By 1887, Seymour needed a second platform and more sidings because of all the traffic generated after the opening of the Goulburn Valley line to Numurkah. In 1910, a twenty-bay locomotive roundhouse was added. Seymour's glory days came to an end when the standard gauge line was opened, running parallel from Wodonga to Melbourne. The freight traffic being handled on the broad gauge was cut substantially.

As many as four hundred people worked at Seymour railway station in its heyday. The workshops were not big, but the repair depot was always busy. There was a ways and works staff under a district superintendent and a traffic superintendent was also stationed there, as was a district engineer to oversee rolling stock maintenance staff. The refreshment rooms employed thirty-five people, a number that rose to fifty during World War II when Seymour became a refreshment stop for troop trains (it was the station that served Puckapunyal military camp). The refreshment rooms are still in existence although the dining room with its parquetry floor is now used as a storage room. The kitchens, with their huge stoves, remain although many parts of the stoves have been stolen over the years. The refreshment servery area is now available for functions. Three broad gauge passenger services stop there each day, in addition to the twelve daily commuter services which run between Seymour and Melbourne. The XPT from Sydney swishes past on the standard gauge line without stopping.

WESTERN AUSTRALIA
Meekatharra

Located 554 km from Geraldton

While not a true railway town in the sense that it owed its existence primarily to trains, Meekatharra was an important railway centre. Between 1910 and 1931, it was the railhead of the line that pierced the inland from the port of Geraldton. It lost that status in 1957 when the extension to Wiluna was closed, but remained a terminus until the line was closed in 1978. Apart from its role as a mining centre, Meekatharra was the end of the road for all the pastoral properties to the north. Cattle from the Kimberleys were driven 1,500 km down the Canning stock route and loaded into rail livestock wagons for the remainder of the journey. When it opened in 1910, one of the first major consignments was that year's wool clip. The town was also noted as a regional labour exchange where property owners came to recruit shearers and other workers.

The then Minister of Railways travelled all the way to Meekatharra in 1931 to drive the first spike in the extension of the line to Wiluna. The workmen in the background seem unexcited by the occasion. *Wiluna Shire Council.*

Mullewa

Located 121 km by rail from Geraldton

The Western Australian town of Mullewa was an important railway centre, with more than a hundred men stationed there in its heyday. Its prominence lay in its position as the junction where the lines from Geraldton and Northam met.

Rail first reached Mullewa in 1894. From 21 November in that year, a train left Geraldton at 7.30 am on Monday, Wednesday and Friday, reaching Mullewa at 11.45 am. However, it looked for a while like Mullewa was going to be just another town that boomed while it was the railhead and then busted as soon as the trains could go further inland. Such was the case when the track was opened to Cue; many of the businesses and residents upped stakes and moved closer to the goldfields.

However, the Northam–Goomalling–Wongan Hills line reached Mullewa from the south, providing a more direct connection with Perth, and saved the day. When that line opened on 5 March 1915, the station and refreshment rooms moved to the present site, the only problem being that the line then separated the town from the station, with several sets of tracks to be crossed each time someone wanted to go to the station. This brought inevitable complaints from the townsfolk.

Once, there was a big community with many railway houses built along the streets around the station. In Burgess Street, for example, there were twelve railway houses. In the 1930s, there was a two-storeyed boarding house owned by a Mrs Twomey who catered for (and mothered) single, young railway workers. To them, she was affectionately known as 'the old general'. At a later

stage, a railway barracks was built for the unmarried men. One storey has since been removed and the remainder of the building is now Mullewa's supermarket.

Colin Browning, who worked for Western Australian Government Railways from 1942 until his retirement in 1990, spent the years 1948 to 1965 at Mullewa. He started in the WAGR as a junior, which in those days meant jack-of-all-trades: answering the telephone, running messages, cleaning and polishing among the duties. He recalls that the traffic and locomotive section at Mullewa reflected the importance of a junction station. There were twenty guards stationed there which meant that the establishment had another forty men who drove or fired the engines which operated out of that yard. Among others on the staff were two porters, the caretaker of the railway barracks, one head shunter and two shunters, while the refreshment room was privately run. The senior stationmaster worked from eight in the morning until four in the afternoon, followed until midnight by the afternoon stationmaster. The night stationmaster came on at midnight.

There were about fifty train crews posted to Mullewa which, with dependants, added between three hundred and four hundred people to the town's population. Three Australian Rules teams existed: the town team, the country tea and the railway team.

While there was always activity at the station, the highlight of each week occurred on Mondays, the only day on which the Wiluna and Perth trains passed through the town. Mullewa had an island platform, and it was thronged as travellers crammed the refreshment room and bar from both trains. There were two trains a week to

LEFT: Katanning became a busy centre because of its role as a junction on the Great Southern Railway in Western Australia. The line running from Beverley to Albany opened in 1889. Katanning had two branch lines running off in opposite directions: to the west to Kojonup (opened in 1907 and closed in 1982) and to the east as far as Pingrup. This latter line, opened in 1923, was shortened in 1957 and Nyabing became the new terminus. This photograph looks across the railway and, from the yard layout and rolling stock in view, would appear to date from c1910. It illustrates the grand buildings which sprang up around important railway junctions and, in the background, the storage silos for the local flour mill can be seen. *Noel Inglis collection.*

ABOVE: The Mullewa was the name accorded the passenger service that ran between Perth and Mullewa via Morawa. The train is behind X1001 Yalagonga during a brief stop at Morawa in November 1970. *John Beckhaus.*

Wiluna but only on Monday did they pass Mullewa.

The closure of the line to Meekatharra in 1978 was a blow, but the railway role really ended with dieselisation. The locomotive crews were transferred to Geraldton and there was no need for locomotive maintenance at Mullewa. Much of the original site has disappeared. However, part of the station was saved after local residents campaigned against its demolition. The section that was saved — the stationmaster's room, booking office and goods consignment office — is now in use as a craft centre.

Wagin

Located 310 km by rail from Perth

Wagin was once an important railway junction, its name deriving from an Aboriginal name translated as 'place of emus'. It was located on the Great Southern Railway which connected Perth to Albany. In 1907, a branch was built to Dumbleyung and, in 1917, another branch in the opposite direction to Bokal. The West Australian Land Company, which built the Great Southern Railway, developed a private town on the site called Wagin Lake which was renamed simply Wagin when gazetted in 1897.

Walkaway

Located 461 km by rail from Perth

Originally known as Back Flats, its present name is a corruption of Wagga Wah, or river bend. It was the point at which the line from Perth operated by the Midland Railway Company met the government system. Walkaway was a station administered by the Western Australian Government Railways, although staff salaries were shared between the two systems. About 1 km south of the station there was a Midland company locomotive depot and crew quarters.

Walkaway's decline began first with the introduction of diesel traction, and then accelerated after the Western Australian Government bought the Midland company in 1964. The Geraldton Historical Society, which now manages the preserved station, describes the style of the buildings (completed in 1888) as showing the influence of the British railways of the late 1870s, with construction being largely of stone with brick chimneys. It also served for many years as the town's post office. In September 1965 WAGR withdrew the stationmaster post, but other staff remained there until 1985 with the goods siding closed the following year.

WHISTLES AND THEIR CODES

ALL RAILWAYS HAD a system of whistles applied by the drivers of steam locomotives, and these varied little between different colonial and then state administrations. On Tasmanian Government Railways, the whistles were:

approaching a station	long whistle 400 yards from station
approaching level crossing	1 long at 400 yards, another at 100 yards from crossing and then continuing until crossing reached
starting a train	1 whistle
entering tunnel	1 long whistle
guard to apply brakes	2 short, distinct whistles
danger	3 sharp, distinct whistles
in need of assistance	long whistles continued until help arrives
in haze or fog	repeated whistles
to recall guard while stopped	3 whistles

View from Railway Bridge, Wagin.

Wagin, Western Australia, about 1912,
showing all the details one would expect at
a busy country railway station: the variety
of four-wheel wagons, bags of agricultural
produce to be loaded, the water hose and,
presumably, the large hotel on the corner.
Author's collection.

TRAINS, GOOD AND BAD

TRAINS IN AUSTRALIA have often borne names, both official and unofficial. Sometimes, as in the case of trains like Sydney's 'The Fish', the unofficial name eventually makes its way into the timetables. Locals often bestowed names on their trains; at Quilpie in Queensland the short train that came down from Charleville was known as the 'Flying Flea'.

It is not possible within the confines of this chapter to recall each of Australia's named trains. But some stand out.

INTERSTATE

In the beginning, there was the Intercolonial Express that ran from Melbourne to Adelaide, later known as the Melbourne Express or Adelaide Express, and today as the **Overland**. The Overland was introduced in 1936 and covers a route distance of 788 km.

Until the Melbourne–Adelaide line was standardised in 1995, the Overland was Australia's only broad gauge interstate passenger train. Passenger services between the two cities started in 1887. Even the Intercolonial was a trendsetter, being the only interstate passenger train that did not involve a change of trains at a border (only locomotive changes being involved) until standard gauge lines were extended from New South Wales into Brisbane in 1930.

In 1936, the title the 'Overland' was adopted by both states. Victoria had actually introduced the title in 1926, but the South Australians — possibly still smarting from their argument over which state controlled the station at Serviceton where the two systems met — refused to acknowledge the name. The agreement on the new name coincided with a new spirit of co-operation with the two railway departments deciding at that time that they would jointly refurbish the rolling stock. It was jointly owned by South Australian Railways and Victorian Railways and steam-hauled until 1952. The broad gauge set was fully air-conditioned, with first class sleeping cars along with first and second class seating. A club car was provided for first class passengers, with economy travellers using a separate buffet car. In the early years of the twentieth century, dining cars were attached between Melbourne–Ararat and Serviceton–Adelaide. These were later suspended and returned only in 1935 as the worst of the Depression came to an end. Also, at this time, the South Australians detached the car at Tailem Bend rather than run it all the way to the border. In 1942, the train lost both its sleeping cars and on-board catering due to wartime economies and passengers reverted to using refreshment rooms. The cars that were used in the latter part of the twentieth century had been built at Islington workshops between 1949 and 1972. The train is now operated by Great Southern Railroad.

In 1917, the building of the great railway project across the Nullarbor opened the way for the introduction by Commonwealth Railways of the **Trans-Australian** between Port Augusta and Kalgoorlie, a distance of 1,689 km. From 1937, the train's run was extended to Port Pirie.

There was a complicated arrangement of connecting services. In the west, a narrow gauge train from Perth met the Trans-Australian at Kalgoorlie. At the other end, passengers from Adelaide boarded a broad gauge train at Port Augusta for the trip as far as Terowie, then transferred to a narrow gauge service via Quorn to Port Augusta, with a further transfer to the standard gauge transcontinental train. In 1937, the standard gauge was extended to Port Pirie. Thereafter, South Australian Railways ran a broad gauge connection from Adelaide to that station.

The Trans-Australian began as an all sleeper train. For much of its life, it offered first and second class sleeping compartments, with both dining and lounge cars attached. Sitting cars were added and withdrawn for periods of the train's life. In its later years, the train was equipped with motor-rail wagons for passengers' cars. In the steam era, the locomotives were changed at Cook, roughly halfway between Port Augusta and Kalgoorlie. These runs to Cook (from either end) were longer than any through running by steam locomotives elsewhere in Australia.

Two new carriage sets were introduced in 1953. Each had a power brake van, one second class sleeper with four-bunk compartments accommodating thirty-two passengers in all, a combined second-class sleeper/lounge car, dining car, a first class lounge car, first class sleeper cars and one first class sleeper/observation car.

The appeal of the train was in decline in the 1980s, with one of the four weekly services eliminated in 1983. Also, second class sleepers were withdrawn and replaced by additional first class accommodation. By 1991, the Trans-Australian was down to one service a week, and ended its life later that year as patronage plunged even further.

The **Ghan** first ran as a narrow gauge train in 1926 to Oodnadatta. From 1929–57, it ran between Port Augusta and Alice Springs via Marree and Oodnadatta. From 1957–80, it ran as a standard gauge train to Marree and narrow gauge train to Alice Springs. From that latter date, it was standard gauge via Tarcoola from Adelaide to Alice Springs, a distance of 1,559 km. In 2004, the train was extended to Darwin, making a total one-way run of 2,979 km.

Commonwealth Railways introduced this train when it took over from South Australian Railways as operator of the Central Australia Railways. The Ghan gained its name from the Afghan camel drivers who ran teams to carry

The Intercapital Daylight was a popular train for those travelling between Melbourne and Sydney, and this interior shows that carriages were well patronised. *John Beckhaus.*

wool and supplies to and from the rail stations along the route. The present-day train has an Afghan riding a camel as its emblem. The narrow gauge train had first and second class sleeping cars, first class sitting, first and second class lounge cars and a dining car.

The train originally started at Port Augusta as a narrow gauge operation but when the new standard gauge line was opened to Marree, the service was provided by two trains; a standard gauge set from Port Pirie to Marree, and narrow gauge thereafter.

In its narrow gauge days, the Ghan was notorious for being late. The first trip through to Alice Springs pulled in five hours late, but that was nothing compared to some of the delays. One driver, Bert Twilley, recalled that one trip of the Ghan, when he was on the footplate, lasted two weeks, the train having become stranded between two flooded rivers. Trips lasting a month were not unknown. Rivers, often dry beds for much of the year, could rise from nothing after rain and wash away bridges or even the track which had been laid on top of the ground often without any proper formation work. There was not much comfort to be had when the trains first started running northwards from Port Augusta in South Australian Railways days, with 'Short Tom' passenger cars attached. These were bogie carriages with interior seating along each wall so that the passengers faced each other. There was a centre toilet and passengers could step out into the fresh air on end platforms.

Commonwealth Railways not only introduced a better standard of sitting car, but coupled sleeping cars onto the train. It also got a dining car. In 1961, several standard gauge cars were converted for use on the Ghan, and it now boasted a club car. German-made dining cars were brought onto the line in 1969. The final trip of the old narrow gauge in 1980 — on which the author travelled — saw Australian National (as it is now) pull out every piece of available rolling stock to cope with the numbers of people wanting to board this historic journey. In anticipation of the new standard gauge route being opened, the track had fallen into considerable disrepair with the train lurching along at slow speed. Not many passengers envied the dignitaries on the trip who travelled in the old commissioner's car. All the wood panelling in the world was no compensation for the fact that the car was not air-conditioned. But it certainly gave one a taste of what it must have been like to sit in carriages in the days when the only form of ventilation was to open windows and let in even hotter air.

The new standard gauge Ghan is a world away, a sleek modern train that seals off its passengers from the hostile environment through which it passes on smooth narrow gauge tracks held in place by concrete sleepers.

In November 1983, after seeing the success of the 'new' Ghan, the State Rail Authority introduced **The Alice**, a train that ran from Sydney to Alice Springs. The decision to provide only first class accommodation limited the appeal of the train; without economy seating it failed to gain a critical mass of patronage. It lasted only until 2 November 1987.

Another prestige train of post-war Australia was the **Brisbane Limited**. It was introduced on the 987 km Sydney–Brisbane run in 1952, being replaced by XPT sets from 11 February 1990. The Limited, after leaving Brisbane, stopped only at Bromelton, Casino, South Grafton, Broadmeadow, Hornsby and Strathfield before easing into Sydney Terminal.

FOR PRISONERS AND GREYHOUNDS

A SURVEY OF NEW SOUTH WALES rolling stock rosters between 1892 and 1938 showed that the government system had available at various stages seven four-wheeler prison and four eight-wheeler prison vans; a four-wheeler invalid car built in 1890; more than 170 four-wheeler and twelve eight-wheeler horse boxes; and four pigeon vans. The fleet in 1935 got an addition by way of DC 1040, a twelve-wheel dental car, in addition to FW 76, a hospital car, and four RG Class eight-wheeler greyhound cars.

119. ADELAIDE TO MELBOURNE EXPRESS

ABOVE: A scene that captures the early steam era. The Adelaide to Melbourne express starts its journey, illustrating not only the power of two locomotives easing through the points before opening up on the main line, but the detail as well: the yard locomotive at left being prepared for another shift; the variety of four-wheeler wagons; and semaphore signals. *Museum Victoria.*

OPPOSITE ABOVE: Locals and their dogs at a stop on the transcontinental line between South Australia and Western Australia. The passengers take the chance to have a look at something other than earth and scrub. The photo dates from about 1940. *By permission of the National Library of Australia.*

RIGHT: A touch of elegance aboard the old narrow gauge Ghan which served Alice Springs until 1980. The passenger in this sleeping compartment had a fold-up basin, wardrobe and water jugs. *Author's collection.*

Until 3 March 1973, the Brisbane Limited had a sister train, the **Brisbane Express** which, for much of its life, ran on two different routes. On Mondays, Wednesdays, and Fridays it departed Sydney at 3.10 pm running via Tamworth and Tenterfield to arrive on the Queensland border at Wallangarra station at 7.23 am. Thereafter, passengers transferred to a Queensland Railways narrow gauge train for the remainder of the journey to Brisbane. On other days, the Express ran straight through to Brisbane on the standard gauge interstate link. It was also unlike the Limited in that the Express belied its own name by picking up and letting down passengers at minor stations. The 1970 timetable allowed for stops out of Brisbane at Beaudesert Road, Bromelton, Tamrookum, Glenapp, Border Loop, The Risk, Kyogle, Fairy Hill, Casino, Leeville, Amarina, Rappville, Banyabba, Gurranang, and Kyarran — and that was before reaching South Grafton! This service was replaced with a Sydney–Murwillumbah train. Both trains had sleeping and seating accommodation.

Then, in 1970, with the standardisation of the transcontinental line, came the **Indian Pacific**. It was originally a Commonwealth Railways train, thereafter passing to Australian National. This service now runs between Perth and Sydney via Adelaide and Broken Hill (a distance of 3,961 km) as a part of Great Southern Railways, a private passenger operator. It has first class roomette and twinette cars, with these passengers eating in the Queen Adelaide dining car. Travellers booking economy sleeping accommodation or sitting cars use the Matilda restaurant car.

Melbourne–Sydney had its share of prestige trains, none more famous than the **Spirit of Progress**. From 23 November 1937, this train ran on the broad gauge section of the Melbourne–Sydney route between the southern capital and Albury. It set a new standard of train luxury, and included an observation car with armchairs. The train, built at Newport workshops, had Australian timber interiors, while the shells of the carriages were made from steel alloy and streamlined. The first class cars sat forty-eight people in twelve compartments per car, while the second class cars could seat sixty-four passengers.

Victorian Railways assigned to the train four powerful S-Class locomotives, which had a winged VR emblem painted on their noses. The engines were named after early figures in the state's history: Matthew Flinders, Sir Thomas Mitchell, Edward Henty and C. J. La Trobe.

The all-blue cars owned by Victorian Railways were remounted on standard gauge bogies when the NSW gauge was extended into Melbourne. The train offered first class sleepers and first and economy class seating.

The **Intercapital Daylight** was added to this run in 1956, brought into service by Victorian Railways after it was realised a demand existed for daytime travel between the two state capitals in preference to overnight journeys on the Spirit of Progress.

An entirely new prestige train began operating between the two state capitals from 16 April 1962, the **Southern Aurora.** During its life, it was the most prestigious of the Sydney–Melbourne trains. Its accommodation was entirely first class sleepers, with both a lounge and a dining car. The rolling stock was built by Commonwealth Engineering and was jointly financed by what were then the New South Wales Government Railways and Victorian Railways.

ABOVE: Another service — and line — that belongs to the past. Here, the Canberra-Monaro Express in the form of a DEB set arrives at Cooma on 26 March 1983. It was a long run from Canberra and, on this day, just a handful of passengers took advantage of the service. *Author's collection.*

LEFT: The country trains in New South Wales always made plenty of stops, even if they were called expresses. The Central West Express pauses at Tarana in 1971. *John Beckhaus.*

OPPOSITE LEFT: Very 1960s, but in 1970, this was the acme of Australian rail travel — the lounge car on the Southern Aurora. *John Beckhaus.*

OPPOSITE RIGHT: And the dining car in 1970. A journey on this train by the author in 1978 invokes memories of surprisingly good food and the pleasure of sipping wine as the train rolled through the night. *John Beckhaus.*

From 4 August 1986, the Spirit of Progress was combined with the Southern Aurora to form the Sydney and Melbourne Expresses. This latter service was replaced in 1993 by XPT operations.

There was a short-lived but brave attempt to bring some European-style elegance to Australian rail travel with the unveiling in February 1988 of the **Southern Cross Express** running between Sydney and Melbourne with some services taking a detour to Canberra. A private company, Victorian Vintage Travel, bought some ex–South Australian broad gauge steel-panelled cars which had been restored for the similarly short-lived Melbourne Limited steam service. They were then converted to standard gauge for the Southern Cross Express. The train included two dining cars, which had been restored with polished timbers and brass-work. Wine was served in crystal glasses and the tableware was Wedgwood. The owner company failed in less than a year and the train was withdrawn.

NEW SOUTH WALES

New South Wales had a vast array of country trains, many of which had official names. Then there were those with unofficial names, but names that stuck and came into wide use.

Express trains

These trains tended to be daytime operations, compared with the mail trains which ran overnight. Many of these expresses were relatively recent inventions, such as the **Canberra–Monaro Express** which came into existence in 1955. It replaced the **Federal City Express** connecting Sydney with the federal capital at Canberra and ran on to Cooma, a total distance of 432 km. The Federal City had been introduced in 1936 as a daylight service in addition to existing night mail expresses between the two cities.

Three years after its inauguration, this service was equipped with the new air-conditioned rail motor sets, although in the mid-1940s, it once again became a working by steam locomotive and carriages. The Canberra–Monaro replacement ran from Sydney to Queanbeyan, then into Canberra before running back into NSW and continuing on to Cooma. It was equipped with DEB railcars from the beginning, whereas the superseded Federal City had been a carriage train. The DEB cars were built at Chullora between 1951 and 1960 and were designed to replace the steam-hauled country trains. The DEB railcars offered first and second class seating, along with meal tray and liquor service. Hostesses also regularly passed through the train with trays containing cigarettes, sweets, ice cream and nuts which passengers could buy. The Canberra–Monaro service was withdrawn from 26 November 1988. A year later, the line from Bredbo to Cooma was closed due to low traffic volumes and the need for expensive bridge repairs. Other trains that carried the 'express' status were the **Central West Express** (Sydney–Orange) and the **Far West Express** (Dubbo–Bourke or Cobar). This run was operated by DEB railcar sets in its latter years, leaving Dubbo four minutes after the arrival of the Western Mail running on Mondays, Wednesdays, and Fridays to Bourke, but on Thursdays to Cobar instead with stops at Miandetta, Hermidale and Boppy Mountain. In the steam era of the 1950s, the Central West Express took on fresh coal at Lithgow and offered a connection at Dubbo by rail motor to Narromine

on Tuesdays, Thursdays and Saturdays. The connection operated to Parkes on Mondays, Wednesdays and Fridays.

Additionally, there was the **North Coast Daylight Express** which hauled passengers the 696 km between Sydney and South Grafton. The **South Coast Daylight Express** ran the relatively short 153 km from Sydney to Bomaderry which was chosen as the terminus to avoid the cost of building a bridge across the Shoalhaven River to Nowra. Another short distance but popular service out of Sydney was the **Southern Highlands Express**, which covered the 222 km to and from Goulburn.

Some expresses that survived into the 1970s, and sometimes beyond, were daytime counterparts to overnight mails. Like them, they were split into two sets at an intermediate junction. Thus the **Northern Tablelands Express** (the daylight equivalent of the North Mail) ran out of Sydney in the 1970s as a DEB set departing at 7.35 am as one train to Werris Creek, then splitting for Moree (666 km from Sydney) arriving at 5.27 pm and Tenterfield (774 km from Sydney) arriving at 8.22 pm. However, in the steam era, the Northern Tablelands Express operated six days a week only to Armidale, with a two-car diesel train offering a connection three days a week to Glen Innes and the other three days to Tenterfield. The **Riverina Express** split at Junee for Albury (643 km from Sydney) and Griffith (637 km) via Narrandera. In the days of steam, the Riverina Express ran only to Albury on Monday to Saturday, with the locomotive taking on coal at Demondrille in both directions. Around 1940, it connected with a railmotor at Harden which ran to Young each day except Wednesday, when the railmotor service was provided on the Boorowa branch.

The Fish

Sydney–Mount Victoria, NSW

Route distance: 125 km

Status: Still operating

In 1882, it was recorded that The Fish was due to depart from Mount Victoria in the Blue Mountains at 5.00 am, stopping at all stations to Granville and then running to Sydney for a 9.16 am arrival. In later years, its afternoon service from Sydney was followed two minutes later by a Sydney–Springwood service which soon, and inevitably, earned the name 'The Chips'. The Fish was probably, by consensus, named after one of the early drivers on the Sydney–Penrith train. In the 1860s, John ('Jock') Heron was known as the 'Big Fish' (his surname having first been corrupted by the locals to 'Herring'). He was a large, burly man in charge of engine No. 15 and the nickname soon became the unofficial title of his train — and stuck long after his death. (Heron was promoted from driving and became Inspector of Steam Sheds.) There was also a regular guard in the train's early days named Charley Pike, a factor which may have given some reinforcement to the title. While it was first just a local name, New South Wales Government Railways did eventually adopt it and even had a headboard attached to the front proclaiming it as The Fish. In the 1950s, the train was described as having a club-like atmosphere where 'regular' seats were closely guarded.

Although the name never appeared in official timetables, the daily Sydney–Emu Plains service was known by the locals as 'The Heron', probably again after the same driver. The Blue Mountains also had a train popularly known as 'the Caves Express' that ran from

LEFT: **The North Mail at Moree in December 1978 behind 4707.** *John Beckhaus.*

OPPOSITE: **The rails reached Moree in 1897 and, while this line eventually went on to Mungindi and a branch opened to Inverell, Moree was the terminus for the express and mail trains from Sydney. The centre train is thought to be the Mail awaiting departure for Sydney and the consist at left an Inverell branch working; on the right, wagons are being loaded at the goods shed. The licence plate on the only motorcar in the scene would be a prized possession today.** *Author's collection.*

Sydney to Mount Victoria, so known because it was the train people caught for part of the journey to the Jenolan Caves.

Mail trains

The mail trains of NSW — many of which were replaced by the XPT sets — offered NSW travellers a cheap and clean form of overnight travel to the farther reaches of the state network. One of the earliest recorded was the **Southern and Western Mail**, which dated from 1869. It left Sydney at 5.00 pm and was timed to reach Parramatta at 5.32 pm. It was then divided into two sets, one travelling to Goulburn with an arrival time of 11.05 pm, the other steaming to Mt Victoria by 9.30 pm. The next morning the two consists reunited at Parramatta for the run into Sydney, arriving at 7.10 am.

Over the years there were many overnight trains whose names disappeared along the way. They either stopped running or were replaced by other trains (the **Albury Mail**, for example, became part of the **South Mail**.) In their latter years, the rolling stock was antiquated by standards in most developed countries. These trains provided first class sleepers, along with first and second class seating. They were not air-conditioned, nor was there any on-board catering. They were not a quick way to travel, but in their time they were a vital link. But passengers did need patience. The **North Mail**, for example, operated from Sydney to Moree (666 km) and Tenterfield (774 km). When this train reached Werris Creek (411 km from Sydney) the consist was split in two; one section was hauled via Tamworth to Tenterfield and the other ran via Gunnedah to Moree. Those travelling to Tenterfield left Sydney at 7.50 pm, travelled all night and next morning to arrive at

their destination at 12.36 pm the next day (the Moree leg arrived at its destination by 9.05 am). Other trains split, too. The **South Mail** left Sydney at 10.30 pm for Albury (643 km) and Griffith (637 km), arriving at Junee at 7.53 am next morning. Then it split with the Albury section arriving more than thirteen hours after departure with the Griffith section completing its journey by noon. The **Western Mail** was formed in 1973 from the combination of two separate trains, the **Forbes Mail** and the **Dubbo Mail**. Its main intermediate stops on the 462 km journey were Lithgow, Bathurst and Orange. As with the other mail trains, there was sleeping accommodation along with first and second class seating but no on-board catering. This Mail departed Sydney at 8.55 pm and pulled into Dubbo at 7.00 am the next morning.

The mail trains had a variety of sleeping cars in their last decades. The VAM cars were used on the western lines and dated from 1903; they had eighteen bunks in nine compartments. The LAM cars were very similar, and were first built in 1907; these were used primarily on the **Temora Mail** and the **Cowra Mail**. EAM cars also had nine, two-bunk compartments and came into service between 1908 and 1912. There was also the FAM carriage which had ten two-bunk compartments.

Sleeping cars might denote comfort, but the sitting passengers on the mail trains recall quite a different image. A. R. Astle wrote the following about going home to Dubbo at the start of university holidays in the late 1950s:

You soon lost the romantic feeling of being on a steam-hauled night train when you were crowded into an often noisy, eight-passenger compartment on a painfully

RIGHT: **DP 104 powers the Silver City Comet away from the station, the travellers preparing themselves for another rocky ride.** *John Beckhaus.*

OPPOSITE LEFT: **One of Queensland's premier trains, the Capricornia, seen at yet another of the state's roofed stations, Rockhampton, on 31 January 1972. Locomotive 1528 is in charge.** *John Beckhaus.*

OPPOSITE RIGHT: **The Sunlander runs along Denison Street, Rockhampton, behind DEL 1515, with a BLC wagon between locomotive and carriages. Note also the signal for the main line (top) and loop to the platform (lower) — a 1970s scene.** *Brian Webber.*

slow, dirty and sometimes freezing trip. I seem to remember that the RRR (railway refreshment room) was open at Orange and you could get at least hot tea or coffee to combat your numbness in the tableland's winter. After Orange, things started to look up — you were on the home stretch; if you were on the later, faster Bourke Mail . . . the sun would be up as you approached Wellington (but if you were on the all stations Coonamble Mail, there was little sun to warm you up before arriving at Dubbo). Going back to Sydney was always a painful business and I usually softened the blow somewhat by missing Monday's lectures and travelling on the 'day train' where I could travel in comfort.

He adds that, even worse than the Coonamble Mail, was the Saturday night paper train which left Sydney at 11.08 pm and did not slide into the platform at Dubbo until 11.31 am on Sunday.

Silver City Comet

Parkes–Broken Hill, NSW

Route distance: 679 km

Status: Withdrawn 1989

The Silver City Comet was the first completely air-conditioned diesel set to run on Australian rails (and, it is believed, within what was then the British Empire), with the first train built in 1936 by Ritchie Brothers of Auburn (and rebuilt between 1953 and 1958). The motive power was provided by two Harland and Wolf diesel engines, with two diesel generator sets providing train lighting and power for the kitchen. It ran three times a week, providing

the link between the terminating Central West Express from Sydney and the Silverton Tramway to Cockburn and then South Australian Railway services. It was also a vital transport link for those who lived in the sparsely populated areas of New South Wales' Far West region. It carried perishable supplies into Broken Hill and would stop at tiny stations along the way for passengers or to drop off bread, milk and other items; stations such as Beilpajah, Darnick and Kaleentha Loop. Back in 1937, it was also a revelation for the seasoned railway traveller used to slow, dirty steam-hauled trains. The Comet was a high-speed service and covered the distance from Parkes to Broken Hill in about eight hours. However, accounts indicate it was not a comfortable ride; the state of the track combined with the light-weight timber frame cars meant that passengers took a few jolts. It was said that no one tried to hold a full cup of tea on the Silver City Comet. The introduction of the Indian Pacific service in 1970 marginalised the Comet but it kept going for almost another two decades. In 2002, State Rail introduced a new train to Broken Hill, the Silver City Xplorer, running once a week from Sydney. The train set has been preserved at the Sulphide Street Railway Museum at Broken Hill.

QUEENSLAND

Over the years, this state has operated trains over the vast lengths of its network. When it started its days on 27 May 1935, the **Sunshine Express** offered one of the longest narrow gauge railway train trips in the world (Brisbane–Cairns 1,680 km). This train was equipped with new wooden body cars with steel under-frames, divided into three first class and three second class sleeping cars, one first class and one second class sitting car, along with a

parlour car and dining car. The interior was finished with varnished timber. During World War II, the train was put on a reduced operating schedule and, to save money and staff numbers, the parlour car was withdrawn.

On the coastal runs, there was the **Capricornian** between Brisbane and Rockhampton (627 km) and the **Queenslander** (Brisbane–Cairns), the premier train in the QR long-distance fleet, taking thirty-two hours to travel between the two cities. First class passengers have the choice of single or double berth cabins, and there is both a dining and lounge car. The **Sunlander** between Brisbane and Cairns was a service that appealed to the dedicated railway traveller, the trip for many years taking thirty-seven hours to complete. Queensland Railways maintained four complete train sets to operate the service, which when introduced offered first and economy class sleeping (the latter having three berths per compartment), first and economy seating, and a dining car. A lounge car was introduced in 1977. Today the train is seen as providing a cheaper train trip than the more luxurious Queenslander. There are first and economy class sleepers, seating cars, and a dining car.

Queensland also had the **Gulflander**, running on its own isolated section, the 151 km between Normanton and Croydon. This service initially survived into the modern era because it was the only form of reliable transport during 'the wet' in this part of northern Queensland. The northern terminus, Normanton, is located 80 km upstream on the Norman River and developed as a port for the cattle business and later gold mining. The line was planned to reach Cloncurry, providing an inland route to the river port for all the cattle country along its route. However, before this

could come about, gold was discovered near Croydon and the decision was made to build the line to that point. It was cleverly designed: hollow steel sleepers packed with mud meant that ballast would not be needed — and that was a considerable cost saving as well as avoiding the difficult task of transporting ballast to the area. The construction method also meant the line was not subject to damage in flooding, remaining intact when the waters subsided. Steam was used exclusively on the line until 1922 when rail motors were introduced.

In the 1970s, author Patsy Adam Smith visited the Normanton–Croydon line and reported that there were eight men keeping it going, four of whom were Thursday Islanders. The ganger each week took his team out on the line, and they camped each night at one of the various sidings along the line. The line's officer-in-charge had to be a qualified fitter, a manager and the paymaster. He also acted as stationmaster at Normanton and train driver. The rolling stock at the time — the AEC and Panhard rail motors — needed maintenance work almost every time they returned to Normanton.

In latter years, the train has achieved fame as a tourist attraction. In the mid-1970s, the Queensland Government considered closing this railway. In 1974, the Gulflander had earned just $3,340 and it was estimated that $63,800 needed to be spent to keep the line in running repair.

The 'Lander' trains

In the early 1950s, Queensland Government Railways revamped the interior long-distance services. New steel cars were built, and the trains were air-conditioned, while buffet cars reduced the time spent at stations for

RIGHT: **The Gulflander at Gitters Camp, 30 August 2000.** *Brian Webber.*

OPPOSITE: **The crew make last minute adjustments behind 1277 as the Westlander is getting ready to depart Roma on 16 February 1972.** *John Beckhaus.*

refreshments. For Queenslanders, it was a welcome change after the wooden, non air-conditioned stock. The trains were:

The *Inlander* (Townsville to Mount Isa), 970 km, introduced on 12 February 1953.
The *Midlander* (Rockhampton–Winton), 864 km.
The *Westlander* (Brisbane–Cunnamulla, with auxiliary service to Quilpie), a distance of 971 km to Cunnamulla and 999 km to Quilpie. The point at which the train split, Charleville, is 777 km from Brisbane. Introduced on 24 August 1954. This train now terminates at Charleville.

Commonwealth Engineering at Rocklea was contracted to build eleven all-steel vehicles to make up the Inlander, with first and second class sleeping and sitting cars as well as a dining car. It was air-conditioned. First class sleeping compartments were provided with Dunlopillo mattresses and special lightweight rugs. Wardrobes included full-length mirrors, a folding perspex wash-basin and a collapsible writing table. Second class sleeping compartments had three bunks, coat hooks rather than a wardrobe, and travellers were expected to bring their own bed linen and blankets as these were not provided.

These three trains provided a reliable, if not exactly fast, service on the three main inland arteries of the Queensland rail system.

Only the Westlander had two destinations. Before the train was terminated at Charleville, the service from Brisbane was split at that station. Two carriages were removed from the main train, then a locomotive, guard's van and power van was attached to these two cars. This small consist then headed off on the branch to Quilpie, and was known by the locals as the 'Flying Flea'. The remainder of the Westlander then proceeded to Cunnamulla. On the return trip, the carriages from Cunnamulla and Quilpie would be reunited at Charleville for the journey to Brisbane. Douglas MacGregor of Cunnamulla remembers that, because the section from his home town to Charleville was laid with light rails, the Westlander travelled at only about 30 mph (48 km/h). It also made stops at many country stations before reaching Charleville. Those stops included Nardoo, Offham, Mirrabooka, Claverton Sidings and Wyandra. In the 1950s, the roads were still not good, so most of the locals used the train for long-distance travel. Passengers who boarded the twice-weekly service at Cunnamulla for the 9.00 am departure made themselves comfortable once aboard because they knew they would be on that train until it rolled into Brisbane about lunchtime the following day. At least, compared to earlier trains, the cars were air-conditioned.

By 1957, the Westlander included several freight wagons as well as the passenger cars. Louvred steel QRX and QLX-T wagons and a diesel-powered MPR refrigerated wagon were regular components of the consist, the latter being attached at Toowoomba to carry perishables to the inland railway stations. Regulations allowed the Westlander to be made up with a maximum of sixteen cars and wagons.

Mail trains

As with New South Wales, the mail trains were the original backbone of the long-distance passenger services. The first of this class of service was the Sydney Mail,

introduced in January 1888, which ran to Wallangarra on the border with New South Wales. Two months later, the Western Mail began operations to Charleville upon the opening of that line. Four sleeping cars were ordered to provide more comfortable accommodation on these long overnight journeys.

The Rockhampton Mail began running between that city and Brisbane in 1904, leaving at 10.00 pm going north, with a noon start on the return leg. Most passengers on this train opted for sitting cars for what was a twenty-hour trip. Later the Townsville Mail was added, leaving Brisbane at 2.20 pm from Roma Street and arriving forty hours after departure. By 1892, Longreach had two mail trains a week.

Second class sleeping cars were added in 1896 with a surcharge of two shillings and sixpence.

SOUTH AUSTRALIA

Long-distance passenger travel in South Australia was dominated by interstate services such as the Indian Pacific, the Ghan, the Overland and the Trans-Australian. There was also the **Broken Hill Express** which ran on the narrow gauge as far as Terowie. It was technically an interstate service as, beyond the South Australian Railways terminus at Cockburn, the train was hauled the remaining distance to Broken Hill by Silverton Tramway Company locomotives.

One of South Australia's better known trains was the **East-West**, the broad gauge connection between Adelaide and Port Pirie. This line was completed in 1937, connecting with the Commonwealth Railways standard gauge line from Port Pirie to Port Augusta and thence Kalgoorlie. The opening of the line south from Port Pirie meant that passengers travelling between Adelaide and

Port Augusta no longer had to use the long, time-consuming narrow gauge route through Riverton, Peterborough and Quorn. South Australian Railways needed a new fast locomotive to work the East-West service and thus was born the 620 Class.

In 1950, the **Blue Lake** train service began running three days a week between Adelaide and Wolseley and thence to Naracoorte. The train left Adelaide at 8.45 pm each Sunday, Tuesday and Thursday, arriving at Naracoorte at 5.27 am, with a connecting train to Mount Gambier with a timed arrival of 9.28 am. The return trains were usually a heavier load for the locomotives with wagons attached containing perishable goods for the Adelaide market. A refurbished sleeping car, the *Angas*, was attached to the Blue Lake service.

Between April 1986 and December 1990, a train known as the **Iron Triangle Limited** was operated by Australian National on the Adelaide–Whyalla run via Port Pirie and Port Augusta using Budd railcars.

TASMANIA
Tasman Limited

Hobart–Wynyard, Tasmania

Route distance: 378 km

Status: Ceased operating 28 July 1978

The demise of the Tasman Limited, which ran from the capital with main intermediate stops at Ross, Western Junction and Devonport, signalled the end of all passenger services in Tasmania. The train was notable for being the only long-distance consist in Australia with articulated cars, and these were equipped with rotating reclining seats. The train began as a railcar operation from Hobart

---

A STATE OF JEALOUSY

IN 1889, VICTORIAN Railways published a new by-law which allowed a rebate on goods transported from Melbourne by train into the Riverina region of New South Wales. The purpose was transparent — to induce farmers in this area to send their produce to Melbourne rather than Sydney and to buy their supplies from Victoria. At this stage, the only broad gauge track into New South Wales was the line to Deniliquin owned by the Deniliquin & Moama Railway Company. In the 1920s, it would be joined by extensions of the Victorian broad gauge into the state to Balranald (192.4 km in NSW), Stony Crossing (62.1 km), and Oaklands (61.5 km), and a short section across the river into Tocumwal. The rebate line ran just south of Jerilderie and toward Balranald. This meant that a Riverina farmer could pay freight charges of 67s 3d for a ton of fencing wire carted from Melbourne against 80 shillings from Sydney. Groceries attracted a freight charge of 72s 6d from Melbourne compared to 86s 8d from Sydney.

ABOVE: Still sitting in Port Pirie's main street although not selling tickets to rail travellers queuing on the footpath. Ellen Street station is now a museum, and a reminder of the days when railway architecture involved more than concrete blocks and aluminium-framed windows. *Brian Gauci.*

LEFT: DA 1574 at Wagin, 19 August 2003. *Don Copley.*

ABOVE: In early 1953, a tropical low disrupted the Central Australia Railways for six weeks. The first Ghan service after the big wet left Port Augusta on 9 February and took five days to reach its destination. The train had to stop at several places to allow sand to be removed from the track and there was a two-day delay at the Finke River while the loco crew waited for the water level to drop. Then they crawled across when the water was still 250 mm above the rails and, as seen here, the river was lapping at the side of the carriages. *Peter Dunham.*

OPPOSITE ABOVE: Goods of all descriptions. At Kamma in 2003, QR's 2814 arrives in the loop to cross 1752D on the Babinda–Cairns molasses train. *Brian Webber.*

OPPOSITE RIGHT: The station at Mullewa is isolated from the tracks by a wire fence, and the goods shed sits far from the nearest set of rails. Only prompt action by locals saw at least part of the station saved from demolition. *Don Copley.*

A buckle in the line to jolt passengers
on the isolated Normanton–Croydon railway
in Queensland. *Brian Webber.*

to Launceston. In April 1954, it was extended along the island's Western Line, and in 1955, locomotive-hauled red and cream carriages were introduced to provide additional seating capacity. There were two factors which doomed the Tasman Limited; first, it was introduced at a time when motorcar ownership was becoming more common and secondly, its route ran parallel to bus services which offered quicker transit times than the train's almost nine-hour trip (it left Hobart at 9.20 am and arrived in Wynyard at 6.05 pm). In 1975–76, the train lost $600,000.

VICTORIA

Victoria, because of its relatively small size, had few of the grand railway journeys. Its top trains tended to be daytime runs, so that trains like the Albury Express, the Gippslander (just 275 km) or the Great Northern Limited between Melbourne and Bendigo never quite achieved the legendary status of some other Australian journeys. The longest, and only overnight, journey within the state for many years was aboard the **Vinelander,** introduced between Mildura and Melbourne, a distance 566 km, from 9 August 1972.

After intensive local lobbying, the overnight train service between Melbourne and Mildura was upgraded with the addition of air-conditioned sleeping cars transferred from the Overland (although two years later there were complaints about the old wooden sleeping cars still being used as they belied the promotion of the 'luxury' train. However, Victorian Railways said it had no alternative when bookings exceeded space in the newer cars). The old cars had been described by a local politician as 'dog boxes', but nevertheless in pre-Vinelander days there was an additional $3 charge for occupying them rather than the sitting carriages. A buffet car offering light

snacks and a bar service was added to the Vinelander in 1977. However, this was a mixed blessing with drunken behaviour being a constant problem and often leading to offending passengers being thrown off the train at the next stop. In the early days, Victorian Railways went to great lengths to promote what was one of their premier passenger trains, the Mildura line providing sufficient distance to justify the use of sleeping cars. The department sponsored a race at one of the 1974 meetings of the Mildura Racing Club, the winner receiving The Vinelander Plate. The timetable altered over the years but the 1975 schedule was typical of the type of trip; the train departed Melbourne at 9.20 pm and pulled into Mildura the next morning at 8.05 am. The train also hauled motorail wagons to allow passengers to bring their cars along. By the 1990s, the service was faltering. The daytime Sunraysia train was withdrawn from the line in 1990 and, after the new Liberal state government failed to attract a private operator, the Vinelander itself ran for the last time on 12 September 1993. Mildura residents have, in recent years, been promised a new train — but there was still no sign of it at time of writing.

WESTERN AUSTRALIA
Albany Progress

Perth–Albany, Western Australia

Route distance: 547 km

This train, which ran overnight on its route, could not compete with modern road transport. It had a weekend sister service known as the Albany Weekender. The Progress pulled out of Perth at 7.15 pm, arriving at its destination the next morning at 8.40 am, with its main

Introduction of buffet cars in Western Australia meant the end for many refreshment rooms. Such a car was AQL 288, seen here in service on the Albany Progress in 1970. *John Beckhaus.*

stops along the way being Northam and Wagin. The train saw considerable changes in rolling stock over the years. Originally equipped with stock dating back as far as 1903, in the early 1960s, Westrail began overhauling its overnight carriages. The Albany Progress had first and second class sleeping cars (the first class ones having wash basins with hot and cold water), sitting cars for intermediate passengers, and a buffet and lounge car.

Australind

Perth–Bunbury, Western Australia

Route distance: 185 km

This train was named after a settlement near Bunbury founded in 1841 by Marshall Clifton, the word 'Australind' capturing his hopes for the establishment of trade between Australia and British-run India. The original train had cars built at the Midland workshops in 1947 and overhauled in 1960. Some carriages (the AYD class) had a central entrance door with a vestibule dividing the saloon from the buffet lounge. In the late 1980s, a new diesel unit was introduced to the run complete with air-conditioning, piped music, individual reading lights and double-glazed windows. The train was capable of speeds up to 140 km/h.

The Kalgoorlie

Perth–Kalgoorlie, Western Australia

Route distance: 611 km

Status: Replaced in 1971 by the Prospector

This train operated as a complementary service to the Westland Express. While the latter was essentially a connecting operation for passengers travelling to and from Kalgoorlie on the transcontinental standard gauge line, The Kalgoorlie primarily served the intrastate traveller.

It had a pre-war predecessor known as The Kalgoorlie Express. Initially, its sleeping cars were configured with either four or six berths, the lack of privacy accentuated by communal hand basins and lavatories. From the 1930s, first class passengers were afforded greater privacy when two-berth compartment cars were introduced.

Its replacement, the Prospector, became Australia's fastest train reaching speeds up to 140 km/h until the XPT trains in New South Wales were cleared to run at up to 160 km/h. It was originally scheduled to travel the 611 km in a little over eight hours, leaving Perth at 8.30 am and arriving in Kalgoorlie at 4.40 pm.

Westland Express

Perth–Kalgoorlie, Western Australia

Introduced: 1948

Route distance: 611 km

Status: Withdrawn 1970

The Westland Express operated on the narrow gauge link between Perth and Kalgoorlie, being superseded when the standard gauge link was opened and the transcontinental Indian Pacific was inaugurated. However, in 1948 when it began running, it was a smart train equipped with newly built carriages from the workshops at Midland with accommodation for forty-eight first class passengers and sixty in second class. The first class sleepers were divided into eight two-berth apartments, with the shower room at one end of the car. It is believed to be the first train in Australia to have hot water provided to hand basins in each compartment. Each compartment had a fan, fluorescent

West Australian trains were notable for their centre-loading cars, as seen here on the Australind between Perth and Bunbury behind U657, some time in the 1950s.
Battye Library.

lighting and refrigerated drinking water. But while the second class compartments had fourth berths, the interiors were lined with polished jarrah timber. The train had a 40-seat dining car and a lounge car with easy chairs and writing desks. Diesel haulage took over from steam in 1954. It was very much conceived as a connecting service for trains to and from the east, with Western Australian Government Railways accepting bookings only on behalf of interstate sleeper passengers.

Railcars, railmotors and diesel sets

On other than main lines, it was often uneconomic to provide steam-hauled carriage sets — there was rarely an occasion when the number of patrons would fill such a train. Then, as road transport started to compete for passengers, the railways looked for ways to replace the most common form of country passenger service — the mixed train (usually consisting of one or two cars at the end of a rake of wagons) — because it was far too slow, with trains stopping to shunt at almost every wayside station.

The answer, and it was a very successful answer for many decades, was the self-propelled rail vehicle — the railcar, and its variants.

Steam railcars

In the age before the modern petrol or diesel engine, steam was the only viable method of propulsion. South Australian Railways operated steam-powered railcars between 1883 and 1924. Its first venture was the importation from Belgium of a double-decked steam railcar. Steam was raised in an area on the lower deck, next to which was placed the baggage compartment. There was also a passenger compartment on the lower level together with an open rear deck, from which stairs gave access to the upper area where longitudinal seating provided accommodation for thirty-six passengers. The car was first assigned to the Strathalbyn–Victor Harbor run. However, the vehicle struggled to climb the grades of up to 1 in 55 and was transferred to Adelaide in 1885, where it ran on the line owned by the Largs Bay Land and Investment Company (SAR provided all rolling stock and services on that private line). In the 1890s, the car was transferred to run between Woodville and Grange. It was scrapped in 1910.

But, in 1906, SAR bought two narrow gauge 22-seater Kitson steam cars. One was placed on the Quorn–Port Augusta run, and was later sold to Commonwealth Railways, in 1926, for use between Port Augusta and Oodnadatta. It was renumbered NJAB No. 1. The other vehicle was assigned to the South East Division of SAR.

In 1923, Commonwealth Railways ordered a Sentinel–Cammell steam railcar and this entered service in October the following year. It was an all-steel car, with one-end control and a lavatory for passenger use. A vertical boiler was mounted in front of the driving cabin. The boiler had a central chute through which coal was dropped on to the fire. It had the capacity for thirteen hundredweight (about 660 kg) of fuel and three hundred gallons (1,364 litres) of water. This car operated between Darwin and Katherine until October 1936. When the United States Army arrived in the Northern Territory it was decided to convert the railcar to run on petrol, planning to install a Ford V8 engine. However, this was never completed. T. Southwell Kelly recalled a journey on the Sentinel, which soon became known as 'Leaping Lena' for the state of its riding

A railmotor of a type that saw service around New South Wales and transported the country people to town. HPC 401 is sitting at the Inverell platform in December 1978 ready to depart for Moree. Inverell was removed from the railway map in 1987. *John Beckhaus.*

ABOVE: The 'Coffee Pot' was more correctly South Australian Railways' Steam Motor Coach No. 1. The locomotive was built in 1905 by Kitson & Co. of Leeds in the United Kingdom, with the coach coming from the Metropolitan Amalgamated Carriage & Wagon Co. of Birmingham. It ran initially between Quorn and Hawker, averaging 35 km/h. *Author's collection.*

RIGHT: Another view of the famed 'Coffee Pot'. *Author's collection.*

OPPOSITE: Leaping Lena, more formally known as the Sentinel Cammell Laird steam railcar which operated on the North Australia Railway. Its wheel arrangement was 0-4-0. Although not used since World War II, it was scrapped by Fujita Salvage Company around 1960. *Noel Inglis collection.*

qualities. He recorded that it pulled out of Darwin station with 'a series of jolts and jerks, which it maintains with unfailing regularity throughout the journey, so that one braces oneself in readiness for the next shattering jar and is disappointed if it does not occur'. He watched ahead as the narrow gauge rails 'stretched out in front through a tapering clearing; not the shining rails of the southern lines, but rust encrusted, for the trains run but once a week. The monotony of the Australian bush, mile after mile of the same type of stunted trees and scrub, is maintained to the terminus.'

Victorian Railways was, like SAR, also interested in steam railcars and by 1883 had imported a Kitson unit. This differed from other contemporaries in that its power unit could be detached from the passenger section and a replacement coupled instead. This vehicle, known as the 'Rowan Car', seated twelve passengers in first class and thirty in second. It made its test run to Bendigo and back but thereafter provided services around Melbourne, including Box Hill and Lilydale. This car was withdrawn in 1892.

Twenty years would pass before Victorian Railways again tried steam railcars, this time importing a Great Western Railways–type Kerr Stuart system. The body was built at Newport workshops and the unit assembled there, with the railcar entering service in June 1913. It had a baggage compartment, along with two first class compartments (one for non-smokers) and, beyond an entrance vestibule, a second class compartment. In all, this car could seat fifty-four passengers. It was clearly not a great success because VR ordered no further cars, and the first was withdrawn in 1924.

In its early years, Western Australian Government Railways did go as far as having a steam railcar designed, but progress went no further. In 1932, however, WAGR committed to a standard, 52-seater Sentinel railcar which initially operated on a variety of lines but from 1939 was used on suburban services between Perth and Armadale to fill the long gaps between steam train passenger services on this line. It was notoriously difficult to fire, and WAGR staff could use only Newcastle coal as no other coals could provide the heat to get the steam pressure up to a sufficient level.

Queensland Railways operated an unusual service, a tram-train in Rockhampton. This ran along a public thoroughfare between Stanley Street and Lakes Creek, a distance of eight miles. A small 4–4–0 locomotive was attached to a bogie and it stopped at all the cross streets in between. In 1923, the steam railcar was replaced by French-designed Purrey steam trams, the service ending when bus operations became popular in the 1930s.

The year 1931 saw Tasmanian Government Railways enter the world of the steam railcar with the purchase of two Sentinel–Cammell vehicles, numbered SP1 and SP2, which had 100 hp capacity. They carried eighteen first class and twenty-two second class passengers on nightly services between Hobart and Launceston, covering the 213 km run in four and a half hours. TGR was pleased with the experience and in 1934 ordered two further cars (SP3 and SP4), which each had two 100 hp engines. These cars took over the main line runs, leaving SP1 and SP2 to be assigned to duties on the other lines. In 1937, five more cars (SP4–SP9) entered service. Parts became a problem during World War II and operations of the steam railcars became intermittent. They were used occasionally after the war.

The diesel era

In 1951, the Commonwealth Railways introduced the Budd RDC air-conditioned railcars which were driven by two General Motors diesel engines. The railcars were capable of speeds above 110 km/h. In fact, in a test run held on 29 April 1951, a Budd set ran from Port Augusta to Kalgoorlie. It completed the journey in nineteen hours with an average speed of 89 km/h, at that time the fastest long-distance speed in Australian rail history. The Budd actually got to 144 km/h on the long straight stretch across the Nullarbor. These cars ran between Port Pirie Junction and Port Augusta, the only two towns of any size and population on the standard gauge Trans-Australian Railway. Some runs were extended to Tarcoola.

But the state systems had experimented very early in the piece with diesel cars. By 1960, more than 1,330 rail motors or railcars were operating in the NSW system.

In 1919, New South Wales Government Railways converted a road lorry to run on rails. Called Rail Motor No. 1, it was formed from a five-ton truck with the front axle replaced by a four-wheel bogie. A new body was built to accommodate thirty-three seated passengers. It made its test run to Waterfall, on what is now the extremity of the Sydney suburban system, and ran at about 40 km/h. From 1 October, it was assigned to Lismore where a light four-wheel trailer was added containing a guard's compartment and space for seventy-two cream cans.

Rail Motor No. 2, named *Kathleen*, was a converted American suburban car FA 1864, equipped with a 100 hp engine and divided into two compartments seating a total of fifty-three people. On 29 April 1921, it was assigned to run on the Barraba branch line from West Tamworth. However, after numerous failures in traffic, this car was

withdrawn and returned to its original form. It was still working in the Newcastle district in 1967.

Rail Motor No. 3 was the first of the memorable CPH rail motors. In November 1923, CPH 3 was assigned to the Riverina where it ran three days a week on each of the Culcairn–Holbrook and Henty–Rand branch lines.

The CPH railmotors carved for themselves a special place in NSW rail history, and several have been preserved in running order. They ran on country lines in most parts of the state, and, in 1929, were drafted to work on parts of the Sydney suburban system which had yet to be electrified; first out of Bankstown and to Cowan in the north and Waterfall in the south. For some of the cars, their last years were spent based at Wollongong before electrification came to that part of the system.

After World War II, New South Wales introduced the 600 Class railcar, notable for introducing driving controls in the trailer as well as the power car (so making shunting unnecessary at journey's end) and also allowing multiple units to be lashed together for single-driver operation. These rail units were designed to run on the higher density branch lines, replacing steam-hauled carriage trains. A variation on this design was the 900 Class that became identified with some of the longer-distance train services such as the Northern Tablelands Express, which provided a passenger service between Sydney and Tenterfield (via Armidale and Glen Innes) and Moree. They were easily split which allowed the train to be cut in two at Werris Creek for runs to the two separate destinations in the north of the state, and then be joined again at the same junction on the return to Sydney.

William Webb, the Commissioner for South Australian Railways, introduced Model 55 railcars in 1924 for use on

Henry Scott, line foreman, and Sid Wilson, linesman, discuss the day's work in 1953 with a Leyland railcar standing on the North Australia Railway line.
Peter Dunham collection.

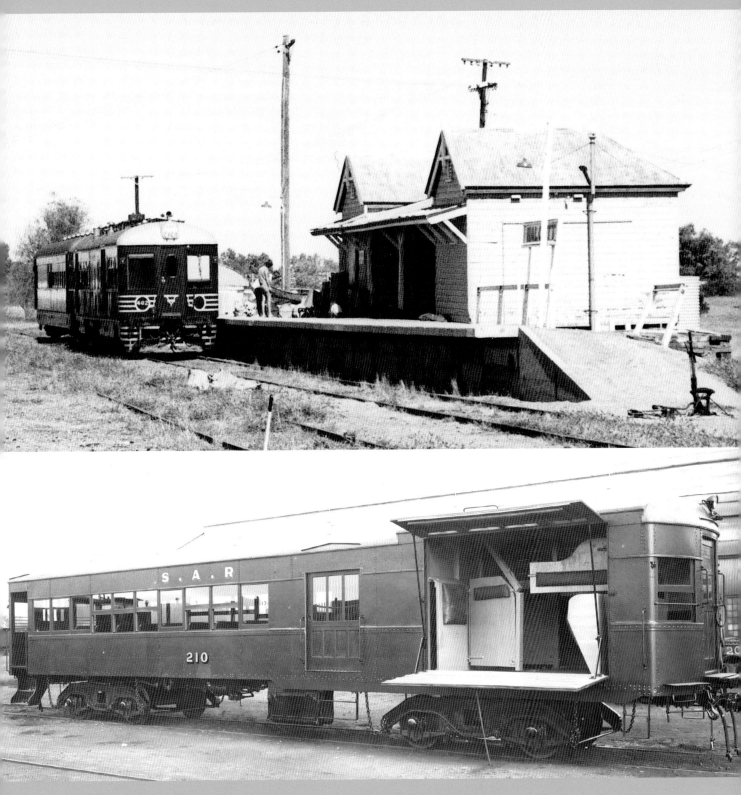

TOP: **Its days were numbered when diesel train 402/503 ran to Walgett station on 26 April 1973. The rail service had gone by the early 1980s, and the line to the station was closed in 1987, freight services thereafter terminating 4.1 km earlier at Walgett wheat terminal.** *John Hoyle.*

ABOVE: **This South Australian Brill Model 75 railcar trailer No. 210 has been modified to carry three horses, with the side open to show the stalls. Passenger seating was reduced to forty-five.** *National Railway Museum.*

Many road vehicles were equipped with flanged wheels to allow them to travel on rails, but they were usually works-related. Here, a Faegol motor coach has been put on the rails, one of several providing passenger services on the isolated Eyre Peninsula system in South Australia. Railcar 109 with trailer has reached the end of the journey, Buckleboo, on 7 October 1959. Usually, conversion resulted in a headlight being placed on the roof, but SAR kept the original ones. *National Railway Museum.*

ABOVE: Between trips at Normanton.
Brian Webber.

LEFT: Out in the far north reaches
of the Queensland system, a railcar awaits
departure from a clearly underused Almaden
station on 6 September 2000. *Brian Webber.*

FOLLOWING SPREAD: Werris Creek. The grand
station is shown to advantage in this
photograph. The four cars on the north-west
platform (left) comprise two cars from the
'Rain Train', the drought relief special, leading
the normal two cars from Moree. On the north
platform, the three-car set from Armidale waits
for the north-west portion to be coupled in the
lead for the remainder of the journey to Sydney.
The small building at the apex of the platform
is the signal box. Recent restoration of the
station exterior has resulted in a much-
improved appearance. *John Currey.*

ABOVE: In a panorama reminiscent of the last days of branch line railmotor services in Victoria during the 1970s, the 280 hp Walker railcar 91RM has just arrived at Bullarto to collect its lone passenger, and will then proceed to Daylesford. *Barry Fell.*

RIGHT: In the early 1970s, Victorian Railways bought two 600 hp diesel railcars to improve some branch line services. In this photograph, DRC40 has just 1 km left to run on the light 60 lb rails, dating from the 1880s, before reaching the terminus at Daylesford. *Barry Fell.*

country lines where there were insufficient passenger numbers to justify a full passenger train. The cars, made by the Brill Company, soon became known as the 'Tin Hares'. They were later switched to suburban running until withdrawn in 1968.

Two years after the Tin Hares appeared, Webb brought in another railcar from the United States, Brill's Model 75. Then SAR went on to build its own version at the Islington workshops. These also operated mainly over country branches and lasted until 1971.

Another innovation, this time in the 1930s, was the introduction of the Faegol railcars. These were to become familiar on the isolated system on South Australia's Eyre Peninsula, where the first line opened in 1907 and tracks reached Buckleboo by 1926. In 1915, South Australian Railways tried a small German-built motor engine on this line but it proved unsuccessful. Passengers using this system had a weekly steam-hauled passenger train from Port Lincoln to Thevenard, and mixed trains to Minnipa and Kimba. As elsewhere in Australia, these services simply could not pay their way. Therefore, SAR decided to convert four Faegol motor coaches that had been used for its road passenger services to Victor Harbor, Gawler and Mannum. At Islington workshops, the buses were given a front bogie and two trailing wheels at the back. After a lavatory had been added, there was seating for twenty passengers and a trailer car was added to carry perishables, mail and parcels. From August 1931, the first of these cars took over from steam-hauled passenger trains from Cummins to Kimba, and later Buckleboo, and Cummins–Minnipa. All four were in service by May 1933, taking over from the Thevenard trains (reducing the 433 km journey time from eighteen and a half hours to

twelve) and also providing a new service to Penola. They were a stop-gap measure on the main run to Thevenard. Some were replaced in 1936 by bigger Model 75 railcars and two Faegols were transferred to work Naracoorte–Kingston. The last Faegol car run on the Eyre Peninsula, with No. 109, took place on 17 August 1961. Earlier, in 1944, 55 class railcars were introduced and the Faegols were kept on at Port Lincoln as back-up vehicles. The cars were numbered 107 (1931–1957), 108 (1933–1959), 109 (1933–1961) and 110 (1933–1961). The cars had a six-cylinder Hall Scott engine rated at 43.3 hp.

South Australian lines were familiar territory for the Bluebird trains, built at the Islington workshops between 1955 and 1959 for South Australian Railways (and were part of the transfer of SAR to Australian National). The cars, painted blue and silver, were named after local bird species. For example, Bluebird 101 was called 'Grebe' and 230 was 'Quail'. They operated to Victor Harbor, Mount Gambier, Peterborough and Port Pirie. First class seating was available on the latter two runs, with economy seating only on other routes. In 1972, SAR converted some of the cars to allow for a buffet section offering light meals and snacks, but by the 1980s these buffet operations had been withdrawn on all but the Mount Gambier service. The last was decommissioned in 1993.

At about the time when the Bluebirds arrived on the scene, SAR introduced a railcar version called the 'Red Hens' for working on Adelaide suburban systems.

Queensland also depended on railcars or railmotors for services on branch and country lines. The most famous was (and is) the Gulflander, on the isolated Normanton–Croydon line in Far North Queensland. In the mid-50s, Queensland Government Railways introduced the 1900

Older suburban travellers in Melbourne will remember the old red rattler cars, with the whine of their electric motors and the comfort of their upholstered seating. No. 128M is seen here in the lead at St Kilda on 21 May 1971. *John Beckhaus.*

Class railcars, the first stainless steel railcars in the Commonwealth. They were fashioned after the Budd cars, built by Commonwealth Engineering and ran on a variety of suburban, inter-urban and branch services. The SCR-1 version could take fifty-eight passengers, while the SEC-2 held fifty people and 2.5 tons of luggage.

Among Victoria's early experiments were two McKeen railmotors, including trailers, bought from the United States in 1912. They were noteworthy for having windows shaped like portholes and rounded ends. Powered by a 200 hp Alecyl engine, they could theoretically make 95 km/h, but they never proved satisfactory when assigned to Warrnambool–Hamilton and Ballarat–Ballan services, starting on 13 May 1912. In 1919, they were converted to ordinary carriages and assigned to the Newport–Altona line.

Queensland Government Railways imported five McKeen cars and in November 1913, the South Brisbane–Sunnybank service was taken over by these rail-motors. They served around Ipswich with one going to Woolloongabba. One of their shortcomings was that, because there was no guard's compartment, milk, cream and fruit were carried in the engine room. They were also heavy on fuel. In 1914, QGR tried to find a better use for them by converting Nos 2 and 5 into tourist cars. They were done out with settees, lounge chairs, tables, lockers, an ice chest and a lavatory. But by 1920, the McKeen cars were rarely used.

A large fleet of railcars served Victoria's busy country passenger network in the 1950s, and had replaced mixed trains on most branches. The 280 hp railcars, painted blue and silver, could carry twenty-eight first class and fifty-six second class passengers as well as 2 tons of freight. These cars operated out of Spencer Street station in Melbourne to Wangaratta, Daylesford, Wonthaggi and Bacchus Marsh. The 153 hp cars plied between Melbourne and Mansfield and Melbourne–Heathcote. Finally, the smaller 102 hp type ran Rushworth–Seymour, Ararat–Avoca–Maryborough, Cobram–Numurkah–Shepparton, Maryborough–Castlemaine, Wodonga–Tallangatta, Yarrawonga–Benalla, Pinnaroo (South Australia)–Ouyen, Horsham–Goroke and Ararat–Hamilton. They served as feeders to the main line passenger trains, enabling country people to get to Melbourne and back in a day.

Suburban trains

Australia's first railways were mostly suburban railways. The first line in Melbourne ran a short distance to Port Melbourne. In Sydney, the first line was to Parramatta. In Adelaide, a private company connected Glenelg with the city. The basis for Perth's suburban railway system was laid when, on 1 March 1881, a 32 km section opened between Fremantle via East Perth to Guildford. Then, in 1883, the line south to Pinjarra was completed, with Armadale being the limit of suburban train operations. In 1885, a small branch was laid from Bayswater to Belmont, the main purpose of which was to carry passengers travelling to and from the Belmont Racecourse.

Brisbane was the notable exception. Queensland's first line ran from Ipswich, and only later was the then colonial capital reached by rail.

In all state capitals, services were expanded to meet the ever-increasing urban population. In all these places, too, the jungle that is their road systems ensured that the railways had a significant transport role, even though, in Sydney's case at least, it came close to buckling under the strain.

OPPOSITE ABOVE: **Charleville's rail ambulance with Nurse Audrey Millington and friend about 1950. They are ready to depart to collect another patient. Note the water bag strapped to the cowcatcher in front of the radiator; the headlight is positioned high on the roof canopy.** *Photo by Mrs P. R. New, George Balsillie collection.*

RIGHT: **An AEC railmotor stands at Red Cliffs station after arriving from Mildura.** *Wilf Henty.*

Expansion has continued over the 150 years since the first rails were laid for steam train services in Melbourne. For example, in Sydney, between 1920 and 1932, much work was carried out extending the suburban system, part of it in anticipation of the completion of the Sydney Harbour Bridge (opened in 1932) that provided a cross-harbour rail link. East Hills and Cronulla were also finally reached by rail in this period. In more recent times, Sydney and Brisbane have added airport railways, with mixed success. Melbourne, eventually, went underground. Brisbane and Perth, eventually, went electric.

Of all the mainland capitals, Adelaide has been the equivocal one. Even in the 1940s, a period when most people still did not own a motorcar, the suburban services were characterised by light traffic loads. Outside peak hours there were two services an hour to Semaphore, one to Henley Beach, one to Port Dock, (although special boat trains ran to Outer Harbour). Under the Webb regime, which began in 1922, South Australian Railways had a policy of discouraging suburban passenger trains and services were consequently reduced. On 4 March 1929, the South Terrace to Glenelg line (that had been built by the Adelaide, Glenelg and Suburban Railway Company) was sold to the Adelaide Municipal Tramway Trust to be converted to a tram line.

The Semaphore branch, closed in 1978, was noteworthy both for the line running down the centre of Semaphore Road as well as having a station located in the street — Exeter consisted of a narrow raised platform around which road traffic flowed. At the Semaphore terminus itself, the main platform had been formed by raising one side of the street to platform level and locating the station in line with adjacent shops.

But many towns and cities around Australia had their own suburban trains, most of them forgotten other than by rail historians or the occasional older resident. There is no space to describe them all, but some examples will do.

In 1882, Queensland Government Railways introduced a shopper's special each Saturday from Westwood and this mixed train became a daily, although short-lived, service for commuters from 1884. However, local trains did return in subsequent years to Westwood, Stanwell and Kabra, the junction of the central and Mt Morgan lines. Rail motors were operating local services by the 1930s, but these had all come to an end by 1967.

Trains leaving Rockhampton for Mt Morgan stopped to pickup and set down passengers at what were suburban stations of the latter town: Waterhall, Baree, Kirkhall and Moongan. At one stage, there were three mixed trains each weekday, a late Saturday night train, and two services on Sunday. By 1907, twelve trains a day were operating to provide transport between Mt Morgan and Moongan, with a special train from town at 9.40 pm to allow people in outlying districts to have an evening in Mt Morgan. By the middle of the 1930s, all these services had disappeared. Trains also provided local services between Rockhampton and the two seaside destinations of Emu Park and Yeppoon.

In Townsville, a suburban service started running out to Brookhill, and then to Stewart's Creek (later renamed Stuart). This section of line was duplicated in the 1930s and tiny shelters (described as 'roofs on stilts') were provided at the various stops. Eighty services a week were operating to Stuart by the 1950s, with additional trains to Partington for workers at Stuart Gaol. Cairns, too, had

BATHING BUSINESS

AT MUCKADILLA, ON the Western line, the Queensland Railway Department diversified into running public baths. Analysis of bore water showed it high in various minerals with curative properties for rheumatic ailments. Once the railway reached the town, people travelled there for the waters. In 1911, the railway department took over the baths from the Queensland Treasury, building four new bath houses and charging visitors sixpence for entry. The department also built a nearby hotel. Concession fares were available to travellers to Muckadilla. The advent of World War II resulted in the end of the special trains run to the station. In any event, the appeal of the baths had been receding and the whole operation was closed on 29 July 1943.

local trains, initially to Aloomba. The AEC railmotors introduced on this run in 1927 were allowed forty-four stops over the 28 km distance — as one writer described it, almost the same spacing as between bus stops. Innisfail and Redlynch eventually got their local trains out of Cairns. The latter run, a distance of 11.3 km, was allowed thirty minutes as there were five wayside stations and an additional fifteen places designated as railmotor stops. Local trains ran from Maryborough to Pialba, Urangan and Howard. From Toowoomba there were short-lived services to Willowburn and Wyreema.

Mildura, in the Sunraysia region of Victoria had a suburban train service between 1922 and 1928. At Red Cliffs, south of the town, soldier settlements had been established for men returning from the Great War. Most of these men continued to live in Mildura, or in Merbein further north, and travelled each day to their land. However, the roads were bad and local agitation began for a better train service around Mildura. From 22 June 1922, AEC Rail Motor No. 1 and trailer, which had been assigned from Melbourne, started services north to Merbein and south to Red Cliffs, supplemented by normal steam services, offering in total up to four services a day to each end. The railmotor stopped at level crossings as well as stations, and soon after a Saturday service further south to Yatpool was added. However, this was a steam-operated service as Yatpool had no turntable for the railmotor, which had only one driving end. Before the service began, small, light-weight turntables had been supplied to Merbein and Red Cliffs so that the railmotor could be turned each trip. One aspect annoyed the locals — Victorian Railways had imposed a higher fare for rail-motor travel than for steam trains. In 1923, the railway

commissioners agreed on one of those compromises that can only come out of a bureaucracy. Those boarding at stations would pay the normal steam train fare, but the higher rate would continue to apply for people joining the railmotor at level crossings and other non-station stops, and special tickets were then printed for issue to the latter category of customer. In another interesting ruling, Victorian Railways allowed the steam train to stop at Red Cliffs Soldier Settlement — not an official station — but passengers could only board or alight using Mallee cars, the type that had very low steps in the American style (where raised platforms were not the norm). The inevitable competition from a local bus carrier began in 1925. This appealed to many people because the vehicles could stop right outside their doors. The railways countered by bringing in a new railmotor, and from 1927, added a second machine to allow more frequent services. A Saturday service was also run from Ouyen and back, which became known as the 'shopping train'. However, the die was cast as the extra services could not compete with buses. Mildura's suburban services ended as of 10 November 1928, although the Saturday service up and back from Ouyen lasted until 1930.

Kalgoorlie was claimed to be the smallest town in Australia ever to have suburban rail services. Yet, in an article published in the *West Australian* in 1975, it was argued with some plausibility that the busiest station in Australia around 1900 was Golden Gate in the outskirts of Kalgoorlie. It certainly handled more trains a day than Perth at that time. The town had a suburban rail service from 1897 when the first section of the loopline was built and the entire line was completed in 1903. The loopline formed an elongated circle that went through eleven

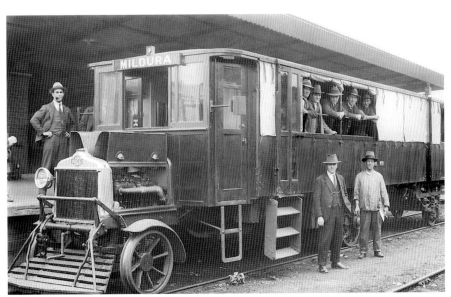

AEC railmotor No. 1 and trailer MT1 are seen here at Mildura station in June 1925. The number of officials posing suggests this was the inaugural run to Merbein. *John Thompson collection.*

stations, the trains ending up back at Kalgoorlie whence they had come. One was Golden Gate where trains would run every ten minutes when there were shift changes at the mines, which worked three shifts around the clock. Up to sixty-one trains a day operated on the loop and the line was also used to bring equipment to the mines (boilers, crushers and winder motors) and also fuel (mainly firewood to be used to keep the mine boilers alight). This wood was supplied to Kalgoorlie on private tramways along a network at the ends of which more than 2,000 men felled trees. Golden Gate had two stationmasters and a large staff of porters and clerks. Boulder City station had three passenger lines, an island platform linked by overhead footbridges and a staff of twelve. Kalgoorlie's electric tram service started in 1904, and most of the passengers who had used loopline trains switched to the new trams. However, the railway still carried freight with train services lasting until 1974.

Trains for all occasions

Over the decades, before motorised road transport and paved highways became ubiquitous, the railway systems were involved in the operation of specialist train services of many types. Some were for communities beyond the main cities, others were to serve the needs of the railways themselves. In the case of water trains it was to serve both; the people struck by drought on the land and the rail workers and locomotives as well.

Rail ambulances

Queensland Railways built ten rail ambulances during the 1920s that were based in outback towns to cope with medical emergencies. They were operated by the Queensland Ambulance Transport Board. Seriously ill people in areas remote from hospitals could often not be transported to a doctor because of the state of the roads. Before the ambulances were built, trains had been used to transport very sick or badly injured people. But they ran to schedules whereas the ambulance could be dispatched in response to a specific crisis. Local districts raised money towards the costs of the rail ambulance. One newspaper account of 1921 advised of a Sunday excursion to a small settlement of Wyandra with tickets at six shillings for adults and three shillings for children, where the excursionists could fish, go boating or shooting.

The rail ambulances were painted white and had prominent red crosses on their sides. The roofs were made of canvas. Their operation required a qualified railways department driver to be in charge, along with one other rail staffer. Charleville got its rail ambulance in 1929. It was 4.72 m in length and powered by a 10 hp Gardner engine built in Enoggera. On the lighter branch lines, the ambulance was limited to a speed of 24 km/h on the straight and 9.5 km/h on curves. The vehicle was very light and would easily have been derailed had it struck any object on the line. When the brakes were applied, the wheels tended to slide along the rails rather than grip them. In 1945, the Charleville ambulance base had two road vehicles, and used the rail ambulance only when the roads were impassable or at night when visibility was poor. It served until 1965 and was subsequently bought by the Charleville District Historical and Cultural Society by whom it was fully restored.

Another is preserved at Mareeba. It was a 45 hp AEC model 506, originally a London bus, which was converted for railway use. Between 1926 and 1940, it ran on the Milla

What is thought to be Ambulance Car 229 (ex passenger car 105) of the South Australian Railways was comfortably fitted out for the patient being transported. Electric fans for the hot daytime, lights for evening and a window so the patient could see the view. This was photographed at Adelaide on a date unknown. *National Railway Museum.*

The Reverend Stanley Drummond is pictured inside one of the baby, clinic cars watching as a baby is weighed by a sister, while mother looks on. *Great Cobar Heritage Centre.*

FOLLOWING PAGES: **This photograph was taken in late 1957 at Byrock Railway Station (between Nyngan and Bourke in northern New South Wales). Sister Godfrey is standing in the carriage while Robin and Rose Mitchell return to their car with baby Lynette.** *Great Cobar Heritage Centre.*

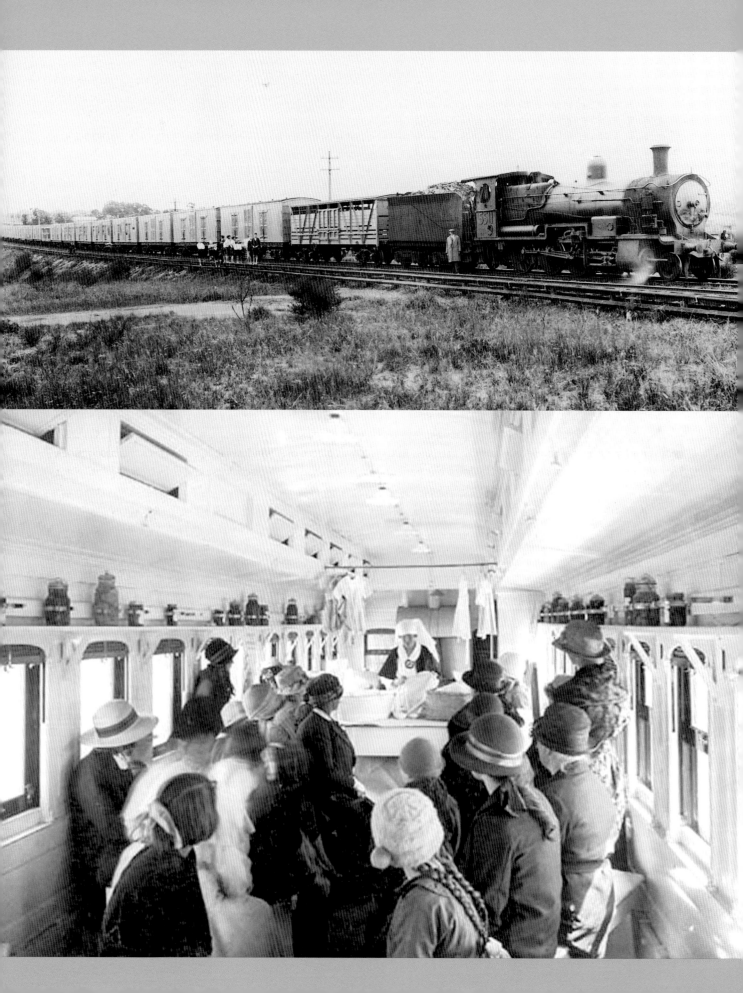

Milla branch transporting cream for the Atherton Butter Factory with a Queensland Railways Department driver. It was then left unused for most of the war years. The Mareeba Hospital Board bought the machine after the war. The engine was rebuilt by the QR locomotive foremen at Mareeba then it went to QR's Townsville workshops where the body was rebuilt. In April 1949, the car was used on lines south and west of Mareeba and by 1964 had clocked a total of 55,960 km. After that year, the ambulance was put into use only when roads were flooded and rail was the only means of transport. Government policy eventually turned to air transport to move sick or injured people, but this Mareeba ambulance did make the occasional foray until 1983. It is now being restored at Mareeba.

In 1939, Newport workshops at Melbourne completed the first ambulance carriage (as opposed to the self-propelled Queensland models). It was built for the Defence Department, the first part of a plan for a complete hospital train of sixteen cars, including staff cars, an operating theatre, dining car and a stores car along with bed space for 360 casualties. This first ambulance car was converted from a side-door excursion Tait carriage, BPL 82, and was fitted out to accommodate forty-one patients arranged in triple tiers along the side walls. The car was painted moonstone grey with large red crosses on the roof and sides.

Children's health cars

This train originated from a scheme developed by a Methodist minister and his wife appointed to the Methodist Far West Mission, a position that brought with it some 145,000 square km of the New South Wales outback. In 1924, the Reverend Stanley Drummond and Lucy Drummond arrived in Cobar where they found many families living in dire poverty due to the closure of the mine near the town. This situation, however, was not unique because children in many parts of rural Australia suffered disease and illness without recourse to medical services.

It was the closure of the Great Cobar copper mine in 1914, followed by other mine failures, that brought economic misery to this outback town. Its population, about ten thousand while the mines were booming, shrivelled to 1,250 by the time the Drummonds arrived. (The Great Cobar re-opened in 1916 but shut again in 1919 because there was simply not sufficient demand for its output.)

The result was the Far West Children's Health Scheme which began operation around 1930. Initially, one railway carriage was converted to be a Travelling Baby Clinic. It was staffed by a nursing sister and part of the car was converted into her living quarters: a bedroom, bathroom, kitchenette and even a refrigerating plant. The rest of the car was fitted out as a consulting room and clinic. Gauze was placed over windows to keep out flies and mosquitoes while shades protected nurse and baby from the sun. No. 1 Clinic Car, as it was designated, began service in 1931 and was sent out on the Bourke, Brewarrina and Cobar lines. Sister Brooks was the first nurse. She would spend between two and ten days in each locality caring for the infants brought from all over the local districts. Apart from the priority of having their babies checked and perhaps treated, the mobile clinics were a major social event for the mothers and a welcome break from the routine and drudgery of their lonely lives. In her last tour in 1934 before she returned to Britain, Brooks saw about

OPPOSITE ABOVE: **New South Wales ran a Better Farming Special, designed to help introduce new methods of wheat production to the man on the land. The train is pictured in 1937 near Sydney and would visit many regional centres including Albury, Tumut, Harden and Gundagai. Locomotive 5511 hauled a BCW wagon, seven BCV covered wagons, seven BSV wagons, water van, dining car and brake van, a total load of 520 tons.** Author's collection.

LEFT: **While the men learned about new wheat varieties and pig husbandry, the ladies boarded the Better Farming Train for a lecture on mothercraft. Apart from anything else, it was a welcome break from the drudgery of life on the land.** Department of Primary Industries.

ABOVE: A lecture on pig farming from
the Better Farming Train. Note how the
sides of the wagon can be rolled up to
expose the pigs in their cages.
Department of Primary Industry.

450 babies. Such was the success of this service that the New South Wales Government Railways agreed to convert two other cars. No. 2 Clinic Car, under Sister Kellie, operated along the lines to Walgett while No. 3 Clinic Car, under Sister McInnes, plied the railway sidings all the way to Mungindi near the Queensland border. The cars, usually attached to goods trains, would be dropped off at a siding as part of normal shunting duties with the carriage later being collected by another train to be hauled to the next wayside station.

One of these carriages has been restored and it's now on display at Cobar's heritage centre.

Farming trains

In the 1930s, Victorian Railways Commissioner Harold Clapp took his campaign to help the farmer beyond selling fresh produce at railways. He established the 'Better Farming Train'. The consist of fifteen vehicles was painted bright orange and the converted wagons or carriages offered displays on the management of both stock and crops: tobacco, pigs, dairying, beekeeping, potatoes and pasture. And the livestock displays meant carrying animals on the train. While cattle had to be taken off the wagon and put in a pen in the station yard, with the pigs, it was a matter of opening up the sides to show the cages. The train toured Victoria between 1924 and 1935, spending a day at each centre. There was something, too, for the farmers' wives; they could attend lectures by nurses about infant welfare, or watch cooking or sewing demonstrations. The *Journal of Agriculture* reported that the food lectures concentrated on simple fare such as dried fruit, soups, casseroles, and how to make pastry. All these would have been vital on farms where there was little spare

cash and the wives laboured from dawn to dusk. Like the mobile baby clinics in the Far West of New South Wales, the Better Farming Train's visit was a welcome break in the humdrum drudgery that both men and women faced on the farm. They could dress up, go to the local railway station, and probably spend as much time talking to other people from around the district as they did attending the lectures and inspecting the displays.

The centenary train

Between February and June 1941, Victorian Railways had in service the Centenary–Jubilee Train, marking the foundation of Victoria, the granting of self-government and the gold rush. Eleven BPL cars were stripped and, with their end doors, formed a line of carriages through which the public could walk from one end to the other. Hauled by locomotive N430, the train carried pictures from the then National Art Gallery, models of goldfields, rare manuscripts and prints covering Victoria's early history, displays for the Air Force, Army and Navy and a display showing the planned Snowy Mountains Scheme. There was also an entertainment unit which provided shows in the towns visited. The train travelled a total of 10,040 km, stopped at 168 stations and was inspected by 548,000 Victorians.

Tea and Sugar Train

This was the name bestowed on the weekly supply train which served the railway settlements along the Trans-Australian Railway. It ran weekly from Port Augusta and provided a shopping service for the railway employees and their families. The train began running in 1915, before the completion of the transcontinental link, and it carried a butcher shop and a van selling fruit and vegetables. A car with a dispensary was also provided in the consist for many years. The problem of lack of refrigeration was overcome by the cartage of live sheep which were slaughtered as the meat was needed. There were, in fact, two such trains until the transcontinental line was completed. One ran from Kalgoorlie to the western railhead while the other was based at Port Augusta. By 1920, one train set was equipped with purpose-built cars rather than hastily converted goods wagons, and these were replaced by even more modern rolling stock in 1944. The existence of the train meant that the railway staff along the line could buy all their provisions at reasonable prices, whereas goods would have been much more costly had they needed to be freighted at the expense of a private merchant. The train also included sitting passenger cars for the use of Commonwealth Railways employees travelling on the line. Its journey of 1,048 km entailed forty-six stops en route. In the 1980s, two Pullman sleeping cars (which had originally been imported from the United States for use on the Melbourne–Adelaide expresses) were converted to stores cars.

Water trains

When drought struck the Australian continent in the main railway age, trains played a vital role. First, they were used to evacuate stock to other regions or for slaughter. But trains also played an important role in the pre-road era of transporting water to the dry areas (and they also had to cart water to stations inland for use by steam locomotives and by their own staff scattered through remote areas of the state). NSW Government Railways initially used D and S Class wagons fitted with a canvas lining for transporting water, but in 1917, they produced special tank wagons each capable of holding 29,000 litres and smaller, 22,700 litre Ka wagons that were used to supply fettlers' tanks and other rail installation. Cobar was one town that depended on water trains in times of drought until it was connected to a dependable supply in 1965 with the laying of a pipeline to the town.

Many track maintenance staff lived in camps with no assured local water supply in dry times. Every third Monday of the month, for example, a water train would travel between Nyngan and Byrock on the Bourke line, and these trains were also a regular feature on the Cobar line. When Broken Hill ran out of water, the tank wagons would fill up from the Darling River at Menindee where a special siding had been laid. Allen Gordon, who was a fireman based at Dubbo in 1945, was sent on loan to Broken Hill to crew water trains to and from Menindee, which involved a round trip of 230 km. He was one of eighty railway crew seconded for the work and at that stage there were seventy-six water trains each week.

On the line inland from Brisbane to Charleville, steam locomotives had attached a water gin, or wagon, containing enough water to enable them to get the sometimes long distances between local water supplies. This practice ended in 1951 when a water source was found at Mungallala and a bore drilled.

The same line was provided with a staff member known as a 'railway water pumper', who lived in a railway house at Dulbydilla. In the 1930s, it was the railway water pumper's job to pump water for the locomotives from the nearby creek. Once a week, he would travel on the train to Angellala station where he pumped water from the creek there into a large steel tank which had a canvas hose that

ABOVE: In times of drought, the railways were pressed into action to move water. Here a train discharges its load at Cobar. The water is being emptied into wood-lined trenches after which it will be loaded into water carts for delivery to the residents of the town. *Great Cobar Heritage Centre.*

LEFT: Last days of steam. Locomotive 1957 is turned at the Port Waratah loco depot on 24 April 1970. This photo gives an excellent view of the typical roundhouse, with the turntable allowing locomotives to be turned to move into their own bay. *John Beckhaus.*

the locomotive crews would insert into their tenders.

Once the line was opened through the Victorian Mallee to Mildura, it was possible to cart water along the rail for the often drought-stricken settlements to the south. At Ouyen, in the 1914 drought, water trains each day replenished two 4,000 gallon tanks in the yard, from which the caretaker dispatched the liquid to locals at sixpence per 100 gallons. The water train on this line consisted of thirty-five wagons varying in capacity between 800 and 2,400 gallons.

Queensland boat trains

During the many years when Queensland had a number of isolated railway systems and before the completion of the North Coast line which linked them all, travellers used coastal steamers to move up and down the coast between the railway networks. The Gladstone Boat Train began running in 1897, leaving Brisbane at 10.00 pm and arriving in Gladstone at 12.30 pm the next day, the train running on to the wharf to allow passengers to board the waiting steamer. At Rockhampton, the boat trains ran onto the wharf at Broadmount to meet the boat from Gladstone or to bring people for the waiting Townsville steamer which was Queensland Government Railways' own vessel, the SS *Premier*. Travellers were able to buy through-tickets incorporating both the rail and sea legs. A new port was developed at Rockhampton and the boat trains operated there until the rail link to Townsville was completed in 1923. Townsville jetty was also connected by railway line. The train that had departed from Charters Towers at 5.30 pm would run on to the wharf at 10.05 pm, where the steamer *Barcoo* would be waiting. The isolated Cooktown section, incorporating a 1.3 km section to the wharf,

opened on 30 November 1885 and lasted until the whole line was closed on 31 December 1961.

Tasmania also had boat trains to transport people to and from Hobart. A 1947 Tasmanian Government Railways timetable shows the boat train leaving Hobart at 8.25 am, with thirteen intermediate stops, running through to Launceston Wharf.

Rack trains

Rack railways date from 1811 when a British colliery owner sought to improve the performance of a locomotive by applying smooth wheels to a smooth steel rail. Thus the rack railway was born. The original involved a cogwheel on the locomotive gripping a series of steel teeth placed between the two outer rails. In 1882, Roman Abt, chief engineer of a Swiss railway company, devised an improved form of rack using an upright blade into which the rack slots were machined. Effectively, it meant a series of teeth attached to the sleepers. In August 1896, a 4.5 km section of the Mount Lyell Railway on Tasmania's west coast was equipped with the Abt system so that trains could climb the 1 in 16 and 1 in 20 grades on the line.

The other rack rail section was used in Queensland, on the Mount Morgan branch that left the Rockhampton–Longreach line at Kabra to serve the mines operating in the Mount Morgan area. The rack section was 36.7 km, including a 1 in 16 gradient; trains climbed 1,223 m over a distance of 2.4 km. The rack section between Moonmera and Moongan was opened on 26 November 1926. Even with the additional adhesion provided by the rack system, trains nevertheless were limited to a load of about 100 tons. In 1950, the decision was taken to replace the cumbersome rack system and its slow moving trains by

ABOVE: Victoria's narrow gauge is still experienced on the Puffing Billy tourist train. No. 7A awaits return departure from Gembrook during a shower in 2001. *Brian Webber.*

LEFT: 200 X30, the now retired Tasmanian locomotive, sits on a section of rail at St Marys, the one time terminus of the branch from Conara that now ends at Fingal. *Brian Webber.*

FOLLOWING SPREAD: QR Citytrain electric multiple units await entry into traffic in the east side stabling area at Caboolture on an early January morning in 2002. *Brian Webber.*

ABOVE: A locomotive of the Victorian fleet has left its train on the main line while it undertakes shunting on the grain siding — a scene still enacted today at scores of locations around Australia. Only the locomotive types and liveries have changed. *Author's collection.*

RIGHT: On a cold, wet and windy morning in November 2001, West Coast Railway's B76 awaits departure at Warrnambool for Melbourne. *Brian Webber.*

Early diesel–electric traction. Locomotive 7920 at Sydney. *John Beckhaus.*

building a deviation, 10.5 km in length, which used more gentle grades. Thus trains could pull loads up to 650 tons at a time. This was opened on 4 April 1952.

There is an existing rack railway. It is located on the Skitube line in the Kosciuszko National Park, New South Wales. This private railway serving the ski fields would not otherwise be mentioned in this book but for the rack system. Swiss technology was used when the Skitube line was built. The cogs underneath the train set revolve and mesh into the teeth-like centre rail, providing the extra traction needed on the line's steep grade. The system is used for braking on the downhill run.

Dieselisation

After World War II, the railway systems of Australia were more run down and exhausted than they had been before the conflict. So it was natural that the various state railways departments began thinking about re-equipping their fleets. And, if they were going to buy new locomotives, then the preference was shown for the new diesel electric models (although plenty of new steam engines were also ordered). For example, the contract tendered by New South Wales was for twenty of the new Alco diesels, to be built in Canada.

Mainline diesel operations became a reality in New South Wales on 30 November 1951 when the first two of the 1,600 hp Alco, 40 Class locomotives entered service. Initially, these engines hauled freight trains between Enfield in Sydney and Broadmeadow on the outskirts of Newcastle. As more locomotives were delivered as part of the contract, the 40 Class were used to pull express freight trains to Albury and South Brisbane on interstate workings, and also inland services to Orange and

Armidale. These locomotives were eventually also used on passenger expresses, including the Newcastle Flyer. On 15 June 1952, 4019 and 4020 hauled the Brisbane Express, the first time this train had left other than behind a steam locomotive. The 40 Class was withdrawn by 1971. (By 1955, the Brisbane–Sydney expresses were doing the journey in three hours less time than had been the timetabled duration with steam.) In March 1955, diesel–electric traction was brought to the Sydney–Albury line express.

From 1943, New South Wales had obtained some shunting engines made by General Electric under the lend-lease program. Numbered 7920 to 7923, these were seen in Sydney yard and at the St Mary's Munitions Factory.

In 1952, Clyde Engineering of Sydney, which had already sold diesel–electric locomotives to Commonwealth Railways and Victorian Railways, established a special school to instruct railwaymen in the operation and maintenance of the new generation of motive power. Sixteen men a month passed through the school. Soon, Victorian Railways announced it would also set up a school for instruction in the new engines. It truly entered the diesel–electric era with the order to Clyde Engineering for twenty-six 1,500 hp locomotives. These had cabs at each end, and the first was named after that giant of Victoria's railways, Harold W. Clapp. The locomotives were initially used to haul the Overland and fast freight trains between Melbourne and the border station of Serviceton. The new diesel locomotives were popular with travellers on Victoria's country trains for both their speed and cleanliness. One service that benefited was the Bairnsdale Express which attracted

Western Australia farewells steam. The last steam locomotive to use the sheds at Albany was a 1951 Beyer Peacock 4-8-2, W 947, seen here in 1973. In 1897, Western Australian Government Railways built this shed to replace a smaller one used by Great Southern Railway. *Noel Inglis collection.*

more customers after steam was retired. It left Melbourne at 8.35 am, arriving at Bairnsdale at 2.35 pm and then returning to Melbourne by 7.45 pm. This train was renamed the Gippslander from 11 October 1954.

South Australia also saw diesel–electric traction on its main lines in 1951 with the introduction of the 1600 hp English Electric 900 Class.

The first train hauled by a diesel–electric locomotive on Queensland main lines ran between Roma Street and Mitchelton on 6 November 1952 (QGR having bought its first small diesel locomotive in 1939). This locomotive was the first of ten 1,100 hp machines ordered from General Electric's plant in Erie, Pennsylvania. This locomotive bore the number 1213, and was subsequently renumbered 1303 and then 1153. Queensland Railways then ordered ten English Electric diesel locomotives. The first in this class, number 1200, was hauling The Westlander on 1 December 1956, when it collided at Wallumbilla with the stationary Roma Mail behind a C17 Class steam locomotive. Five people were killed, all of them passengers on the Mail. The crew members of both trains escaped injury. On a brighter note, the diesel–electric locomotives immediately allowed freight train tonnages to be increased. For example, out of Mitchell on the section to Roma, a 1700 Class diesel could haul 330 tons compared with 195 tons behind a PB15 steam goods engine.

In 1955, Western Australian Government Railways placed what was, until then, the single largest order for diesel–electric locomotives, forty-eight in all of the 1,150 hp X Class. This at last dispensed with the bugbear of running steam locomotives in bad water country. However, sixteen of the order were modified to allow multiple unit working and they were called the Xa Class.

In 1964, Tasmanian Government Railways became the first Australian system to become nominally all-diesel. A small number of steam locomotives were retained and even by 1965 these were occasionally hauling some services. But, for all intents and purposes, Tasmanian railway trains were basically diesel–electric hauled in almost all instances by this date. The state's early move to diesel power was triggered by an acute shortage of motive power in 1945 (it had been getting steadily worse for twenty-five years, but the war delivered the crunch point). By late 1948, the Hobart and Launceston yards received four 200 hp Drewry diesel mechanical shunters, allocated as the V Class. In 1950, TGR took delivery of the first of thirty-two English Electric 600 hp diesel–electric engines, known as the X Class. Even by the mid-1950s, steam was still king; only 51.5 km of the system was completely dieselised, being the New Norfolk–Florentine section. Some Hobart peak hour suburban workings were also handled by steam engines at this time. However, by 1957, TGR began significant reductions of its steam capacity and these locomotives disappeared from the Launceston–Devonport section. Soon after, other parts of the TGR network saw their old steamers disappear.

Steam traction retained its dominance throughout Australia during the early years of dieselisation, as demonstrated by the fact that steam and diesel–electric locomotives were still being ordered in the late 1940s and into the 1950s. But when steam's end came, it was relatively quick. Overnight, whole sections would be totally dieselised. On 27 July 1968, K 164 performed the last steam shunting duties in Geelong's yard that spelled the end of steam on the Victorian system apart from some broad gauge locomotives being retained for special

workings. The previous December, South Australian Railways' broad gauge saw its last steam working with Rx 214 shunting at Tailem Bend. At this stage, SAR still retained steam engines on some of its narrow gauge lines. Sydney metro was steam-free by June 1971. Yet, just the previous October, Eveleigh Running Sheds had on its roster ten 19 Class, seven 30 Class and four 30T Class locomotives. A month later, on 24 July, the railways promoted the final steam-hauled passenger train, the 6.04 am from Singleton to Newcastle behind 3246. After all the photographs were taken at Newcastle station, 3246 headed away from the platform, stopped and then ran onto a Broadmeadow working, taking it there and back — and only then was steam finished on New South Wales' tracks behind passenger trains.

Diesel traction meant a new lease of life for the railway and a chance to compete with road, not always pursued to the full by the often sclerotic bureaucracy of the state rail departments. But it was the end of an era and the success of steam preservation groups has been testimony to the enduring appeal of steam. A farmer living near Gerogery in New South Wales, L. F. Holmes, wrote in 1965 of how times had changed on the railway near him:

> What is it like to live where there is no steam? Mighty lonely, I say, as there is little incentive now for me to dawdle along beside the main line with the car, hoping to spot a 38 Class hurrying along with the 'Mail' or, perhaps, to see No. 54 Mixed loping away behind an unkempt 55 Class 2–8–0, with untidy movements of its Southern valve gear — these things do not happen any more.

Electrification

It took almost six years for Melbourne to complete its first electrification due to delays caused by World War I. Work began in 1913 and in 1916 there were trial operations between Newmarket and Flemington Racecourse. Then on 28 May 1919, scheduled services started to Essendon, quickly followed by Flinders Street to St Kilda (31 August 1919) and Port Melbourne lines (26 October 1919). On 27 August 1920, the Williamstown and on 2 December 1920, the Fawkner lines were electrified. From 2 October 1920, electric trains started running on the Bendigo line as far as St Albans. In 1921, Princes Bridge–North Carlton, Clifton Hill–Reservoir and Essendon–Broadmeadows were added. The most recent extension of the electrified suburban network was to Sydenham, opened on 23 January 2002 (although the new station was called Watergardens). At present, there are 308 km of electrified lines with trains serving 208 stations.

The first electrification outside suburban services was the conversion of the 155 km track between Melbourne and Traralgon in Victoria. In 1952, Victorian Railways ordered twenty-five electric locomotives from English Electric that were capable of hauling 275 ton trains on the newly electrified Dandenong–Traralgon sectional. This section received an allocation of seven million pounds as part of the overall plan to develop power and fuel industries around Yallourn and Morwell. However, in 1985, wiring was scrapped beyond the outer limit of suburban running at Warragul.

In February 1926, the lines on platforms 18 and 19 at Sydney Central were electrified and the first scheduled

LEFT: **No more manual destination indicators, and even these electric signs have now been superseded by electronic models — although the technology has not helped Sydney's suburban trains run on time. A typical consist, including trailer car T4867, was seen at Bondi Junction on 1 November 1979. T4867 is also now part of history, one of the Tulloch cars withdrawn from Sydney's rails by 2004.** John Beckhaus.

electric train service ran to Sutherland on 1 March. Platforms 21 and 23 were then electrified and by 1 August 1928, electrification was completed as far as Hornsby. However, by this stage, too much traffic was converging on the few platforms with wiring so platforms 12 and 13 of the steam station were wired. By 1932, all the suburban platforms were wired with trains running to Liverpool and Parramatta. However, for some years electric parcel vans continued to use the wired lines at the steam station.

In 1952, the New South Wales Government approved, as part of a £100 million upgrade of services, the installation of overhead wiring radiating out from Sydney to Goulburn, Newcastle, Port Kembla and Wallerawang. By 1955, progress was being made. That year, the 11.2 km section from Parramatta was electrified. The following year, work was completed on the rails above Circular Quay in Sydney, creating the City Circle and ending the days when trains from the outer suburbs terminated underground at either St James or Wynyard.

On 22 June 1957, the first electric train service operated over the Blue Mountains as far as Lithgow. Electrification was opened in 1959 to Bowenfels on the Western Line across the Blue Mountains (158 km) and Gosford (80 km). By 1986, the overhead wires had reached Newcastle, 168 km to the north, and Wollongong, 83 km to the south, with electric services later being extended to Port Kembla and Dapto. An extension of 24 km was opened to Kiama in November 2001.

New South Wales' first main line electric locomotive, 4501, ran a trial journey between Chullora and Liverpool on 19 June 1952. It had six 450 hp motors. An order was placed in England for an additional forty locomotives as they were more powerful, being equipped with six 630 hp motors.

Electrification of the Queensland suburban system began in 1979 and continued until 1986, the 25 kilovolt alternating current being chosen. On 8 May 1979, the overhead between Roma Street and Corinda was energised and several months later, on 17 November, the inaugural electric train service ran. Then the system was gradually extended. Shorncliffe to Kingston was opened in October 1982, while the line between Corinda and Yeerongpilly was electrified to cater for rail traffic during the Commonwealth Games.

Then Queensland turned its attention to electrifying a part of its non-urban network so that by 1990 it had overhead wires above 1,707 km of track. In 1983, it was decided to electrify the Blackwater–Rockhampton–Gladstone corridor and almost all the branches around Blackwater. While the main impetus was to provide electric motive power for coal trains, by 1987 grain and general freight trains were being hauled to Emerald by electric locomotives.

On 5 August 1990, power was switched on in the overhead wires above Perth's suburban rail tracks and a month later electric units began full operations on the Armadale, Fremantle and Midland lines. An extension to Currambine was opened in 1993.

UNDERGROUND RAILWAYS

THE SYDNEY UNDERGROUND system opened in 1926. The busiest underground station is Town Hall, through which all suburban workings operate. Trains approaching from the south go underground after leaving Central and emerge on the approaches to the Harbour Bridge if destined for the Northern Line. Otherwise they traverse the City Circle via Museum, St James, Circular Quay (where the rails briefly run above ground), Wynyard and Town Hall before surfacing again on the approach to Central.

In 2000, a 10 km-long underground line opened to serve Sydney Airport, and four stations on this line were operated by a private venture, Airport Link Company, until it struck financial difficulties. This line starts at Central and runs via Green Square, Mascot, Airport Domestic Terminal, and International Terminal, and rejoins the suburban network at Wolli Creek. The line's viability was affected by the high fares charged to passengers and the fact that trains consisted of standard suburban sets without any special provision for luggage.

DEATH ON THE RAILS

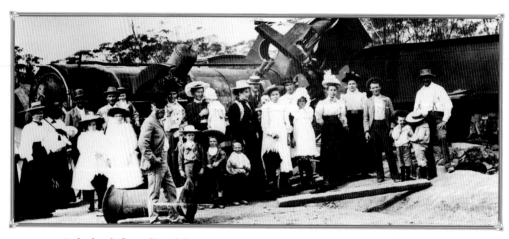

In the days before radio and cinema, a railway accident was an interesting diversion from the
routine of daily life. It was worthy of dressing up and going for a picnic at the scene. Here, an O Class Dubs 2-8-0
locomotive has come to grief near Kalgoorlie. It is thought to have occurred on one of the private lines which supplied
timber for the boilers and pit props at the Kalgoorlie mines. The accident probably occurred when the track spread;
that is, the two rails were pushed outwards by the weight of the train. *Noel Inglis collection.*

The last fatal railway accident occurred at Waterfall, NSW, in 2003, when seven people were
killed. Before then, the worst incidents were:

Granville, NSW — 18 January 1977 A suburban electric train set derailed and struck an overhead
bridge. The structure collapsed on top of the train. In all, eighty-three people died and another
eighty passengers were injured.

Sunshine, Victoria — 20 April 1908 Forty-four people were killed and 431 injured when an Easter
Monday special from Bendigo headed by two locomotives passed multiple stop signals and ran
into the back of a passenger train from Ballarat which was standing at Sunshine station.

Murulla, NSW — 13 September 1926 A collision occurred after several wagons and a brake van
became uncoupled from their train and ran back down the grade, colliding with a mail train.
Twenty-seven were killed and forty-two injured.

Hawkesbury River, NSW — 20 January 1944 A train struck a bus at a level crossing. Seventeen
people on the bus were killed.

Camp Mountain, Queensland — 5 May 1947 A train travelling at excessive speed derailed, killing
sixteen of those on board and injuring another thirty-eight. The working was a special excursion
train heading for Dayborough.

Exeter, NSW — 16 March 1914 The Temora Mail passed a stop signal and collided with a goods
train reversing into the passing loop, killing fourteen people and injuring thirty-two.

Redfern, NSW — 31 October 1894 A head-on collision between two trains saw eleven people
killed and twenty-seven injured. Redfern was then the Sydney terminus. The accident occurred
when a Goulburn-bound passenger train proceeded along the wrong line in spite of a stop signal.

It collided with a train arriving from Parramatta, in the first carriage of which most of the fatalities occurred due to scalding steam escaping from the locomotive.

Traveston, Queensland — 9 June 1925 Ten people were killed and twenty-eight injured when a mail train heading for Rockhampton was derailed; one carriage fell off a bridge into a creek.

Berala, NSW — 7 May 1952 An electric train passed a stop signal after leaving Liverpool with permission but in heavy fog, and did not proceed as required with caution. It ran into the back of another electric train from Bankstown standing at Berala platform. Ten people were killed and eight-one injured.

Violet Town, Victoria — 7 February 1969 Nine people, including the drivers of both trains, were killed in a head-on collision at 7.10 am between the Southern Aurora and a freight train. The passenger train had passed a stop signal, where it was meant to have waited until the goods train got off the main line into the loop.

Cootamundra, NSW — 25 January 1885 In what was at the time the worst railway accident in the then short history of New South Wales railways, seven people died when the Albury Mail crashed on its way to Sydney due to the embankment at Salt Clay Creek having been washed away. Apart from the locomotive, the train was made up of two Redfern carriages (one first, the other second class), a Hudson sleeping car, a four-wheel mail van and the brake van. An inquiry found that the culvert under the embankment was too small to handle any large rush of water in the creek.

In Tasmania and Western Australia, the worst accidents involved the deaths of four people in each incident. On 15 February 1916, a train derailed at Campania, Tasmania, while travelling at excessive speed. A passenger train and a motor section car collided at Rawlinna, Western Australia, on 25 July 1960.

Locals pose with a derailed PB15 locomotive on Queensland's Western line in the 1920s.
George Balsillie collection.

4

THEY RAN
THE TRAINS

IN THE ONE HUNDRED AND FIFTY YEARS of railway operations in Australia, the wheel has turned full circle. Private companies sprang up at the start, inspired by the example of Britain where railway building and operation was the sole prerogative of the private sector. Few flourished here, mainly because there was not the size of population to provide what is now termed 'critical mass'. Moreover, the population was scattered over vast distances rather than in the concentrations of the big English cities, each of which was located relatively close to the next one. Making the Birmingham–London route pay is a good deal easier than an operation between Kalgoorlie and Perth, or Rockhampton and Longreach. The colonial governments either initiated construction, as in Queensland, or were forced to rescue and absorb failing private companies — as occurred in New South Wales, Victoria and Tasmania, for example.

In the past decade, the role of the public sector has shrunk in most cases to no more than maintaining the infrastructure. Only Queensland retains public ownership of all the railways; New South Wales, South Australia and Western Australia have held on to suburban operations. Privately owned passenger trains connect Sydney and Perth, Adelaide and Darwin, Melbourne and Adelaide. Tasmania's system is entirely in private hands, as is all interstate freight on the mainland. Victoria and Western Australia have leased out all their non-metropolitan lines. Even Queensland's state government monopoly is now under threat due to the introduction of third party access.

The following is a list of the most important and more interesting operators over the years. It is by no means exhaustive. Small companies that came and went with barely any impact are not included, nor are the peripheral operators who were more correctly considered tramway operators. In the case of Queensland, the choice was made to concentrate on two private rail builders simply for reasons of space — the Aramac Shire Council and the Chillagoe Railway and Mining Company — although local governments throughout the state often took the initiative to lay track that was later taken over by the government.

INTERSTATE
Asia Pacific Transport Consortium

Status: Operates the transcontinental railway from Tarcoola, South Australia, to Darwin

This group of companies built the 1,420 km rail line from Alice Springs to Darwin. One of the incentives offered under government participation was that it would also gain control of the existing section north from Tarcoola where the line leaves the east–west transcontinental route. The cost of $1.3 billion included the purchase of four locomotives and one hundred and thirty-five articulated container wagons. Additional wagons were to be leased from the South Australian arm of Australian Railroad Group, itself one of the consortium members. The consortium's freight arm, FreightLink, had the task of selling space on the five-day-a-week train service.

Australian National Railways

Formed: 1978

Status: Assets sold 1997; wound up October 2000

Australian National Railways (ANR) came into existence on 1 July 1975, taking over the operations of Commonwealth Railways in the Northern Territory, Western Australia, the Australian Capital Territory and South Australia. That year also saw ANR take over Tasmanian Government Railways and South Australia Railways (except for metropolitan passenger services in Adelaide). Many critics of ANR believed it was doomed to failure because it did not address the main problem in Australia — the fractured nature of the railway system with lack of co-operation between operators. Sir Henry Bolte, the Premier of Victoria in the 1970s, refused to hand over

the state's rail system to what he saw as the socialist Whitlam government in Canberra. By the time Rupert Hamer succeeded Bolte, the government in Canberra had changed and Prime Minister Malcolm Fraser had no interest in taking on Victoria's non-metropolitan railways which he saw as potentially a huge financial drain on the Commonwealth.

The corporation, based in Adelaide, was unique in Australia for having three gauges under its control: the standardised transcontinental line to Kalgoorlie; narrow gauge in Tasmania, South Australia and the Northern Territory; and broad gauge in South Australia. Substantial changes took place on its watch. All remaining country passenger services ended in South Australia under Australian National's management. On the positive side of the ledger were the completion of standardisation of lines between Adelaide and Crystal Brook in 1982, its role in standardising the Adelaide to Melbourne route, the introduction of double-stacking of containers, the laying of concrete sleepers to upgrade main lines and several new wagon concepts.

Ronald Fitch, the former Commissioner of South Australian Railways, recorded in his memoirs, *Making Tracks*, that Australian National came about because of the:

centralist policies of the Whitlam Government; a power-hungry Commonwealth bureaucracy; a Federal Minister of Transport [Charlie Jones] who was prepared to agree to any number of concessions in order to swallow up the state railway systems; and the gutlessness of the South Australian and Tasmanian

OPPOSITE: **Another NM locomotive on the Central Australian Railway, this time No. 21, with the driver and fireman clearly aware of the photographer.** *Noel Inglis collection.*

Labor governments who, unwilling to face up to the long overdue pruning of their respective railway networks in line with a changed transport pattern, saw the take-over offer as a golden opportunity to free themselves for all time of their responsibilities.

To some, Australian National made a key, fateful mistake; it saw only long-haul interstate freight as its future. As a result, it neglected the rural branch line business in South Australia and even pulled up some branches. This meant that it had only one string to its bow while just over the horizon were third party access and competition on the main lines.

In 1997, the freight arm on the mainland was sold to privately owned Australian Railroad Group, the Tasmanian services to another private consortium, and the passenger services (the Ghan, the Indian Pacific and the Overland) to Great Southern Rail. The Australian Rail Track Corporation was formed to take over management of Australian National's standard gauge network. The organisation carried on for another three years to tidy up all the loose ends, including litigation and insurance claims, before finally being dissolved in 2000.

One of the casualties of the sale of Australian National was the small Nullarbor rail settlement at Cook, South Australia. A visiting newspaper reporter wrote in 1998 that the rationalisation of the rail system by the new private operator had seen the end of Cook, once home to families where every man worked for the railway. The staff was relocated and the township left with empty houses, a school and hospital.

Australian Railroad Group

Formed: 1997

Status: Operating

This company, owned by Genesee and Wyoming and Perth-based Wesfarmers, has two separate rail arms: Australia Southern Railroad (ASR) and Australia Western Railroad (AWR). In 1997 it acquired the freight assets in South Australia of the federally owned Australian National, and then in late 2000, it added the Westrail freight business from that state's government railway. In 1999, ASR won a $33 million contract from the then BHP to operate that company's rail network serving the steel works at Whyalla. It provides interstate rail services, South Australia main network freight and also trains on the isolated Eyre Peninsula network centred on Port Lincoln over a total rail network in 2003 of almost 10,000 km. Its main depots are Whyalla, Port Augusta (where there are also workshops), Port Pirie, Dry Creek and Port Flat in Adelaide (and workshops at Islington) and Tailem Bend. The company is also part of the consortium building and operating the Alice Springs–Darwin railway.

Commonwealth Railways

Founded: 1911

Status: Merged with South Australian and Tasmanian systems to become Australian National

The Federal Government had become involved in the railway business when it took over ownership of the narrow gauge Darwin–Pine Creek and Port Augusta–Oodnadatta lines, although both continued to be operated by South Australian Railways until 1926. The latter railway line was losing about eighty thousand pounds a year at the time the

The NM Class were Commonwealth Railways locomotives based on the Queensland C17 Class and worked the Central Australian Railway to Alice Springs. Here, NM19 is shown.
Noel Inglis collection.

Commonwealth took over ownership in 1911. The Commonwealth undertook to connect the two lines and so provide a north–south transcontinental line. In the event, only the extension from Oodnadatta to Alice Springs was built by 1929. It was not until 1980 that the new standard gauge line to The Alice was opened. It would not be until 2004 that the Darwin promise would be honoured, ninety-three years late, and then only because of the foresight of the consortium developers.

Its first major operation was the building and commissioning of the Trans-Australian Railway. It was conceived primarily as a defence measure rather than a commercial undertaking. Its subsequent success and importance to Australian transport should give pause to those critics who have written off the much later north–south transcontinental railway to Darwin. The joining of the isolated Western Australian railway network with the systems of the eastern states was an inducement to persuade that colony to join the new federation in 1901. It was quite a leap of faith given that the two termini — Port Augusta and Kalgoorlie — were comparatively unimportant economic centres. It cost £5,532 per mile to build.

It was decided to construct the line from each end and meet somewhere in the middle of the route; gangs were on the job at Port Augusta in 1912 and the following year work began at Kalgoorlie. Four years later, on 17 October 1917, the two railheads met at a point between Ooldea and Watson. Five days later the first through passenger train pulled out of Port Augusta.

While the chosen route presented few engineering problems (there being no need for tunnels or bridges over deep valleys with few grades steeper than 1 in 100), the main problem was the shortage of water. There was no surface water on the entire 1,690 km route; there was also a stretch of 541 km where no bore water was available either. Where there was underground water, it was rarely close to the surface; the deepest bore sunk was 448 metres. Many of the underground supplies proved to be unfit for human consumption, as well as being unsuitable for locomotive boilers, and its use resulted in very high rates of locomotive break downs along the track. It was only in 1928, when Commonwealth Railways began treating the water with barium carbonate, that much of the water could be used in the locomotives. In fact, the problem was not satisfactorily resolved until diesel–electric locomotives became available after 1945, and the reliance on steam traction ended in 1951. During construction, the workers and locomotives used 42,251,000 gallons of water, of which 31,500,000 gallons were considered to be of inferior quality. This resulted in the cartage of water to stages along the line to provide both for rail staff and rewatering locomotives. Hundreds of tons of food and water had to be carted to supply the 3,500 men and 750 animals employed on the construction task; fuel and water also had to be supplied for the locomotives and steam shovels. Postal, banking, medical and educational services had to be provided; special trains complete with butchers' shops, grocery and clothing stores, ran to the ever-shifting railheads.

Camels were used to pull equipment and were involved in preliminary formation work before the steam shovels did their part. Completion was ten months late, mainly due to the shortage of labour during World War I.

Commonwealth Railways, when deciding on motive power for the Trans-Australian line, opted to copy New South Wales' locomotives. The first goods engines were based on the NSW 50 and 53 Classes; the Commonwealth's C Class was based on the NSW 36 Class 4–6–0 locomotive. In 1942, it imported eight of what became known as the CN Class from Canadian National Railways and the following year two Ca Class engines were added, having been bought from the New York, New Haven and Hartford Railway.

Like the Central Australia Railway before it, the Trans-Australia was not properly ballasted, a mix of earth, sand and ashes being applied over the sleepers. It was not until 1940 that conventional stone ballasting was completed along the full length of the railway. The men who built the line endured extraordinarily hard conditions, with unbroken heat and little protection from insects. In 1937, the line was extended to Port Pirie to allow connection with South Australia's broad gauge system.

Commonwealth Railways had its head office in Melbourne, but operational staff and the workshops were located in Port Augusta.

Until 30 June 1975 (its last day before becoming Australian National), Commonwealth Railways controlled only five routes, although they added up to 3,505 km in route length. Those lines were:

Australian Capital Territory Railway. Queanbeyan, NSW–Canberra, ACT. Total 8 km standard gauge. This line was opened to goods traffic in 1914, with passenger services nine years later. Commonwealth Railways never ran its own trains on this line, all rolling stock being provided by NSW Government Railways although CR did provide local staff. NSW took over full operation of the line in 1985.

Central Australia Railway. Stirling North, SA–Alice Springs, NT. Total 350 km standard gauge and 869 km narrow gauge, with break of gauge at Marree, SA.

North Australia Railway. Darwin, NT–Birdum, NT. Total 511 km narrow gauge.

Whyalla line. Port Augusta, SA–Whyalla, SA. Total 75 km standard gauge. When this line was built in 1972, it was the first main route to be laid with concrete sleepers.

Trans-Australian Railway. Port Pirie, SA–Kalgoorlie, WA. Total 1,782 km standard gauge.

At one stage, Commonwealth Railways operated under four time zones: the Commissioner's office in Melbourne on eastern standard time; South Australia and the Northern Territory on South Australian time; the line between Parkeston and Rawlinna on Western Australian standard time; while the fourth time zone existed between Tarcoola and Rawlinna which was midway between the Western Australian and South Australian time zones.

Great Southern Railway

Operator of what were Australian National's long-distance passenger services. Its trains are: the Ghan running from Adelaide to Darwin; the Indian Pacific, travelling thrice-weekly between Sydney and Perth, via Adelaide; and the Overland, running on the now standardised Melbourne–Adelaide line and operating in one direction as a daytime service, overnight in the other.

Nearing the end of a long trip from Perth, a North British P Class 4-6-2 is seen about 1935 approaching Albany station.
Noel Inglis collection.

National Rail

Founded: 19 September 1991

Status: Sold in February 2002 along with FreightLink to a consortium operating as Pacific National

Established by the Federal, NSW and Victorian governments to take over interstate rail freight operations. The corporation possessed its own locomotives and rolling stock; in the latter case, some 5,700 wagons obtained from NSW State Rail, V/Line in Victoria, Australian National and Westrail. Its main businesses encompassed: containerised operations based in Adelaide, Alice Springs, Brisbane, Melbourne, Perth and Sydney; bi-modal haulage on the transcontinental artery; and carrying steel products out of Port Kembla and Newcastle, NSW. Critics claimed that National Rail suffered the same fundamental shortcomings found in publicly run train systems in that it failed to pursue new business with sufficient energy, and was better at cutting services than creating them. However, it is also credited with having stemmed the flow of freight to trucks, even though it took four years for all the interstate rail services to be transferred to its ownership.

NEW SOUTH WALES
Commonwealth Oil Corporation

Line opened: 27 December 1907

Status: Services ceased 1932

This company's track ran from the Great Western line in NSW from Newnes Junction to the company's oil refinery and Newnes itself, a distance of 51.6 km. The company was founded in 1905 to exploit shale oil deposits in the Wolgan Valley, near the ghost town of Newnes, located north-east of Lithgow. The London publisher, Sir George Newnes, was the driving force behind the enterprise's establishment. He saw a market for benzene, a by-product of the oil shale extraction process, at a time when motor-cars were growing in number. By 1906, the company began work on a railway needed to provide access to the site. It was difficult terrain, with a drop of more than five hundred metres from a plateau. Two tunnels were built, the longer being four hundred metres. The shale operation itself had a chequered record. A strike in 1911 sent the company into financial crisis and the works closed in 1912. It re-opened in 1915 but by the 1920s, was unable to compete against cheap kerosene imports from the United States with high production costs. It closed again in 1927, was re-started briefly in 1929 and again in 1931 (on the latter occasion by the state government) but closed finally in 1932. Passenger trains were operated by Commonwealth Oil. The longer tunnel is now home to glow worms, a popular attraction.

Deniliquin and Moama Railway Company

Line opened: 4 July 1876

Status: Bought by the NSW Government on 1 December 1923

The northern railway between Melbourne and Echuca was opened by the Victorian Government in 1864. By this time, Echuca had become an important and busy centre based on the Murray River boat trade. Victorians wanted the rail to cross the river and penetrate the Riverina, but the NSW Government was jealous of its territory and did not want to hand any further trade to Melbourne. Surprisingly,

OPPOSITE ABOVE: **It was known as the Belmont branch and the passenger services were operated by New South Wales Government Railways, in this case rail motor CPH 17, seen here at Belmont on 3 April 1971. However, the line near Newcastle belonged to the New Redhead Estate and Coal Mining Company.** *John Beckhaus.*

OPPOSITE: **The pride of the fleet. Locomotive No. 1 of the Deniliquin and Moama Railway Company with the company's rolling stock coupled behind.** *Deniliquin and District Historical Society.*

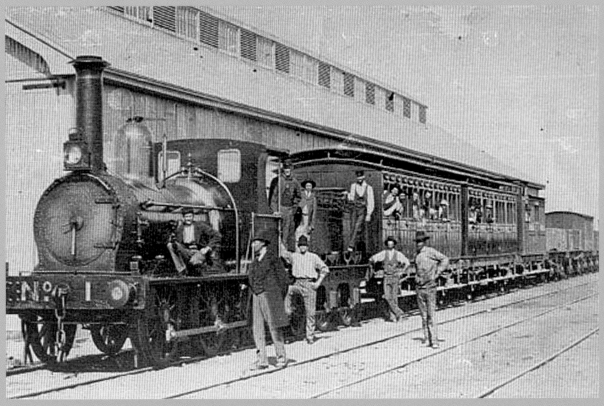

however, in 1874, the authorities in Sydney relented and approved a railway to be built from Moama to Deniliquin, a distance of 72 km, by a syndicate based in Melbourne. Although the company was required to terminate the line well clear of the Deniliquin township, it ignored that provision, taking the lines right into the town. There it built a station, workshops, engine shed and loading sidings.

Apart from crossing the river (the company erected a temporary wooden trestle bridge), few engineering difficulties presented themselves, the line being laid on almost flat country. There was no formation work and the track was laid on the surface. Throughout the length of the line there were only five curves. The wooden bridge was later replaced by an iron road–rail bridge erected at a cost of £81,825. The iron bridge was welcomed by the locals, many having crossed the river by boat rather than enduring the slow, swaying rail trip across the creaking wooden structure which preceded it.

The company bought two Beyer Peacock 0–6–0 tender locomotives similar to Victoria's T Class engines, with a further two later added to the fleet. The carriages were similar to those built for Victorian Railways, and the company eventually owned six cars and sixty-one goods wagons.

While the company's assets were acquired by NSW in 1923 for £165,000, operationally the line was an extension of the Victorian system and control of it was passed to Victorian Railways. There were four staffed stations on the line at this time: Echuca, Moama, Mathoura and Deniliquin.

Having gained control of the line, in 1926 Victorian Railways proceeded to build a branch to Balranald that left the original line at Barnes, just north of Moama.

Hunter River Railway Company

Founded: 1853

Status: Bought by New South Wales Government on 30 July 1855

This company was incorporated to build a line inland from Newcastle to Maitland, to be called the Great Northern Railway. This was opened on 30 May 1857 (two years after the company had collapsed and the government taken control) and ran 27 km to what is now East Maitland. But in mid-1855, the company found itself in financial trouble with the Newcastle–Hexham section nearing completion and the government was forced to intervene and take over the project, paying £307,054 for what was still a going concern. It also took over the operations of the Sydney Railway Company at this time (see below) and thus NSW saw the first nationalisation of railways in the British Empire. The original terminus in Newcastle was located near the present-day Civic station, but this was too far from the centre of the town and the line was extended to the present-day Newcastle station site in March 1858. In fact, the same mistake had been made as in the case of the Sydney Railway Company: the terminus was located away from the centre of the city and the wharf.

New Redhead Estate & Coal Mining Company

Line opened: September 1892

Status: Passenger service ended 8 April 1971
Line closed: 19 December 1991

This company owned a 15.5 km line between Adamstown (near Newcastle) and Belmont to serve three collieries operated by Broken Hill Proprietary including Burwood and Redhead. The company maintained the line, but all

OPPOSITE: **The crew members watch to see that the turntable stops in line with track as 4521 and 4444 are turned at Broadmeadow loco depot in December 1969.** *John Beckhaus.*

traffic was operated by New South Wales Railways, which also provided staffing. It was named the Belmont branch in government passenger timetables. An account of the line published in 1941 revealed that coal dust and ashes were used as substitutes for ballast on the line, which resulted in the suburban passenger cars from Newcastle lurching and rolling badly for almost the entire length of the line. The station buildings were badly in need of painting and the entire line had a general air of neglect. By this time, passenger services had already been reduced due to a competing bus service along with increasing coal traffic on the line.

The last official steam-hauled passenger train on the branch departed Belmont at 1.38 pm on 13 May 1967, to be replaced by railmotor CPH 33. However, a few days later, the railmotor had a mechanical failure and some services that day were locomotive-hauled.

NSW Government Railways (NSWGR)
Status: Officially the Department of Railways from its inception; renamed Public Transport Commission in the 1970s; renamed RailCorp in 2003

The government railway department was formed in 1855 and existed until 1988, when it became the State Rail Authority, and more recently RailCorp.

Fortunately, the NSW rail system attracted a giant of a figure in its formative years — John Whitton. He was appointed engineer-in-chief in 1856 and, in his thirty-four years in the post, the colony saw nearly 3,330 km of new railway lines. These included the 620 km Sydney–Albury link completed in 1881, the lines to the far north of the colony terminating at Bourke (in 1885) and Wallangarra (in 1889), and the completion of the Hawkesbury River bridge which allowed direct rail connection between Sydney and Newcastle and linked the latter to the colony's rail network. All these lines surmounted difficult terrain over some of their length but the Wallangarra line in particular included Australia's highest section of railway, the 1,376 m elevation at Ben Lomond. The line to Albury proceeded only after the construction of a bridge 2.3 km in length over the Murrumbidgee River at Wagga Wagga. In 2004, interstate trains are still required to slow to 20 km/h over the nineteenth-century structure that spans that river. Whitton was employed at a salary of £1,500 a year when there were just 37 km of operating track in New South Wales, with another 27 km out of Newcastle under construction. When he retired at the age of seventy, in bad health, he was granted an annual salary of the modest sum of £657.

Given that they are now closed, it is worth recalling that the Bourke and Wallangarra links were considered trunk lines — the former for opening up the northern hinterland and linking with the upper reaches of the (Darling) River; the latter for forging the first connection with the Queensland system, although it was a break of gauge junction.

But the greatest engineering works were close to Sydney — the now vital rail links to Newcastle, Wollongong and Lithgow. The former involved the Hawkesbury River bridge, for many years the largest rail bridge in the country, and the continent's longest tunnel, the 1,770 m bore at Woy Woy. The line south to the Illawarra also required considerable engineering works around the cliffs; his towering achievement was the Zig Zag rail works on the Blue Mountains.

Whitton's longevity in his post came to give him an

authority and influence that few other Australian railway heads came close to achieving, although both Webb in South Australia and Clapp in Victoria were towering figures in the history of this country's railways. His approach was that the NSW railway system was to be developed on the standards then operating in the United Kingdom. Thus the colony avoided the short-sightedness that came back to plague other parts of the continent, especially South Australia, due to the construction of cheap, lightly railed lines that could cope with neither heavy trains nor fast ones. This is not to say that his approach was unopposed; there were politicians who wanted to do things on the cheap, and the lobby for horse tramways was still vocal. However, penny-pinching in Sydney did lead to some compromises and Whitton, although he stood firm on the question of standard gauge lines being the only ones built, did not always win the battle to build them to as high a standard as he would have wished. Even today, New South Wales continues to pay the penalty in terms of tight curves and steep gradients on its main lines. In fact, it was not until late 2003 that New South Wales finally acknowledged the inadequacies of its main lines and handed control of the main interstate routes to a federal track authority for upgrading.

The next priorities for the NSWGR were the branch lines to Cooma, Gundagai, Jerilderie, Mudgee, Molong and Narrabri. Hay was reached in 1882. By 1888, the colony's railway system was carrying more than fourteen million passengers a year and 3.4 million tons of freight. The decade from 1880 to 1889 saw track opened at the average rate of 231 km a year. Then, in the final decade of the nineteenth century, the rail network was extended to the South Coast at Bomaderry, branches to Cobar, Condobolin,

Corowa, Finley, Forbes, Gravesend, Manilla and Temora, an isolated section between Lismore and Murwillumbah and extensions of the Sydney suburban system (Milsons Point–Hornsby and Sydenham–Belmore).

Over the first two decades of the twentieth century, NSWGR oversaw an extensive branch line-building program so that, by 1920, the state's system totalled just over 8,100 route kilometres. The line to Broken Hill was also commenced during this period. Then followed a decade largely dedicated to extending the Sydney suburban system, although during the 1920s and early 1930s, some important country lines were opened including that linking Moss Vale with Wollongong via Robertson and the completion of the Clarence River bridge at Grafton which provided a standard gauge link between Sydney and Brisbane. This North Coast line was a landmark in the twentieth century because, after several decades of construction on new branch lines, it marked a return to main line development.

There ended the period of aggressive railway construction. In the decades that followed, more emphasis was placed on improving the existing system through engineering easier grades (the most spectacular of which was the building of tunnels that bypassed the famous Zig Zag railway on the western side of the Blue Mountains) and track duplication.

After the Great Depression of the 1930s, New South Wales, like most other Australian rail systems, started to rejuvenate its fleet, much of which was aged or had fallen into bad shape. As just a snapshot of the re-equipment program, the months of October and November 1938 saw the New South Wales Railways take delivery of Rail Motor 404 out of its own workshops, twelve all-steel cars from Clyde Engineering (BS 2162–BS 2173) and five MHO brake vans from Ritchie Bros.

Silverton Tramway Co Y Class No. 17 built by Beyer Peacock in 1888 and used by STC on the main line to Cockburn and for shunting duties at Broken Hill until 1960. *Sulphide Street Railway Museum.*

Silverton Tramway Company

Founded: 1888

Status: Ceased the Broken Hill–Cockburn service in 1970; now provides locomotives and other services within the deregulated rail system

Based at Broken Hill, the company came into being when the NSW Government would not allow South Australia to build its line from Port Pirie beyond the border between the two colonies, leaving a 56 km gap to Broken Hill whence was to flow the valuable traffic of ore and concentrates from the mines. The most economic route for transport of the silver and lead concentrates from the Broken Hill mines was across the border into South Australia, to a smelter.

Rather than allow South Australian Railways over its border, New South Wales opted to allow a private company to make the vital connection from the SAR railhead at Cockburn. The *Silverton Tramway Act* of 1886 stipulated that the gauge of the track would be 3 ft 6 in, compatible with the line from Terowie, but with the provision that the New South Wales Government could, at any time, require that gauge to be changed, although that was not to happen until 1970 when the transcontinental standard gauge link was completed. After that time, the Silverton Company continued as the shunting authority on the lines running into the mine properties. It is interesting to note that when the New South Wales standard gauge line reached Broken Hill in 1927, this made no difference to the Silverton Company. In fact, New South Wales Railways had Silverton operate the 61.8 km narrow gauge line north from Broken Hill to Tarrawingee after the government had taken over

ownership from the Tarrawingee Flux and Tramway Company in 1899. It could hardly do otherwise, given that there was no narrow gauge rolling stock within the New South Wales system. Silverton provided a weekly train on this line which had been built to haul limestone to Broken Hill, where it was used as flux in the smelters. When the smelters were moved to Port Pirie in 1898, there was no further use for the tramway and the Silverton Company refused to buy it. However, Silver City residents created a political issue because, without the tramway, they could not travel to their favourite picnic spots at McCulloch Park and Stephens Creek. The New South Wales Government gave in and paid the tramway company £15,000 for the line, then spent another £36,000 upgrading the track. The government contracted Silverton to run a weekly train leaving Broken Hill at 9.40 am and reaching Tarrawingee at 2.15 pm, hauled by a Y Class locomotive. There were also specials for picnics and race meetings where the company used open wagons to transport the large crowds. The line closed in 1930, was briefly re-opened to carry stone from a quarry to a new power station project, and then closed again. However, a short section in Broken Hill remained as the Vacuum Oil Company siding.

The company's shareholders received generous dividends from the profits made hauling the concentrates destined for Port Pirie and, on the reverse run, hauling fuel and other supplies needed to keep 'the Hill' in business. Just how fast the company grew is shown by traffic figures for 1913; in all, 844,477 tons of mining output. By 1939, the company owned 660 wagons, although the company's rolling stock was interchangeable with SAR wagons on the service between Broken Hill and Port Pirie. SAR passenger

Silverton W 22 Beyer Peacock at Silverton
in 1958 with the Broken Hill–Adelaide
Express which operated until the narrow
gauge was lifted in 1970. These locos ran
main line trains between 1950 and 1960.
Sulphide Street Railway Museum.

stock was hauled from Cockburn to Broken Hill on a mileage charge. What was called 'the express train' came from Terowie with day and sleeping cars, but Silverton would attach wagons at Cockburn rather than waste locomotive energy. The wagons were detached at Railway Town station in Broken Hill and the passenger cars went on the short distance to Sulphide Street station. Silverton operate two main mine branches around Broken Hill and a spur to Broken Hill racecourse.

In 1953, Silverton hauled 760,590 tons and had 202 wagons in service. The company ran no passenger services of its own but its locomotives hooked and pulled the South Australian Railways expresses the final 56 km into Sulphide Street station at Broken Hill. Over its lifetime, the tramway carried 3.5 million passengers and 54 million tons of silver–lead–zinc concentrates.

The original 1886 Act included a formula for compulsory purchase of the Silverton operation. However, the powers that be dodged this liability by building the standard gauge on a different route, although as it turned out, a small amount of compensation was paid to Silverton which had been left with an isolated narrow gauge system.

The most extraordinary event in the life of the Silverton tramway era at Broken Hill was the 1915 picnic train tragedy. On New Year's Day, the company assembled forty of its wagons that normally carried concentrate across the border and fitted them out to accommodate 1,200 people for the Manchester Unity picnic at Penrose Park, Silverton. This was just a few months after the start of World War I, in which one of Australia's enemies was Turkey. As the train passed over the level crossing at Rakow Street, two men opened fire on the train with Snider and Martini Henry rifles. Gool Badsha Mahomed and Mullah Abdullah, who had an ice cream cart to which the Turkish flag was attached, killed two passengers and wounded another seven. After a subsequent gunfight with police and local riflemen, the two Muslims were found behind an outcrop, one dead, the other dying.

South Maitland Railways

Founded: 22 November 1918

Status: Now exists only as line owner, although at time of writing the closure by fire of the Southland Colliery resulted in the withdrawal of rail traffic on the company's track

This company was formed to take over the running of two coal line operations in the Hunter Valley, the Stanford Methyr and a branch to Cessnock, which were separately operated by collieries. This private system joined the government line at East Greta Junction, near Maitland. These lines were primarily for the haulage of coal, but trains also carried passengers and general freight. The company was formed by the amalgamation of the East Greta Coal Mining Company and the Hebburn Coal Mining Company (which had absorbed the coal operations of the Australian Agricultural Company and the Abedare railways) and their rail systems. The East Greta Company had begun running passenger trains in 1902.

The first great disruption to the operation came with the 1929–30 strike on the Hunter coalfields. With train crews refusing to move 'black' coal, the company lost almost all its revenue and stopped all services. Motor omnibus operators soon took advantage of this and started running through the coalfields areas. The chances of the South Maitland Railway winning back the business after the strike were undermined by a fire on 1 March 1930, when the depot housing the company's twenty-seven carriages and four brake vans was destroyed by fire, an event that was thought to result from arson.

Nevertheless, once the strike was over, the local people agitated to have a rail passenger service once more and so New South Wales Government Railways provided locomotives, carriages and crews for operations to Cessnock. In 1940 came the Cessnock Express, a train providing a through service to Sydney. In 1961, the South Maitland Company bought three Tulloch diesel–hydraulic railcars that sat eighty people apiece, although in somewhat cramped conditions. These were not a great success and by 1967 the Tulloch cars were withdrawn.

South Maitland struggled to cope with the sudden upsurge of traffic at the outbreak of World War II. The company had sold off a considerable number of locomotives during the Great Depression as revenue dropped, and so was in desperate need of motive power as the war approached. Soon the lines were busy with more than forty coal and nine passenger trains a day. The end of the war did not see any respite; on 11 November 1946, it was recorded that more than sixty trains hauled coal down the system that day: twelve from Hebburn Colliery, twelve from Erlington, nine from the three Abermain pits, two from Neath, eight from Abedare, another eight from Abedare Extended, two from Cessnock No. 2, nine from Bellbird, three from Pelton, two from Kalingo, four out of Stanford Main, two each from Millfield Greta and Maitland Main. And then, of course, the traffic and signals staff had to handle all these trains returning empty for another load.

In 1955, however, the operations had been reduced to one double track line of 26 km running from Cessnock to join with the main line near Maitland. The company owned its own locomotives and brake vans (most of the wagons did not have air brakes), but hauled stock owned either by individual collieries or the government railway.

State Rail Authority

Founded: 1988

Status: Operating as RailCorp

The State Rail Authority was established to replace the departmental control of NSW railways. The authority was divided into three separate operating groups:

CityRail had responsibility for the suburban passenger train operations within Sydney and on the Newcastle, Blue Mountains and Wollongong corridors, as well as trains to Goulburn, Kiama and the Hunter Valley. In all, CityRail services extended over 900 route km. Its fleet consists of a variety of electric multiple units (the newest being the Tangara consists and the Millennium trains) with diesel railcars running on non-electrified lines (to Goulburn, Bomaderry, and in the Hunter Valley services out of Newcastle to Scone, Maitland and Dungog).

Countrylink operates country train services within NSW and interstate services to Melbourne and Brisbane. Its rolling stock consists of the high-speed XPT sets and Xplorer cars; the former operate with XP locomotives. The XPTs run from Sydney to Melbourne, Brisbane, Dubbo and Murwillumbah, with the Xplorers radiating from the state capital to Canberra, Moree, Armidale and Broken Hill.

FreightCorp (the freight arm privatised in 2002) had three-quarters of its revenue coming from coal haulage, mainly from the Hunter Valley. Its other businesses were grain haulage from country depots and general freight (such as ore from Cobar, cotton along the Warren branch and superphosphate).

Sydney Railway Company

Founded: 1849

Status: Taken over by the New South Wales Government in 1855

An Act of the New South Wales Parliament incorporated this company on 10 October 1849 with the purpose of building a railway between Sydney and Goulburn. The first sod on the project was turned the following 3 July at Cleveland Paddock, followed by the letting of a contract to construct the first 7.2 km of line as far as Haslem's Creek, now known as Lidcombe. This contract was in the amount of £10,000. But work did not get far before the labourers deserted their jobs and headed for the new gold discovery at Bathurst. Finances were a constant problem. An initial £24,520 was subscribed but the company was able to continue only by means of several loans from the colony's government after shareholders displayed a marked reluctance to honour calls made on their shares which had initially been only partly paid.

By 1852, the government had come to the rescue and brought 500 navvies from Britain to work for the replacement contractor. The company ordered four locomotives from Robert Stephenson & Co, and let other contracts in England to cover twenty-eight carriages and fifty-one wagons. Costs had risen to £389,000 by early 1854, at which time the contractor had completed seven bridges, twenty-five culverts and fourteen and a half miles of fencing. The 1849 estimate of costs had allowed £2,348 for each mile of line. By the time it was finished as far as Parramatta, the costs had ballooned to £40,000 a mile.

As with some many other early private projects, in 1855 the Sydney Railway Co had to be rescued by the government to prevent its collapse. On 2 December 1854, the Governor signed an Act which provided for govern-ment construction of railways and the acquisition of both the Hunter and Sydney railway companies. When the government took over, only 5.6 km of the 21.7 km of double track line had been laid.

The Railway Commissioners of NSW were in charge of the line when, on 26 September 1855, a train drawn by two locomotives and consisting of eleven carriages plus luggage van made the first public service between Sydney and Parramatta. First class passengers paid four shillings, second class three shillings and third class passengers two shillings.

QUEENSLAND
Aramac Shire Council

Opened: 2 July 1913

Status: Closed 31 December 1975

This shire council owned a 66.6 km line laid to Queensland's narrow 1,067 mm gauge. Although called a tramway, it is included here because it was effectively a branch line of the state's network. It was worked by ex–Queensland Government Railway (QGR) locomotives while the goods rolling stock which ran on the line belonged to QGR. Moreover, QGR supervised all track maintenance on the branch line and this work had to meet government rail standards, even though shire workers did

THE SHORTEST-LIVED GOVERNMENT RAILWAY

ON 24 AUGUST 1922, Western Australian Government Railways purchased the 26.6 km line built from Waroona to Lake Clifton, which branched off the Perth–Bunbury route. Just eighteen months earlier, the Swan Portland Cement Company had constructed the track to carry lime from the terminus. Soon after the government had made its purchase, however, the limeworks closed and thereafter the line had little purpose. It was closed on 31 December 1924, and some of the materials were used on the Lake Grace–Newdegate line.

ABOVE AND OPPOSITE: Three views of the Aramac shire tramway shortly before it closed in 1975: passengers alight under the roofed station; a view of 'Aunt Emma' standing at the Aramac terminus; and the railmotor crossing the main bridge on the line. *Brian Webber.*

the actual repairs. The stationmasters were hired from the ranks of the QGR, but other employees were engaged locally. Running repairs on rolling stock were undertaken by the QGR fitter at Alpha, while heavy repairs and overhauls required the services of the government's railway workshops at Rockhampton.

The tramway ran between Aramac and the QGR line at Aramac Junction, near Barcaldine on the Central line (579 km from Rockhampton). The shire trains carried passengers, general freight and livestock traffic. The line ran over twenty-four bridges, the longest a 30-metre wooden trestle. No significant earthworks were required due to the relatively flat nature of the country; the deepest cutting was just over one metre below the surface. The main operating problem was that the track and sleepers were laid on the ground surface and, in the wet season, the tracks tended to spread because the surface was a sea of mud.

The shire ended up owning its own rail line because of its failure to persuade the government in Brisbane that it deserved a branch line. After a poll of ratepayers in 1908, the shire decided to go ahead and secured a loan of £66,500 from the Queensland Treasury. Timber sleepers came from as far away as Bundaberg. By 1915, the line was making a slight profit. Records show that in the second full year of operation, the trains carried 4,079 tons of general goods, 53 tons of timber, 23,267 bales of wool, 265,058 sheep, 578 horses, 475 cattle, 133 dogs, 117 bicycles along with 1,414 first class and 5,227 second class passengers. However, in 1917, the shearers' strike hit the tramway very badly with not a single bale of wool being carried. The line was back in profit by 1919 but from 1930, when both the Great Depression and increasing road

transport affected the tramway, it battled to make ends meet. The figures for 1938 contrast sharply with those for 1915. In this former year, only 1,747 passenger tickets were sold and the tramway carried 130 horses, 620 cattle and 6,670 sheep. Eleven people worked for the tramway at this time. In 1958, the shire had to undertake a costly upgrade of the line because QGR had threatened not to allow its rolling stock on the line unless it was upgraded.

The Aramac Shire trains used the QGR platform at Barcaldine and ran a short distance along government tracks before turning off on the tramway. The main intermediate station along the line was Bowyer, which was staffed in the early days. The station building there had a ticket office and a ladies' waiting room; there were also sidings and a stock ramp. Aramac station was staffed (by two men in the 1950s) and the station roof extended over the main line. There were stock races and sidings. The motive power on the line was initially bought from the government: ex-QGR B12 No. 31 and B15 308. In 1924, however, the shire had built a new locomotive, No. A1. It was a standard QGR Pb15 4–6–0 engine. Passengers usually rode in the smaller of the tramway's two carriages, the ex-QGR 613 second class, side loading car. It had three compartments, the centre one being for female passengers, with total seating for thirty. The other carriage, which seated seventy passengers, was rarely used because of its much greater weight. The tramway also owned Fairmont petrol quadricycles that were for the use of the gangers. However, each Monday, an open four-wheel flat top trailer was attached to one of these quadricycles and offered a passenger service known as the 'motor train' along the line, the journey being described as 'no joy-ride'. On Wednesdays (at 5.00 am) and Thursdays

(at 10.00 am) a more conventional train service was offered, a mixed goods and passenger train behind one of the steam locomotives. These trains took three hours to cover the distance to Barcaldine, due to the shunting along the way, where they connected with either the Midlander or a QGR mixed train. The fare one way was six shillings and sixpence; the tramway did not sell return tickets. Two diesel locomotives were bought by the shire in the latter days of the tramway, a 16-ton Cummins in 1960 and a 19-ton Caterpillar in 1968. In 1963, the council bought a second-hand railmotor, QGR's RM28. This machine had entered service on government lines on 11 May 1928, having been built at the North Ipswich railway workshops. Its initial assignment was to work the Maryvale branch near Warwick. In 1955, it was transferred to the Rockhampton area and then, in 1963, was written off by QGR and sold to Aramac Shire for £100. It then spent the next twelve years providing a passenger service on the tramway and was soon named 'Aunt Emma' by the locals. (Aunt Emma has now been fully restored by Queensland Railways' heritage team.) Aramac Shire borrowed QGR goods rolling stock as required.

The end for the tramway came with the sealing of the road from Barcaldine. The last passenger service using RM24 ran on 21 December 1975 and the line closed ten days later.

Aramac Shire was one of several Queensland local bodies to take railway matters into their owns. In what is now metropolitan Brisbane, the Belmont Shire constructed a 6.9 km line from Norman Park on which Queensland Government Railways operated services until the branch's closure in 1926. Beaudesert Shire

owned tow lines which fed into the QGR system at Beaudesert itself, the 33.2 km line to Rathdowney and a 14.9 km branch off that to Lamington. The Glengallen Shire Council built the 5.4 km Tannymorel Tramway and used horse-drawn wagons. In 1910, QGR took over operations with its own steam engines and rolling stock. In 1917, QGR took over the 60.8 km length of track from Proserpine to Bowen Junction that had previously been operated by the Bowen Proserpine Joint Tramway Board. Cairns Shire Council got into the rail business in 1897, laying a 22.7 km length of track south to Gordonvale; then in 1898, 1903 and 1910 progressively extending it as far as Babinda. It would be almost another three years until the government line reached that same town from the south, although by then QGR had taken over the shire's section. The Ayr Tramway (Ayr–Stuart, on Townville's outskirts) was another section of what would become the main North Coast line. It was 69 km long and opened in 1901, with QGR running trains over it three days a week and the tramway providing tea rooms at Cromarty for refreshments. This section was taken into government ownership in 1911.

The Pemberton branch from Bundaberg was constructed on the initiative of Woongarra Shire but by 1 January 1918, became the property of QGR (with part surviving until 1995). QGR built a branch inland from Mackay that reached Pinnacle by July 1902. Then Pioneer Shire Council built a line out to Kirkup, 11.7 km away in 1903, and opened a second line to Finch Hatton, a distance of 9.2 km, on 21 September 1904. These were both absorbed by the government in 1910 and extended further to Netherdale. (Finch Hatton lost its railway in 1990; Kirkup's had gone in 1967.)

OPPOSITE LEFT: **Not too much had changed on the old Chillagoe line when this mixed train behind a PB15 was photographed in 1961 sitting at Mareeba.** *Brian Webber.*

OPPOSITE RIGHT: **The Chillagoe Company built its lines to government standards, so that when the lines were absorbed into the state system no great amount of upgrading was necessary. A more modern scene of the Mareeba–Chillagoe goods at Lappa.** *Brian Webber.*

Chillagoe Railway and Mines Limited

Established: Enabling Act passed 1898

Status: Lines taken over by government on 20 June 1919

By 1893, Queensland Government Railways had completed a line from Cairns as far as Mareeba. Then a syndicate in mining wanted a line to go on to where the operations were based, and eventually the Chillagoe Railways and Mines Ltd was formed. On 1 October 1900, the company opened its first section of railway to what would be Lappa Junction, a distance of 89.6 km. Fourteen months later, the project was completed with Mungana having been reached. In the following year, a 52.4 km branch was opened to Mount Garnet. The company's other line was an altogether more ambitious undertaking; 229.3 km from Almaden to Forsayth, making a total of 446.7 km built by this private company.

The track was laid to a high standard using 60 lb rails so that it could be used by the QGR's standard locomotive at that time, the B15 4–6–0. Government locomotives worked the Mungana line until its completion; then the company bought its own motive power (although wagons continued to be interchangeable). QGR trains worked the Forsayth line from its completion. In 1914, the government bought the Mount Garnet branch, and then in 1919 took over the rest of the company's track. The Chillagoe smelter had closed in 1914.

Among Chillagoe's motive power were four B15 locomotives along with two A Class 2–6–0 engines bought from Western Australian Government Railways, one ex–South Australian Railways X Class 2–6–0 and a tank engine. At the time of the government's takeover, the company had nine locomotives in service.

Queensland Government Railways

Established: The Railway Act of 1863 authorised the spending of £1.23 million for railway construction

Status: In operation, now known as QR

The first sod of the 34 km line from Ipswich to the Little Liverpool Range was turned on 26 February 1864 and in July the following year, the line from Ipswich to Bigge's Camp (now Grandchester) was opened to traffic. This line also had the first railway bridge — actually, a combined road–rail structure — across the Bremer River. In 1867, Toowoomba was reached, followed by Dalby the following year. In the other direction, the Ipswich–Roma Street (Brisbane) was not completed until 1876 with the opening of a bridge over the Brisbane River at Indooroopilly. By 1875, there were 405 km of track laid in Queensland.

Within the next few years a number of lines had been opened that radiated from Roma Street to Ascot, Caboolture and Sandgate. Meanwhile, work continued on the Darling Downs, and the Queensland narrow gauge reached the NSW border at Wallangarra by 1887. But a year was to pass before the standard gauge line on the other side of the border reached the town, thus making possible the interchange of passengers and freight. By that time, rails had pierced the western areas as far as Charleville, 776 km from Brisbane.

The early pattern of railway building in Queensland was typified by the construction of isolated sections. The effect of this pattern of rail development (that is, being built from three original points of origin: Brisbane, Townsville and Rockhampton) was that the colony's transport system did not become focused on one hub; nor did Brisbane become economically dominant in Queensland. Unlike

New South Wales or Victoria, Queensland's was a decentralised rail system. Within the first decade of construction, lines reached out from Brisbane to Mill Hill, and from Rockhampton to Westwood. Then the third trunk line, 137 km from Townsville to Charters Towers, was opened to traffic on 4 November 1882. It took some time for these disparate systems to be united; in 1900, there were still eleven isolated sections making up Queensland's railway. The rail between Brisbane and Rockhampton was not completed until 1897 and the great coastal route — all 1,680 km of it — was not completed until 10 December 1924 when the final Lilypond-Feluga and Innisfail–Dardgee sections were opened to traffic, a year before Townsville finally had been connected with the state capital. After all, there had been no great pressure to link the rail systems within the state. There was a very efficient coastal shipping industry along the length of Queensland, and these vessels provided an adequate service for both passengers and freight. It was the beginning of the Pacific war in 1941 that effectively ended the coastal shipping business, not competition from the railway.

On the builders pressed; a line reached out to Forsayth from Cairns, 422 km away. This involved a section which climbed 303 metres in just 24 km. Then branches radiated out to serve mining, agricultural and timber traffic.

Dajarra, 935 km from Townsville, was reached in 1917 on the Great Northern Railway, and that terminus became one of the major cattle shipments centres in the world. The 686 km from Rockhampton to Longreach was built by 1882 and, in 1928, this line was finally linked to the Great Northern via Winton. A decade earlier, in 1917, this trunk had been enhanced with the opening of the 271 km Jericho–Yaraka branch which carried huge volumes of agricultural traffic.

This left the Normanton–Croydon route as the only isolated section under Queensland Railways' control, a situation that continues to this day. Construction petered out in 1933, by which time the state had 10,422 route kilometres. The Normanton to Croydon line, all 152.6 km of it, was laid between 1889 and 1891 and steel sleepers were laid into the often muddy soil in an attempt to make the track flood-proof in the wet season.

SOUTH AUSTRALIA
Adelaide, Glenelg & Suburban Railway Company

(also the Holdfast Bay Railway Company and the merged Glenelg Railway Company)

Founded: 1871

Status: Taken over South Australian Railways on 15 December 1899

Persistent demands from settlers at Glenelg for a rail link with Adelaide, which the new colony's government could not afford to meet, led to the passing in 1871 of the *Glenelg Railway Act* which provided for private interests to build such a line. The government required the company to lay the track to the broad gauge of 5 ft 3 in (1,600 mm), that it operate a minimum of three trains a day in each direction and that the trains travel at no greater a speed than 30 mph (48 km/h).

The company was floated with a nominal capital of £22,000. Its plan for the line of 11.7 km aroused some public opposition when it was disclosed that trains would run down the centre of King William Street in Adelaide

OPPOSITE ABOVE: **Roofed stations were not unusual in Queensland. Here 2313 hauls a freight train out of Winton bound for Longreach in early 2003. Note the typical old goods crane at right.** *Rob McQueen.*

LEFT: **The line to Dirranbandi just north of the border with New South Wales was constructed primarily to secure the region's trade rather than have it go south. The line was opened as far as Goondiwindi in May 1908, and the arrival of the first train was captured for posterity.** *Author's collection.*

FOLLOWING SPREAD: **The owner by this time was South Australian Railways — its K57 is in the lead — but the look is still that of the Adelaide, Glenelg and Suburban Railway Company, which laid the track down Adelaide's King William Street. This photograph dates from 1914.** *National Railway Museum.*

and Jetty Road in Glenelg. When laid, the tracks were flush with the road surfaces to allow horse and other traffic to pass over them without danger. The guard rang a hand bell while trains were sharing these public roads. However, the authorities of Adelaide could not be moved on the subject of allowing the company to install a turntable at its Victoria Square terminus; instead, engines were turned at the South Terrace station.

The first scheduled revenue service ran to Adelaide on 4 August 1873. The line had no loops as it was initially intended that only one train would ever be operating at any time, and so the line had neither signalling nor any safe working regulations. Operations began with two small 2–4–0 tank locomotives built by Robert Stephenson & Co (numbered 1 and 2) and two end platform four-wheeler carriages. The company ran six return services a day, the first train leaving Glenelg at 8.50 am and the last arriving back at 8.30 pm. By 1874, the company had four carriages and the increasing frequency of services made the laying of a loop near the middle of the line necessary to allow trains to pass each other.

Glenelg became a popular seaside resort once the railway line was opened. For one shilling, you could buy a ticket from Adelaide that would allow you return travel and admission to the pool owned by the Glenelg Bathing Company. Trains also hauled some goods from ships, especially overseas mail landed at Glenelg Jetty. By 1875, the company had eight wagons that could be attached to the rear of the passenger trains; occasionally they were also used for passengers, with planks added to provide seating. In 1876, the company was operating four locomotives and eighteen carriages. That year, a profit of just over twelve thousand pounds was reported to

shareholders. A fifth locomotive was added to the fleet in 1875, a sixth in 1879. Back in 1873, its services connected with the line along the coast owned by the Glenelg and South Coast Tramway Company.

But the company was facing increasing criticism about its trains running in the middle of public streets. Complaints about the noise and soot were received with increasing frequency. There was also strife with the government of South Australia. The newly formed South Australian Railways wanted to build a line out of Adelaide to Nairne that would involve crossing the Glenelg Company's track. Initially the directors asked the government for a fee of more than twenty-five thousand pounds, but this was later negotiated down to eleven hundred and fifty pounds.

The Glenelg Company had become widely known as the 'vexing monopoly'. It was said to treat its customers badly. People complained about normal services being cancelled on race days, trains sometimes not stopping at halts, and some trains accommodating passengers without a roof. Punctuality was apparently not always something of which the company could boast.

Into being sprang the Holdfast Bay Railway Company which built a competing railway. In 1880, the Glenelg Company lowered its fares, with the Holdfast Bay directors countering by the introduction of low-priced excursion fares. An important source of revenue for Glenelg was the carriage of traffic to Morphettville Racecourse and it prohibited passengers travelling on Holdfast Bay trains from walking across its line to the racecourse entrance. That year, for the first time, Glenelg failed to pay a dividend, the profits being badly eroded by the competition. Because its trains had to crawl along sections

In the 1920s, South Australian Railways adopted a policy of building more powerful locomotives. Here, a goods train is seen powering through a peaceful Mt Lofty station in 1925. *Author's collection.*

at either end that ran down public roads, the Glenelg trains took twenty-five minutes to run the entire route compared with twenty minutes on the Holdfast Bay line. The government had a working relationship with Holdfast whereas relations were obviously not good with Glenelg. Thus South Australian Railways timetables included the Holdfast Bay schedule but not that of its competitor; SAR also allowed Holdfast Bay to run over a section of its rails at nominal cost.

Glenelg was also disadvantaged in that it had to maintain, above ordinary weekday needs, two extra locomotives and ten carriages for the racecourse and holiday traffic to the beach. This was calculated to cost about £1,130 in interest costs a year on loans to buy that equipment. By contrast, Holdfast Bay had an arrangement with SAR under which it could rent locomotives for thirty shillings a day and carriages at nine shillings a day each — a total annual cost of £141.

The competition was too much for either company to endure and, in 1881, they merged to become the Glenelg Railway Company.

The end came in 1898, when the South Australian Government, as provided in the original Act authorising the Glenelg line, decided to exercise its right to purchase the railway. It wanted the Victoria Square–Glenelg track but not the now unprofitable route built by the Holdfast Company. The offer was £75,000. The company arranged for a wagon containing that sum in gold sovereigns to be transported from the Bank of Adelaide to the company's premises in Glenelg, complete with armed guard and order of compulsory purchase. However, the directors rejected the delivery and the gold sovereigns were returned to the bank vault. The government finally had its way when

the directors gave in and accepted £120,000, the amount being paid on the day of the takeover, 15 December 1899.

Two other small sections of rail in Adelaide were built by private interests. First, the Largs Bay Land and Investment Company laid 2.1 km of track from Glanville to Largs in 1882 which was taken over by South Australian Railways in 1891 and closed in 1908. Secondly, the Grange Railway and Investment Company built a 5.5 km route from Woodville to Grange in 1882. SAR took control of this section in 1893.

Broken Hill Proprietary

Status: From 1999, lines operated by Australian Southern Railroad

The 'Big Australian' built a 1067 mm line a distance of 55 km between Iron Knob and Whyalla, with a 66 km branch to Iron Duchess. The lines were used to carry iron ore from mines to the blast furnace at Whyalla or for shipment from Whyalla to Port Kembla or Newcastle, New South Wales. BHP employed two 2–8–2 locomotives (the largest narrow gauge steam engines in Australia) to haul trains of up to 2,100 tons, but in 1956 the company changed over to diesel traction. In December 1999, BHP signed a five-year contract allowing Australian Southern Railroad to take over the operation of the company's railway network.

South Australian Railways (SAR)

Founded: 1856

Status: Merged into Australian National Railways

The department came into being with the construction by the colonial government in Adelaide of the 12 km broad

gauge line from the city to Port Adelaide. It was the first totally government-built and operated railway in the British Empire. The first significant expansion came in 1860 when a line was built to Kapunda, initially to serve copper mining but subsequently to carry grain. Ten years later it was extended to Burra by which time the South Australian Parliament had declared that no farmer should be farther than fifteen miles (24 km) from a port or railway. Perhaps SAR's most ambitious project was the Great Northern Railway which opened between Port Augusta and Quorn in 1879, and reached Oodnadatta in 1891. It also was responsible for the Darwin–Pine Creek railway in the Northern Territory until it was passed into the control of the Commonwealth.

By 1917, SAR had grown almost to its full extent, with about 5,300 km of track crossing the state. However, the department never satisfactorily resolved the question of gauge. The South Australians built their first lines to the broad gauge, and subsequently converted some narrow gauge tracks to the wider system. Many lines in rural areas, along with those to Oodnadatta (and then Alice Springs), Cockburn on the New South Wales border and the isolated system on the Eyre Peninsula, were all laid to narrow gauge. The many breaks of gauge, with the need to handle all freight from wagons of one gauge to that of another, was inconvenient in the early days but deadly for rail's competitive edge when trucks started running in competition. The introduction of standard gauge with the Trans-Australian line from Kalgoorlie to Port Augusta (and Port Pirie in 1937), and then to Broken Hill in 1969, further confused the picture to the extent that there arose that peculiarly South Australian phenomenon, the triple gauge station (Gladstone and Peterborough).

The narrow gauge network was built to serve pastoral and mining interests: the line to Cockburn which allowed the development of Broken Hill; the agricultural network on the Eyre Peninsula; the central region of South Australia and Mount Gambier; and, of course, to the north via Quorn and Oodnadatta. The broad gauge network was based on Adelaide, and it was intended to connect that city to the Murray River and the Victorian rail system.

Just as there had been John Whitton in New South Wales and Harold Clapp in Victoria, so SAR had its own giant figure: William Alfred Webb. He was appointed Commissioner in 1922 as SAR was facing a multitude of problems which cast doubt over the department's ability to continue to provide a function through the state system. The rolling stock was ageing and traffic was declining due in part to the lack of new investment over the period of World War I and after. His policy was to provide SAR with new and much more powerful locomotives to replace the large fleet of small engines that simply could not provide economic train operations. The powerful new locomotive fleet, along with large capacity wagons, helped the railways at a time when the road transport industry was beginning to grow (although the repeal of the *Road and Railway Act*, which allowed much greater road business, effectively negated the new economies wrought by Webb). He also expanded the Islington workshops, where new and large freight wagons were built. Part of the solution to having trains with larger goods capacity, apart from new wagons and more powerful locomotives, was to convert many lines to broad gauge.

SAR ceased to exist on 1 March 1978, in its one hundred and twenty-sixth year. Although it had effectively been absorbed into the State Transport Authority of South

OPPOSITE: **While private narrow gauge tramways were built for carrying freight — usually timber, coal or other minerals — they did play their part in providing passenger transport in the era before motorcars. Here, a wood-burning Krauss compound 0-4-0+0-4-0 is seen in Tasmania around World War I. The 762 mm railway, operated by Magnet Silver and Lead, connected at Waratah with the Emu Bay Railway.** *Noel Inglis collection.*

Australia two years previously, it was not until 1978 that its non-urban operations were formally taken over by Australian National.

TASMANIA
Emu Bay Railway Company

This company, which was acquired by the Australian Transport Network (owner of Tasrail) in 1998, owned a 141 km stretch of narrow gauge railway from the mining town of Zeehan which ran to the port of Burnie on the northern coast of Tasmania. There were two spurs, Guildford to Waratah over 16.5 km, on which operations ceased in 1939 due to lack of traffic after the effects of the Great Depression had led to the closure of the Mt Bischoff mine, and a 8.5 km line off from Rayna Junction. In 1989, the company laid a line to the Hellyer mine that closed in 2000. The section from Burnie to Waratah had been constructed by the Van Diemen's Land Company to a three-foot gauge, operating with two Beyer Peacock saddle tank locomotives. The Emu Bay and Mt Bischoff Railway Company converted the line to 3 ft 6 in (1,067 mm) on 14 July 1884. In 1897, the Emu Bay Railway Company of modern times was formed by a group of businessmen who acquired the railway with plans to extend it to serve the Mt Lyell mine. Mining operators there had to get their supplies by sea, the boats coming to the harbour of Strahan which was noted for the dangers of a land sand bar at the entrance and a vicious ebb tide. They then started laying the line from Guildford which became Guildford Junction when the new section was opened. The line was opened as far as Zeehan, where the company was granted access from 15 April 1901 by Tasmanian Government Railways to its station there on that isolated government section.

This meant that a traveller could travel between Burnie and Queenstown on three different railway systems: the Emu Bay as far as Zeehan, by TGR for the next 47.3 km to Regatta Point, and finally the last 27 km by the Mt Lyell Railway to Queenstown.

The railway was originally laid to serve the historic Mount Bischoff and Mount Magnet tin mines, but in the post-war years, carried out the concentrates produced by the Electrolytic Zinc Company. However, even though its origins were as a mining line, the company was heavily involved in passenger transport. During the Great Depression, the company introduced railmotor services to keep the costs down on what was then the Waratah branch. In the 1950s and early 1960s, Emu Bay operated fifteen locomotives including three large 4–8–2 + 2–8–4 Beyer Garratts.

An account of a trip along the line written in 1943 shows that the line was still extensively staffed. Those places that had declined in status — Renison Bell, Ridgely and Rayna Junction — had by this time lost their staff, but stations at Hampshire (where a woman was in charge), Guildford (where there were refreshment rooms for passengers, the guard telephoning orders ahead from Hampshire) and Primrose still had Emu Bay employees located there, as did Farrell which was the transhipment point for the 610 mm gauge tramway operated by the North Mount Farrell Mining Company. Rosebery was the most important station along the line, deserving a stationmaster. The terminus at Zeehan was on Tasmanian Government Railway land. At this time, Emu Bay was operating a 150 hp Gardner diesel railcar, two AEC railcars with trailers and passengers could also travel in cars on goods trains. Guildford was the first raised platform after Burnie and it

was also, at 617 metres, the highest station in Tasmania (the line reaching its highest point of 620 metres just beyond the station). So cold was it there that fires were usually kept alight in the refreshment rooms even in January and February. Boko was an important point on the line; although an unattended siding, it was the main crossing point for trains and at busy times an up service might wait while four down trains went through.

In 1960, the company suspended passenger trains between Rosebery and Zeehan, although people were allowed to travel in a compartment in the guard's van on goods trains. Because of the fact that the road network was not then complete in this region of Tasmania, the Emu Bay Company owned flat trucks which transported motor vehicles over the gap in the road system; this traffic regularly included a Pioneer Tours coach with passengers aboard. In 1961, the company tried to recapture passenger traffic by launching the West Coaster, made up of locomotives 6 and 8 along with three overhauled carriages, all decked out in two tones of blue. The Pioneer coaches stopped using the rail in the 1960s.

A rail fan's visit to Burnie resulted in the recording of yard activity at Burnie one afternoon in 1960. Emu Bay No. 19, a 2–6–0 locomotive, was the station shunter. At 4.10 pm, a goods van arrived from Zeehan down the Emu Bay line behind the Standard Garratt G18. There was a Devonport passenger train sighted and, at 5.15 pm, locomotives X23 and X12 pulled in the Tasman Limited from Hobart. Five minutes after this, Emu Bay railcar M8 arrived from Zeehan. Locomotive H4 arrived with the Devonport goods, was turned and left at 7.00 pm with a return working. The day's activity ended at 7.05 pm when the Emu Bay diesel–hydraulic PVH1

arrived from Primrose with an ore train.

In 1998, the then owner, the mining company Pasminco, sold the railway to the Australian Transport Network for $7.8 million after just ten days of negotiations. At that stage, the rail line employed about sixty people, including its own engineering maintenance staff. Emu Bay was carrying 630,000 tonnes a year out of Pasminco's Rosebery mine, Aberfoyle's Hellyer mine, and the Mt Lyell mine operated by Copper Mines of Tasmania. When the line became part of Tasrail, it was renamed 'the Melba branch'. The fleet of eleven G diesel locomotives was replaced by new motive power rebuilt in the workshops of Tranz Rail in New Zealand, which was the operating shareholder in Tasrail.

Launceston and Western Railway Company
Established: 1865

Status: Went bankrupt in September 1873 and railway taken over by government on 31 October of that year
Founded in 1865, this company built Tasmania's first railway — the 72.5 km broad gauge route between Launceston and Deloraine — which was opened to traffic on 10 February 1871. The Tasmanian Government did not want to be involved in railway construction and declined to contribute any money to the building of this line, although it passed an Act in 1865 authorising the project. In 1868, the Duke of Edinburgh added his prestige to the enterprise by turning the first sod. From the start, the company adopted the same 5 ft 3 in gauge as existed in Victoria. In fact, the company bought locomotives from Victoria to haul its trains. When the company went bust, the government went after the 2,259 landowners who had

voted to support a guarantee under which the line had been built. Riots occurred when bailiffs attempted to seize landowners' property and the government in Hobart was voted out after some months of disturbances.

Mount Lyell Mining & Railway Company

Founded: Incorporated on 29 March 1893

Status: Line closed 10 August 1963, due to high maintenance costs

This 27 km narrow gauge railway was completed in 1899 from the company's copper mine near Queenstown to Regatta Point on Macquarie Harbour at a cost of £216,000. The first section, from Teepookana on the King River to Queenstown, was opened in 1897 with Regatta Point being reached three years later. Trains took concentrates down the line, returning with coal and other supplies. Passengers were also carried. Steep grades near Regatta Point necessitated a rack system for almost 5 km to cope with a grade of 1 in 20 on one side of the saddle and 1 in 16 on the other.

In 1960, this line became an isolated section after Tasmanian Government Railways closed down the Zeehan–Regatta Point line. It lasted only another three years, made redundant after the area was connected to Tasmania's highway system, as well as facing high costs to keep the railway running.

The Abt Railway Society was formed in 1994, named after Dr Rowan Abt who designed the system whereby locomotives negotiated the severe grades by inserting a cog in the 'teeth' of the middle rail. Its intention was to restore the railway line. This would prove to be a substantial task as much of the railway had been lifted after closure and the thirty or more wooden bridges and two steel ones had been allowed to deteriorate. In 1999, the society obtained federal government backing and a grant of $20.45 million was made to the project. In 2001, the project was bought by the Tasmanian Government and leased to a private operator.

Tasmanian Government Railways (TGR)

Established: 1872

Status: Absorbed into Australian National Railways 1978

The Tasmanian Government's involvement in railways was not of its own choosing. A decision had been made to leave railways to private capital. It was only the failure of the Launceston and Western Railway Company in 1872 that left it with an existing and operating railway on its hands. The department then built several branch lines off the narrow gauge Tasmanian Main Line Railway Company track and bought the company in 1890. It also extended the Launceston and Western line to Devonport before going on to absorb the Marrawah Tramway, a 41.6 km section in the far north-west of the island.

Meanwhile, the government became distracted by the many rail and tramway proposals generated by the mining boom on Tasmania's west coast. By 1897, it was possible to travel from Hobart to Queenstown by rail. But not only was it a circuitous route, but also a slice of Tasmanian history. The traveller would have left Hobart on track laid by the Tasmanian Main Line Railway Company; travelled from Western Junction on a route built by the Launceston and Western; then as far as Burnie on rails laid by the TGR itself. South from Burnie,

Class B13 233, a 4-6-0 locomotive, taken in Charleville yards about 1900. The driver was probably the man in the bowler hat. *George Balsillie collection.*

the traveller would then be on an Emu Bay Railway train as far as Zeehan, where he or she would have been deposited at the start of an isolated TGR section. After sitting once again in a government-owned carriage on a government-operated train, our traveller would have reached Regatta Point and then relied on the Mt Lyell Railway to complete the journey to Queenstown.

After World War II, the TGR — like most of the other Australian rail systems — was in the situation where most of its motive power was either obsolete or needed substantial repairs. It ordered thirty-two new diesel–electric locomotives from English Electric and diesel mechanical shunters from the Drewry Car Company. But it still needed steam; eighteen new locomotives were also ordered, comprising eight 4–8–2 H Class heavy goods and ten 4–6–2 M Class mixed traffic locomotives. During the desperate shortage of motive power in the 1945–50 period, TGR also resorted to taking over surplus locomotives from other parts of Australia. It purchased four ex–Commonwealth Railways Nfb Class 2–6–0 locomotives that had originally been built for South Australian Railways between 1890 and 1892 and six Standard Garratts from Queensland Government Railways. The department was looking at ways to free up locomotives and in 1945, the Launceston–Wynyard fast train, the Western Express, was taken over by four-car diesel sets.

Tasmania's rail system thus survived but, as in the pre-war years, it was not possible to say that it prospered.

When the Whitlam Federal Labor Government offered to buy all the state rail systems, Tasmanian politicians could not believe their luck in getting rid of a department that had drained state finances for decades.

Tasmanian Main Line Railway Company

Founded: 1871

Status: Tasmanian Government took control on 1 October 1890

Authorised by an 1869 Act of the Tasmanian Parliament, this company was founded to build a narrow gauge line between Hobart and Launceston. The government also made provision so that, from Western Junction on the final 18 km at the Launceston end, the company could lay a third rail on the existing broad gauge track built by the Launceston and Western Railway Company. Building of the line was started in 1873, the 3 ft 6 in narrow gauge having been adopted by the company. The TMLR line began operations on 1 November 1876. The main Hobart station was opened on 15 March of the following year. The express service, started in 1876, called for trains to leave what was then called Hobart Town at 7.45 am, stop at Campania, Oatlands, Antill Ponds, Ross and Campbell Town before reaching Evansdale Junction at 1.00 pm, whereupon passengers changed trains for the completion of their journeys. The government built several branch lines off the trunk route and then acquired the company's assets in 1890.

RULES, RULES, RULES

IN 1920, SOUTH AUSTRALIAN RAILWAYS ruled that no dogs could travel in brake vans, and that the Trans-Australian could carry a maximum of sixteen crates of pigeons. By 1924, snakes could be transported by rail provided they were in special boxes and paid for at double the normal livestock rate. Guards were required to provide a specified amount of drinking water for live poultry and ensure they had enough space in each cage.

When the Spanish influenza epidemic struck in 1918, the Trans-Australian along with trains on the Broken Hill, Melbourne, Pinnaroo border and Mount Gambier border lines, were required to travel with all carriage windows opened to keep the cars properly ventilated. In 1933, South Australian Railways instituted pillow hire at one shilling (ten cents) for passengers travelling on the Melbourne Express. Some passengers must have departed with the pillow sheets because, several weeks after the pillow service came into being, staff were advised to check that the covers were also handed in at the end of the journey along with the pillows themselves. By contrast, in 1972 Victorian Railways decided that it would no longer charge sitting passengers for cushions on the overnight service to Mildura and that, henceforth, guards would provide them free on request.

TOP AND ABOVE RIGHT: The Tasmanian Transport Museum Society has preserved several of the state's railcars. DP 26 was one of the articulated long-distance batch of cars built for Tasmanian Government Railways. The seating seems adequate for the relatively short distances of the island's rail network. *Stuart Dix.*

LEFT AND ABOVE LEFT: DP 15 was designed for suburban services in Tasmania, and the seating reflects that intent. *Stuart Dix.*

TOP: Tasrail locomotive 2118 at the Derwent River near Boyer in 2001. *Brian Webber.*

ABOVE: Three Tasrail locomotives cross the bridge at Deloraine. Private ownership of the state's railways has seen the system claw its way back to being a viable operation. *Peter Mackenzie.*

OPPOSITE: Tasmania's premier service, the Tasman Limited. No passenger trains now run in regular service on the island. *Peter Mackenzie.*

ABOVE: After World War II,
Victorian Railways set about
replacing the remaining country
line passenger carriage trains,
and old wooden body rail
motors, with modern railcars.
Several examples have been
preserved and now run through
the same rural scenery as they
did 50 years earlier. Rail Motor
No. 63, with diesel-electric
traction, is seen here with Motor
Trailer No. 26. *James Brook.*

RIGHT: Queensland coal
power — 1307 and two 1270s
haul empty coal wagons near
Blackwater in 1970. *Brian Webber.*

ABOVE: A memory only for Tasmanians: a passenger service about to depart from Hobart station in the guise of railcars DP 27 and DP 24 on 8 November 1973. *John Beckhaus.*

LEFT: DP 22, owned by the Don River Railway, was a country railcar although, like the articulated cars, it ended its days on Hobart suburban services after all country trains had been withdrawn. The seating is basic. *Stuart Dix.*

Tasrail

Formerly Tasmanian Government Railways

Founded: 1978 as a division of Australian National Railways

Status: Sold 1997 to the Australian Transport Network; operating

In November 1979, when the Federal Government finalised the sale of Tasrail, it signified the ambitions of a consortium led by Wisconsin Central to expand from its New Zealand beachhead into Australia. The new owners set about winning traffic back to rail, and also expanded with the purchase of the Emu Bay Railway from Pasminco. For the first time, Tasmania now had an integrated rail network. The single largest traffic was hauling cement between Railton and Devonport, followed by coal, logs and containers. The new owners also moved quickly to re-open the line from Burnie to Wiltshire Junction, and then upgraded motive power with locomotives rebuilt at Tranz Rail workshops in New Zealand. In 2004, Tasrail was again sold, this time to Pacific National, one of the two large mainland rail freight operators. At this time, Tasrail had 780 km of track, thirty-nine locomotives and 668 wagons.

VICTORIA
Freight Australia

Incorporated: 1998 (initially known as Freight Victoria)

Status: Taken over by Pacific National in 2004
This company was a fully owned subsidiary of RailAmerica, a short-line specialist based in Boca Raton, Florida. The company leased about 4,000 km of track from the Victorian Government and took over the state's rail freight service known as V/Line. The company made several large investments in rolling stock and lines including, in 2001, spending about one million dollars upgrading the important freight track between Inglewood and Eaglehawk, near Bendigo. Freight Australia's business was dominated by grain haulage, a fact which led to it, in late 2002, having to lay off staff as traffic volumes plunged due to the drought. To diversify, the company sought business in New South Wales and acquired contracts for the movement of rice, cement and petroleum. It also began an express freight service between Sydney and Melbourne.

Geelong and Melbourne Railway Company

Incorporated: 1853

Status: Taken over by Victorian Government in 1860
This company turned the first sod of the planned Melbourne–Geelong line on 20 September 1853 with construction beginning at the Geelong end. The government granted it a land corridor as well as space for a terminal at Geelong. Running rights were granted over the Melbourne, Mt Alexander and Murray River Railway Company's line from Williamstown Junction into Melbourne. However, due to the collapse of the latter company (see below), there was a delay completing the railway into Melbourne. Initially, the Geelong Company's trains ran only to the mouth of the Yarra River, with passengers using a ferry in and out of Melbourne. The first train ran on 25 June 1857. This situation continued until the railway was completed, with Geelong Company trains

SYDNEY'S CENTRE

SYDNEY'S FIRST CENTRAL station comprised of a primitive galvanised iron train shed, about 30 metres by 10 metres, served by a single rail track. Staff worked in a lean-to iron-roof building. It was replaced in 1874 by Sydney's second station, a more substantial red brick building with two through platforms and two bay platforms. Sydney's third and present station, now known as Sydney Central, was opened in 1906 and was built for the extraordinary sum, in those days, of £693,364. The station was erected on the site of the Devonshire Street Cemetery after the removal of all human remains. In 1921, further stories and the clock tower were added. Then, in 1926, Central Station opened with an additional seven platforms to service suburban electric trains. With that development, the interstate and country platforms were known as Sydney Terminal, although the general public tended to refer to both stations as Central.

able to run into Spencer Street, Melbourne, by January 1859. However, the company was unable to make its operations profitable and they were taken over by the government in 1860.

Kerang Shire Council

Line opened: 19 July 1889

Status: Taken over by Victorian Railways 1 February 1952; closed 1 March 1983

This 21.7 km line was built by the Swan Hill Shire Council (later the Kerang Shire) and ran from the town of Kerang to the Murray River at Koondrook, which lies between Swan Hill and Echuca. Known as the Kerang and Koondrook Tramway, it qualifies for inclusion because scheduled passenger services ran over the line as did Victorian Railways rolling stock; it was a designated common carrier.

The local body had decided to build the line to allow Koondrook to capture its share of the river traffic on the Murray that was transhipped to rail for transport to Melbourne. Its northern terminus was in the main street of Koondrook and a passenger platform was built in that same street, the line running several hundred metres before it ran into its own right-of-way.

In 1938, Guy Bakewell visited the operation and some years later committed his memories down to paper. At that time, the tramway was serviced by an ex–Victorian Railways T Class 0–6–0 built at Ballarat's Phoenix Foundry in 1884, the train consisting of a guard's van, one carriage (the interior of which included a small booking office, with all tickets sold on the train) and several wagons. A return ticket was four shillings. This train was limited to

29 km/h. It stopped at three stations — Yeoburn, Hinksons and Gannaworra — along with other places where passengers needed to join or alight. There was a tramway manager and twelve staff, including drivers, firemen, gangers, an engineer, a guard and clerical workers. Minor repairs were undertaken at Koondrook, but heavy work meant the locomotive or other rolling stock being sent to Victorian Railways' Bendigo workshop. Most wagons were VR stock that ran through without transhipment at Kerang. During Bakewell's visit, there was also a D Class 4–4–0 locomotive parked in the yard at Koondrook as well as a disused Sentinel–Cammell steam railcar. Apart from the carriage in use, the tramway owned an ex–South Australian Railways four-wheeler car that was used only in emergencies.

Melbourne and Essendon Railway Company

Incorporated: 1859

Status: Acquired by Victorian Government August 1867

After acquiring running rights on the government line from Spencer Street to Essendon Junction (later North Melbourne), this company built a railway to Essendon and opened for business on 21 October 1860. The following year, a branch line was opened between Newmarket and Flemington racecourse, making 8 km of track in total. Locomotives and rolling stock were hired from the government but the company was unable to sustain its services beyond July 1864. The lines remained unused until acquired by the government three years later, but even then it was not until 1872 that scheduled trains ran on the

Wagons being built as far as the eye can see. These grain wagons were one of the range of rolling stock that came out of railway workshops across the country, this scene taken in Melbourne in the early 1900s. *Author's collection.*

company-built section. The government, by that time, had extended the line northwards to Seymour and Longwood, reaching Wodonga in November 1873.

Melbourne and Hobson's Bay Railway Company

(incl. St Kilda & Brighton Railway Company)

Established: August 1852

Status: Absorbed St Kilda & Brighton in 1865 to become Melbourne and Hobson's Bay United Railway Company; taken over by Victorian Government on 1 July 1878

This company constructed the short line from the south side of Flinders Street to Sandridge (now Port Melbourne) on Hobson's Bay which opened on 12 September 1854, thus becoming the first steam-operated railway in Australia. The line was 4 km in length if you added the extension to Station Pier opened in 1916. The company was given a land corridor for the railway.

The Act establishing the railway was passed in January 1853 and the company launched itself with capital of £100,000. However, the money raised soon proved inadequate with prices of most goods spiralling upwards following the start of the gold rush.

Because of delays in delivery of locomotives from England, a local company, Robertson, Martin & Smith, was contracted to build an engine. This 2–2–2 locomotive was built in ten weeks but it lasted only six days. Eventually, the company suspended operations until locomotives arrived from Robert Stephenson & Company. The company operated both routes until 1865.

However, the opening day had been a great success, with Lieutenant-Governor Sir Charles Hotham being presented with a copy of the railway's by-laws and its timetable printed on silk. Passenger services were soon running smoothly between the city and its port, with departures every half hour between 8.30 am and 8.00 pm. A restricted timetable operated on Sundays, including no trains during the hours of morning church services. It cost one shilling and sixpence to buy a one-way ticket. In the period between 1 November 1856 and 30 April 1857, the company recorded the sale of 232,973 passenger tickets and the booking of 43,173 tons of freight. Wool bales were carted for a charge of three shillings and sixpence, general freight cost ten shillings a ton and gold was transported 'by arrangement'.

In May 1857, the company opened a 5.6 km branch line to St Kilda passing through what is now South Melbourne.

Melbourne, Mount Alexander & Murray River Railway Company

Founded: By Act of Parliament passed on 8 February 1853

Status: Taken over by trustees in 1856, and then placed in the hands of the Board of Lands and Works in 1857

This company had its origins in the early desire, once Victoria was established as a separate colony in 1851, to have a railway link between Melbourne and Echuca on the Murray River. The government gave the company a corridor of land just over 90 metres wide and 20 hectares for a terminal at Batman's Hill (later Spencer Street station). The first sod was turned at Williamstown on 12 June 1854 for the line that was to be a 342 km railway costing £7.72 million.

In what was to become a familiar story with early private railways in Australia, the company soon struck financial problems and was taken over by the Victorian Government

T 383 on a country passenger train at Korumburra, Victoria, on 17 December 1971. Note the typical variety of rolling stock in the sidings. *John Beckhaus.*

in 1856. By that stage, only one contract had been let by the company for some fencing work. But some earthworks had also been undertaken between the planned Melbourne terminus and the Maribyrnong River.

Melbourne and Suburban Railway Company

This company's trains operated from its station at Princes Bridge first to Richmond, then to Prahran where it connected with a private line built from St Kilda. The first section was opened on 8 February 1859. In 1860, a short branch was built from Richmond to Picnic Platform on the Yarra, being extended to Hawthorn the following year. The company never prospered. In 1862, it was taken over by the Melbourne Railway Company, and ended up in 1865 as part of the Melbourne and Hobson's Bay Railway.

St Kilda and Brighton Railway Company

This company was established to construct an extension to the existing railway between Melbourne and St Kilda, with the new section to Brighton via Prahran. This was opened on 19 December 1859, with an extension to Brighton Beach opened two years later. In 1865, this company was purchased by the Melbourne and Hobson's Bay Co, whose line it joined, and became part of the enlarged Melbourne and Hobson's Bay United Railway Co.

Victorian Railways

Formed: The Victorian Railway Department came into existence on 19 March 1856, after the colony's government had been forced to rescue the Melbourne, Mount Alexander and Murray River Railway Company which was building a line to Williamstown

Status: In 1997, split into V/Line passenger and V/Line freight arms; the latter was sold to Freight Victoria (later Freight Australia); suburban passenger services now operated by privately owned trains

After acquiring the Mount Alexander Company, and its incomplete line to Williamstown, the department called for tenders for the railway to be built to Echuca on the Murray River and border with New South Wales and for a separate line to Ballarat. Echuca was reached in 1864, and the 1862 purchase of the privately built Geelong line gave Victorian Railways a route to Ballarat via Geelong, the direct line through Bacchus Marsh not being completed until 1889. Wodonga had been reached in 1873, followed by the north-western line to Dimboola. South-west to Camperdown, the line ran via the Goulburn Valley to Cobram on the NSW border while the Gippsland line to Sale and Portland was connected to the colony's rail network.

The gold boom of the 1850s had been the first real trigger for building a train network in Victoria, and the expansion phase lasted until the 1930s. A rail building boom in the 1880s, with sixty-six lines authorised in 1884, saw a complex network built in Victoria, totalling 4,666 km by 1892.

During the depression of the 1890s, Victoria sought to save money by building some lines at 2 ft 6 in (762 mm gauge) but they could never have been successful when rolling stock was not interchangeable with the broad gauge network. The last of these lines closed in 1962. Newport workshops were called upon to provide much of the rolling stock for these rail services. The 49.1 km Wangaratta to Whitfield route, opened on 14 March 1899, was equipped with one passenger carriage, one brake van,

The 762 mm narrow gauge lines built by Victorian Railways were an attempt by the governments of the day to extend the railway system without having to spend too much money. When the 42 km line from Moe to Walhalla was opened on 3 May 1910, the citizens of Walhalla found their excursion train provided rudimentary comforts. *Author's collection.*

thirty open wagons, one cattle wagon, one louvred van and one insulated van. Over the life of this line (it closed 12 October 1953) Newport built a total of 298 vehicles. By 1916, there was a weekly mixed train and a motor tricycle which ran up the line three days a week to carry mail.

In the early years of the twentieth century, Victoria had a higher route mileage than the much geographically bigger New South Wales, a testament to the rail frenzy which had gripped the southern state. More lines were laid until the early 1930s, so that by 1933 the Victorian system had 7,585 route kilometres. This included lines to NSW between Barnes and Balranald, Murrabit and Stony Crossing, Yarrawonga–Oaklands and the purchase of the Echuca–Deniliquin line from the Deniliquin and Moama Railway Company.

The railway system, notwithstanding the appalling state of the equipment by 1945, struggled on until petrol rationing was abolished in 1950. A long strike on the railways that year did the rest. As car ownership and road trucking increased, there was little incentive for successive governments to maintain or repair much of the network. It was cheaper to close lines. Since 1962, more than 2,100 km of track has been closed in Victoria.

West Coast Railway

Incorporated: 1993
Status: Operating
This company came into being in response to the Victorian Government's decision to privatise long-distance services. West Coast operates several daily services between Melbourne's Spencer Street station to Warrnambool, a distance of 267 km, with stops at Geelong, Winchelsea, Birregurra, Colac, Camperdown and Terang. It restored B-

Class and S-Class carriages, dating from the 1950s, for the new service. The company has its office at Geelong and a maintenance depot at Warrnambool and Ballarat East. In 2001, it bought a half-share of long-distance passenger rail services in New Zealand.

WESTERN AUSTRALIA
Great Southern Railway

Founded: Signed contract with government in 1888
Status: Taken over by the Western Australian Government in 1896 for £1.1 million
This company built 389 km of railway from Beverley to Albany. The latter was the colony's main deepwater port until the development of Fremantle but Western Australians were frustrated by the fact that it took five days by road coach to get there from Perth. The government therefore decided to entice a private company to build a railway from Beverley south to the port.

A Sydney businessman, Sir Anthony Horden, established the Western Australian Land Company in London with the intention of building the line, but he died in 1886 on the ship returning to Australia. Eventually, by 1888, the company was in a position to sign an agreement with the government which allowed it to claim 12,000 acres for every mile of line built. The company was also contracted to bring five thousand immigrants from the United Kingdom to help populate the lands along the route.

The first sod was turned on 20 October 1888, and the work was relatively easy as the route ran through mainly undulating country. The first train ran from Albany to Mt Barker in April 1889, and the whole line was ready for traffic by 1 June. Mail trains took eleven hours to get from

FROM BUFFER TO COUPLER

NEW TECHNOLOGIES were not always adopted quickly in the Australian railway systems. Victorian Railways advised its staff in 1953 that, from 1 January 1954, buffers and transition chains would be removed from all freight rolling stock, thus completing the first phase of the changeover to automatic couplers, a phase begun in 1926.

Beverley to the southern port. The company provided comfortable bogie carriages that were missing one vital facility — a lavatory.

As it turned out, the company could not find enough people wanting to lease the land and, inevitably, the railway ended up in government hands.

Midland Railway Company

Founded: 1890

Status: Purchased by the Western Australian Government in 1964

This company was floated in London and subsequently completed a 445 km line between Midland Junction (near Perth) to Walkaway, where it connected with an isolated section of track owned by Western Australian Government Railways. Like other Western Australian ventures, this private railway was dependent upon land grants. Midland acquired 3.3 million acres (about 1.34 million hectares) from the government in Perth.

Construction had begun on the line from what was originally called Guildford under the control of a private syndicate. However, by 1887, the government had completed the line south from Geraldton to Walkaway but work on the private section up from Guildford had ceased because the syndicate ran out of money. There was little the government could do until 1890, the contracted date for the syndicate to have completed its part of the deal. Thus the Midland Company came into existence. By April 1891, the company managed to open the 80 km section from Guildford to Gin Gin, and a few months later trains could go south 96 km from Walkaway to Mingenew. Work continued while the company battled several financial

crises, resolved only when the government guaranteed a £500,000 bond issue. The first through train to Walkaway made its journey on 2 November 1894.

Nevertheless, as a commemorative publication by the Australian Railway Historical Society explains, the company's troubles were far from over. A parliamentary select committee in 1901, investigating the company after many complaints had been received, turned up facts which showed that all was not well within the Midland operation. Stationmasters were not always experienced in their jobs, some stations were left in the charge of gangers' wives and some drivers had no proper certification. But the company's presence did bring benefits to the communities along the way, and not just by providing a reliable form of transport to Geraldton or Perth. In 1909, the goods shed at Three Springs served as a cinema for the town's first silent motion picture shows while the Gin Gin station was used as a meeting place by local groups. Its headquarters were located at Midland Junction.

The bulk of its revenue over the company's lifetime derived from the haulage of agricultural products, but the opening of the Murchison Goldfields brought other types of freight as well as a surge in passenger traffic. The government responded by introducing a steamer service from Perth to Geraldton with passengers moving on WAGR lines to the goldfields. Then, in 1915, the govern- ment completed its near parallel line northwards to Mullewa, giving the WAGR its own route to Geraldton from Perth. In 1915, the Midland Company added three sleeping cars to its existing seated carriage stock, the new vehicles having been ordered from WAGR's Midland Workshops. Eventually, as road operators sprang up and started to drain away Midland's passenger business, the company bought its

Busy days on the narrow gauge. In this West Australian scene, PMR 732 (with banking engine at the rear) hauls an ore train while a diesel-hauled passenger working passes in the opposite direction. The passengers would have been contemplating the peaceful countryside one moment only to be startled by the passing of the black steaming beast and then the clickety-clack of its wagons over rail joints.
John Buckland collection, by permission of the National Library of Australia.

own buses as well as road express freight services.

It remained a relatively busy operation to the end. In 1960, Midland trains carried 265,000 tonnes of freight. But the company struggled to make ends meet. Midland was put out of its misery by the government in 1964, when the latest of several approaches for a government buyout was accepted in Perth at that time. This was effected by the Midland Company going into liquidation and its assets transferred to the Crown. The line remains in use today under the management of the Australian Railroad Group.

Western Australian Government Railways (WAGR)

Founded: Preceded in 1877 as Department of Works and Railways. WAGR founded in 1890 and, between then and 1949, took on tramways, ferries and electricity supply. After 1947 reverted to WAGR.

Status: The name finally disappeared in 2003 when WAGR was merged with regional bus services.

Western Australia's first government line preceded the department's creation. This was the 52.4 km line from Geraldton to Northampton, built over five years and opened on 26 July 1879. Then, in 1881, building began on a line from the port of Fremantle to the inland regions. By 1897, the tracks reached Kalgoorlie on what was known as the Eastern Goldfields Railway. Another main line to Bunbury was completed in 1893. The Western Australian government had decided that no farmer should be further than 25 km from a railway line. The result? Within twenty years, track mileage in Western Australia more than doubled with 3,200 km of rail line being laid by the Railway Construction Branch. Between 1894 and 1899, more than one thousand miles (1,600 km) of government railways were laid and opened to traffic. Yet any of what became a comprehensive network of country lines were not opened until well into the twentieth century: Bonnie Rock was reached in 1931, Pingrup in

1923, Newdegate in 1926 and Wiluna in 1932.

Whitton, Clapp and Webb were all names that dominated the railways of New South Wales, Victoria and South Australia. Western Australia's giant figure was C. Y. O'Connor. Appointed as the colony's chief engineer, his responsibilities included the rail system. What he found — and set about rectifying — was a situation where railway workshops were not properly tooled to cope with the demands on them, in addition to which much of the network needed urgent attention to replace light rails with ones that could carry the traffic.

As country rail passenger services were phased out, WAGR expanded its road coach operations. Even as late as 2000, the route map bore a considerable resemblance to the map of the Western Australian rail system before many of the lines were closed and lifted. Westrail's coaches radiated from Perth and other cities to Kalbarri in the north, inland to Meekatharra (going via Mullewa, Yalgoo and Mount Magnet, just as the expresses had done decades earlier), to Hopetoun on the Great Australian Bight via Wagin and on many routes criss-crossing the south-west of the state.

As late as 1955, WAGR was ordering new steam motive power in the form of the 2–8–2 V Class locomotives. The twenty-four machines, numbered 1201 to 1224, were the first with that wheel arrangement owned by WAGR. The first loco to arrive, 1201, showed its paces by hauling a 1,250 ton coal train from Brunswick Junction to East Perth.

In March 2000, the Western Australian Government announced it was selling Westrail's freight operations to the Australian Railroad Group for $585 million. At this time, Westrail had produced five consecutive annual operating profits and in fiscal 2000 had reported a record 31.1 million tonnes of freight haulage for the year, along with 29.5 million passenger journeys on Perth's suburban network while the three country services, Prospector, AvonLink, and Australind, carried 258,000 passengers between them.

OPPOSITE ABOVE: **This is a classic view of the Albany railway station in 1900 showing the rather small, short and narrow shunting yard with the waters of Princess Royal Harbour lapping at the edges. A set of carriages is parked on No. 4 road opposite the station, presumably to clear the platform line for another arrival. The scene today is much different, with massive reclamations having taken place for the modern port.** *Noel Inglis collection.*

OPPOSITE: **An ADE Class diesel–electric railcar is seen leaving Perth's Central Station probably in the late 1930s — the date indicated by the absence of a trailer. The trailers were built later at Midland Workshops to increase the capacity of the six ADE railcars purchased from the United Kingdom. The ADE Class bore names of former West Australian governors and, along with the larger ADF 'Wildflower' Class imported in 1949, saw service on the Great Southern line. They would run between Perth and Albany and also on the southern branch lines to Ongerup and Pingrup.** *Noel Inglis collection.*

First railways

Grandchester, located 76 km east of Brisbane, acquired its status as the terminus for Queensland's first railway line, laid from Ipswich in 1865. The settlement had been called Bigge's Camp, but Governor Bowen felt that the new railway town needed a more impressive name — and a railway station was built to match that status. The Grandchester railway station, built in 1866, was later listed by the National Trust. The station staff, seen here about 1900, are clearly proud of their station and its impressive wooden platform. The man at left in uniform is thought to be the stationmaster. *John Oxley Library.*

A TRAMWAY USING iron rails was laid in Newcastle in 1827 and used by the Australian Agricultural Company. But, while this is the first recorded use of rail transport in Australia, it was not a 'railway' in that it did not act as a common carrier, nor did it operate scheduled services. The same has to be said for the convict tramway opened in 1836 at Port Arthur, Tasmania. There was also a horse-drawn tramway which started operating in 1854 at the mouth of the Murray River between Goolwa and Port Elliot, a distance of eleven kilometres. All worthy of note, but not railways as we know them.

For the purposes of this book, the first railway in Australia opened in Victoria one hundred and fifty years ago. It was steam-hauled, the first such train on the continent.

Victoria pioneers steam rail

That first steam-hauled railway service ran between Melbourne and Sandridge (later Port Melbourne) on 12 September 1854. The first train pulled out of Flinders Street station at 12.20 pm and consisted of a third class open car carrying the band of the 40th Regiment, a first class car for the Lieutenant-Governor, Sir Charles Hotham and the directors of the Melbourne and Hobson's Bay Railway company, and two second class cars for other guests. This line now serves as a light rail route.

New South Wales

A year later, the Sydney–Parramatta line was opened (on 26 September 1855). The Sydney Railway Company had begun on 10 October 1849, to build a line from the colony's capital with the intention of going as far as Goulburn, but was unable to continue as a viable business. In

1855, the company was acquired by the New South Wales Government, which completed the 22 km section to Parramatta.

South Australia
On 21 April 1856, a broad gauge line was opened between Adelaide and Port Adelaide by that colony's government to the 5 ft 3 in (or 1,600 mm) broad gauge. Construction started in 1853 after the government had taken over responsibility for the project from the original promoters.

Queensland
The first line (between Ipswich and Bigge's Camp, now Grandchester) was opened on 31 July 1865. In the early years of the new colony, goods moving between Brisbane and Ipswich went by river, and the remainder of the transport link inland was served by coaches and bullock teams. The privately owned Moreton Bay Tramway Company had drawn up plans for a horse-drawn tramway between Ipswich and Toowoomba but could not raise sufficient capital. The new colony's government interceded and decided to build the project as a mechanically powered railway.

Tasmania
Private enterprise in the form of the Launceston and Western Railway Company built the island state's first line, the 72 km route between Launceston and Deloraine. It was built to the broad gauge and opened on 10 February 1871. A banquet of forty dishes was held at Launceston Town Hall to celebrate the opening of the line.

Western Australia
The first government-owned line was opened in 1879 between Geraldton and Northampton, a distance of 53 km. It was built to serve lead and copper mines inland from the port at Geraldton. The government's first plan was to lay the line to a three-foot (914 mm) gauge as a cost-savings measure. But privately owned timber lines that had already started operating were all laid to 3 ft 6 in (1,067 mm) and it was subsequently decided to adopt that for the government lines, a change which added £18,000 to the cost of construction.

Northern Territory
A rail line between Darwin and Pine Creek opened on 1 October 1889. This was to become the North Australia Railway extending to the desolate spot known as Birdum. It was to have been the first stage of a north–south transcontinental railway, but this isolated section closed in 1976. The rail link between Darwin and the south only became a reality in 2004.

Australian Capital Territory
A line of 10 km in length was built from the NSW system at Queanbeyan on the Goulburn–Bombala branch line into Canberra in 1914 with the first train running on May 25 of that year. Passenger services began on the line on 15 October 1923. There were also plans drawn up to build a line linking Canberra and the separate part of the ACT — the reserve at Jervis Bay on the coast — to provide the nation's capital with its own port.

5

THE GAUGE
QUESTION

Broad gauge: 5 ft 3 in or 1,600 mm
Standard gauge: 4 ft 8¹/2 in or 1,485 mm
Narrow gauge: 3 ft 6 in or 1,067 mm

The 'gauge' is the distance between the two rails which make up the track. 'Dual gauge' lines involve the laying of a third rail to allow trains of different gauges to operate over the same piece of track. 'Break of gauge' denotes a station where the gauge changes and passengers and goods have to be transferred between train sets.

The question of railway gauge has bedevilled Australia for more than a century; over 150 years, twenty-two separate breaks of gauge have existed. Three different gauges were selected by the colonies for their main systems. New South Wales was alone in selecting what is now known as standard gauge, although it looked initially as though broad gauge was going to be selected. Tasmania started with broad gauge, then switched to narrow. Victoria plumped for the broad, although some lines were laid to the very narrow 2 ft 6 in, or 762 mm, gauge. South Australia laid its main lines around Adelaide to broad gauge but then skimped on some rural lines by making them narrow gauge. Western Australia and Queensland were at least consistent by selecting only narrow gauge, although the 1872 Royal Commission on Railways in the latter colony recommended a 2 ft 9 in, or 787 mm gauge. It was Queensland's good fortune that this suggestion was never adopted.

Over the many decades since these initial decisions were taken, railway administrators grappled to overcome the obvious logistical problems when people and goods had to be moved over more than one system. For example, in 1910 it was suggested that a third rail be laid on the broad gauge line from

Wodonga, on the border with NSW, so that standard gauge trains from the northern state could run through to Melbourne. This issue was still being discussed in 1939 at the outbreak of war. Instead, a large transhipment centre was developed at Bandiana, just inside Victoria, to handle all the arms and equipment transferred between the two rail systems. On the other side of the border, the NSW authorities for many years refused a Victorian request that broad gauge track be laid into the Albury yard.

A vast amount of manpower was required to transfer goods at break of gauge stations from one train to another. One answer Australia developed was bogie exchanges, where the wheels were changed to allow wagons to continue running on a different gauge. Also, engineers devised a way to lay one set of tracks within another. For example, at Wodonga, on the Victorian–New South Wales border, a wagon coming from Melbourne on the broad gauge would be shunted into the exchange and then lifted off its bogies. The broad gauge sets of wheels would be taken away and standard gauge ones rolled in underneath. The wagon would then be lowered on to these new bogies and off it would go on the standard gauge line to Sydney. Other bogie exchanges were located at South Dynon, Melbourne, Peterborough, Adelaide and Port Pirie. The last mentioned was to allow interchange of wheels between standard and broad gauge rolling stock, and the exchange was opened in November 1965. In its first year, it handled 9,067 vehicles and by 1966, the exchange was changing bogies on twenty-five vehicles a day.

At least from 1950 it became the practice to pack goods moving between the two states in rudimentary containers, which could then be transferred between wagons by crane at Albury. It was not until 1962 that a standard gauge line was built alongside the broad gauge track from NSW to Melbourne.

Narrow gauge

Queensland has always been the premier narrow gauge system, with 10,144 km of track in 1986. It seemed that, when Queensland first contemplated building railways, there was no consideration of a future connection with NSW. The first engineer-in-chief of railway construction, Abraham Fitzgibbon, advised the colonial government that the narrow gauge was perfectly adequate provided trains were limited to a speed of twenty miles an hour.

While Tasmania's first line (Launceston–Deloraine) was constructed by private interests to the broad gauge, the government decided to build its lines to the narrow gauge for reasons of economy, and this applied from the extension built in 1885 from Deloraine to Devonport, when private companies were taken over by the government. Rural lines in South Australia, along with the line north to Alice Springs and between Birdum and Darwin, were built to the narrow gauge.

Standard gauge

In 1986, standard gauge had reached all states and territories except Tasmania. Queensland had the lowest mileage of this gauge at 111 km (the section from the NSW border to South Brisbane opened in 1930, extended to Roma Street), with all trains on that section being operated by NSW trains. There was an additional 19 km of 1435 mm trackage located at Weipa on Cape York in far north Queensland owned by the aluminium producer, Comalco. All the private iron ore mining lines in Western Australia were laid to the standard gauge.

Another gauge nightmare—Gladstone, in 1973—one of two places to earn notoriety from being triple gauge stations. In the centre, two gauges are usable, but just look at the four-rail arrangement on the right! *John Beckhaus.*

A 1956 report on rail standardisation in Australia was the catalyst for the expansion of the 1,435 mm system. The determining factor in the decision to promote this gauge was that most of the transcontinental corridor from Sydney to Perth was already laid to this width. By 1962, the drive to uniformity had seen the laying of a parallel standard gauge track to the existing broad gauge route between Wodonga and Melbourne, thus ending a break of gauge at the Vic.–NSW border with all the associated costs and delays of transhipping goods and passengers at Albury.

In January 1970, the transcontinental line was converted to the new uniform gauge. In 1968, the first of the two non-standard gaps was converted (Kalgoorlie–Perth) followed by Port Pirie–Cockburn (on the NSW border).

Broad gauge

Adopted by Victorian Railways and South Australian Railways, broad gauge also existed in New South Wales due to Victorian lines running across the border into the Riverina region. In 1986, Victoria had 5,448 km of broad gauge track, including the lines into NSW, while Australian National operated over 2,001 km of broad gauge in South Australia.

The broad gauge was also used in Tasmania, by the Launceston and Western Railway Company, which built the seventy-two mile line between Launceston and Deloraine. However, when the Tasmanian Government became involved in railways, it decided that the island would have a narrow gauge system and other gauges would be converted. The last broad gauge train in Tasmania ran on 19 August 1888.

2 ft 6 in, or 762 mm gauge

In an effort to save money, Victoria adopted this very narrow gauge for certain rural lines; all but one closed. The remaining line is the 28.7 km track from Upper Ferntree Gully on the outskirts of Melbourne to Gembrook, which is used by the famed Puffing Billy tourist steam railway. The other lines were the 41.9 km Moe–Walhalla line in Gippsland, the 49.1 km from the main line at Wangaratta in the north-east region of Victoria to Whitfield and 70.8 km of line from Colac to Crowes on the scenic Victorian coastline. It was on this latter line that the spectacular G Class Beyer Garrett locomotives were employed.

As with inter-colonial breaks of gauge, inefficiencies were built into the system in order to save money, by constructing cheap, very narrow gauge lines. At Colac, for example, there were special tracks for the transfer of goods to and from the main line broad gauge trains; there were two stations, with a footbridge connecting them. At the main intermediate station, Beech Forest, trains had to run through a balloon loop before proceeding as the tracks from each end of the line came in from the south west, which meant the up and down home signals faced in the same direction. The 1942 timetable allowed for a mixed train leaving Colac each Friday at 11.30 am, not reaching Crowes until 6.15 pm that evening, the return trip taking place on Saturday. Several freight trains ran during the week, and a postal motor trolley went down the line on Saturday to deliver mail.

Initially, New South Wales had decided to build its first line to the broad gauge that had already been adopted by Victoria. Had there not been a last minute change of mind in Sydney, it is just possible that the Australian colonies

T 395 is seen at Tocumwal with a short passenger train in 1970. *Public Record Office.*

might have all built their railways with the two rails 1,600 mm apart and the century-plus nightmare of different gauges avoided. Even Tasmania initially decided on the broad gauge, before opting for the cheaper narrow 1,067 mm gauge. South Australia, too, built its first lines at 1,600 mm. Of course, South Australia adopted the narrow gauge for its many grain lines where speed was less important than construction cost. At one stage, South Australia alone contained breaks of gauge at Terowie, Hamley Bridge, Gladstone, Port Pirie, Port Augusta, Wolseley, Mount Gambier and Marree. The advent of standard gauge on the main east–west transcontinental line created a new monster: the triple gauge stations at Peterborough and Gladstone.

When Western Australia began laying its first line between Geraldton and Northampton that opened in 1879, work began using the extremely narrow 914 mm gauge but common sense prevailed and those rails laid were broadened to 1,067 mm during the course of construction.

The breaks of gauge became one of the bugbears of rail travel. Passengers arriving at a break of gauge station would have to rush across the platform to another waiting train. For those travelling between Sydney and Melbourne, changing at Albury, this meant a changeover in the middle of the night, especially inconvenient for sleeper passengers.

Such inconvenience endured until as late as 1980 on the old Ghan service. Passengers travelling from Adelaide to Alice Springs hopped aboard a broad gauge car at Adelaide in the morning, transferred to standard gauge at Port Pirie, and then to narrow gauge at Marree in the late evening. By contrast, the modern-day Ghan runs smoothly from Adelaide to Darwin via Tarcoola and Alice Springs on standard gauge

track all the way. Standardisation also made possible such famous services as the Indian Pacific (Sydney–Perth) and Southern Aurora (Sydney–Melbourne). The inefficiencies of break of gauges were no better illustrated than at Albury on the New South Wales–Victorian border. When the standard gauge line was extended through to Melbourne, about six hundred jobs were lost at the border station as there was simply no longer any need to transfer the freight.

Another break of gauge station on the New South Wales–Victorian border was that at Tocumwal. Ron Haley started work at the station (in the employ of Victorian Railways) in 1943 as a sixteen-year-old junior porter. Although he did work elsewhere in Victoria, he also ended his career at Tocumwal upon retirement in 1987. There were two separate workforces at Tocumwal and Victoria paid four-sevenths of the station's wages bill with New South Wales picking up the remainder. New South Wales track gangs maintained the station lines and undertook all the shunting operations. There were rest huts beside the station yards for New South Wales train crews. It was always a busy station with the traffic between Melbourne and the Riverina, but the construction of a vast aerodrome for American and Australian air forces in 1942 added to the already considerable war traffic going through Tocumwal. Each item of freight had to be unloaded from the wagons and transferred to those of the other gauge. The station yard had five eight-ton gantry cranes to help shift freight. Even in later years, the station workers met the freight train that arrived each weekday morning from Seymour, followed in the middle of the day by a roadside train (one that stopped and shunted at intermediate stations) from Victoria. Working in gangs of two men, the Victorian employees transferred every item by hand (from potatoes

to cement) on those two trains to New South Wales wagons sitting on adjacent, standard gauge sidings. Ron Haley remembers that the job took all day, with the New South Wales train pulling out in the late afternoon when the transhipment task had been completed. The incoming train from the New South Wales side arrived about 5.30 pm, and its load was transhipped ready for departure the following morning. At some times of the year, there could be as many as four stock trains a week. Again, all the animals aboard had to be transferred from one train set to another for the onward journey. The only dual gauge line in the yard was the spur which ran into the local flour mill. The station yards were equipped with floodlights for night-time freight handling, and New South Wales railways employed an electrician at Tocumwal to maintain those lights. Passengers also had to cool their heels at Tocumwal. If they came up the line from Victoria, there was an hour's wait until the New South Wales rail-motor left for Narrandera, where passengers transferred to a locomotive-hauled train for Sydney, arriving seventeen hours after pulling out of Tocumwal. The station had a refreshment room for passengers to fortify themselves during the wait. During the war and at times after, two ticket windows were opened to cope with the numbers of people travelling.

On the Queensland border with New South Wales, the town of Wallangarra existed only because it was the site of another break of gauge. The obduracy of colonial thinking ensured that the railways were built to different gauges — 1,067 mm to the north of the border and 1,435 mm to the south. The farmers of the Darling Downs were opposed not only to a single gauge connection with the southern colony but to federation itself. They wanted the customs duties at the border to remain to discourage competing produce from the other Australian colonies. From 1888, when both sets of rails ran into Wallangarra, every passenger and all goods had to be transhipped from one train to another. In 1930, a standard gauge route was built from the border right into Brisbane connecting with New South Wales' north coast line.

But the 'Father of Federation', on his way to deliver the famous speech, could not have been other than struck by the inanities of the gauge question in 1889 when, as New South Wales Premier, Sir Henry Parkes took the train from Brisbane to Wallangarra. There he crossed the platform to another carriage, this time on a New South Wales train, thereafter travelling to Tenterfield to deliver his Federation Oration. It has been remarked that the change of train he made at the border would have reinforced in his mind the need for federation but, of course, that event in 1901 by itself did almost nothing to advance the case for a standard railway gauge in Australia. At Wallangarra, the grand old Victorian station remains, and in 2001 the railway precinct was restored as part of the Federation centenary celebrations. But no Queensland trains now run beyond Stanthorpe, 8 km from the border on Queensland's side, while on New South Wales' side the track is still there, but closed to traffic beyond Armidale. An oddity of Wallangarra was that, in spite of its importance as a station where trains terminated, there was no turntable. This necessitated dual gauge track being laid in the station yard and meant that engines had to use a triangle.

Even after the coastal standard gauge connection to Brisbane, traffic continued to pass through Wallangarra. The Sydney Express ran into the 1960s, leaving Sydney at 2.00 pm, reaching Wallangarra after 9.30 am the next day,

LEFT: **Another variety of wheat hopper, FWH 32157, pictured at Rozelle in Sydney in late 1972.** *John Beckhaus.*

OPPOSITE LEFT: **No more sacks of wheat. Instead the grain is transported in modern hoppers. This wagon, WTY 35982, was photographed in 1977.** *John Beckhaus.*

with the narrow gauge train pulling into Brisbane at 7.30 pm that night.

The fact that breaks of gauge persisted into the modern era gave road transport an unfair advantage; transhipment of freight put rail at an acute disadvantage against the newer, larger lorries owned by road transport companies. This was particularly so in South Australia where there were so many break of gauge situations. In fact, the standardisation program of the late 1960s threw up further complications. When the line from Broken Hill to Port Pirie was converted to standard gauge in 1970, it meant that trains could run from Sydney to Kalgoorlie on the same gauge. But while Port Pirie changed from a three-gauge station to one having two gauges (broad and standard, the narrow gauge from Broken Hill having been converted), matters were made more complex at Peterborough and Gladstone — going from one gauge and two gauges respectively to triple gauge each! Until 1968, Peterborough had been the hub of a narrow gauge web: the line north to Quorn; the Broken Hill–Port Pirie line; and the track south to Terowie. Now it had the east–west main line converted to standard, the Terowie line converted to broad gauge with the Quorn track remaining on narrow gauge. Gladstone went from two gauges (broad and narrow) to three with the standard gauge line from Broken Hill, the broad gauge from Balaklava to the south, while the Wilmington line to the north remained on the narrow gauge. Why the Wilmington line was left as an isolated narrow gauge operation remains one of the riddles of this whole saga, when the savings that could have been made over the next thirty years (it closed in 1990) from not having that break of gauge would have more than paid for moving one of the

rails out to make it standard gauge. One of the side effects of the standardisation program has been the increased complexity of a three-gauge state — another depressing development in the chequered story of Australian rail.

As this was being written, Victoria was about to embark on standardising many of its branch lines. Queensland remains a stronghold of narrow gauge, but the proposed inland railway linking Melbourne and Darwin via the interiors of NSW and Queensland will be a standard gauge line if built and completed. This, in turn, is bound to raise operational questions in the northern state.

Many attempts were made over the years to address the problem of the gauge nightmare. In 1921, the Commonwealth Government established a Royal Commission on the subject. Its recommendation was unequivocal; there should, ideally, be one gauge and that should be 4 ft $8^{1}/2$ in — the so-called standard gauge. The prime tangible result from this inquiry was the construction in 1930 of the standard link from NSW (via Kyogle and Richmond Gap) into South Brisbane, which shortened the Sydney–Brisbane journey by about 160 km. That nothing else eventuated was due to the fact that Victoria and South Australia remained obdurate on the question of converting their broad gauge networks, a factor which has led some to argue that one of the great missed railway opportunities was that railways were not placed under the control of new Commonwealth Government at the time of Federation. Had this happened, it is likely that much of the network would have been standardised in the first three decades of the twentieth century, not to mention the use of interchangeable rolling stock right across the nation.

In 1944, the Labor Government in Canberra asked Sir

Victoria's broad gauge line crossed the Murray River into Tocumwal in 1908, but it was not until 1914 that New South Wales' trains could run as far south as that town. In 1913, during construction, the two railway administrations tested the third rail where the gauges met. Victorian Railways' DD 604 is seen on the right with a New South Wales locomotive. Today the broad gauge remains open to Tocumwal, but the authorities in Sydney have remained obdurate on the question of re-opening the mothballed standard gauge line from Narrandera. *Public Record Office.*

The break of gauge at Tocumwal meant transhipping freight between the Victorian and New South Wales rolling stock. Ron Haley, who spent most of his working life at this station, is seen here with the station tractor, 41 RT. *Public Record Office.*

Harold Clapp, formerly Victoria's Railway Commissioner and from 1942 the Director General Land Transport, to come up with a plan for unifying the nation's railway systems. This mission had partly been triggered by the Army, which had experienced many problems during the war caused by the gaps in Australia's rail networks and the breaks of gauge. The military men wanted the Port Pirie–Broken Hill line to be standardised, a standard gauge line laid alongside the existing narrow gauge section between Perth and Kalgoorlie, the standardisation of the Victorian system and South Australia's broad gauge and extension of the existing standard gauge line between Sydney and Bourke into Queensland as far as Mount Isa with a spur to Townsville (shades of the proposed inland rail route now under consideration). Incidentally, in 1940, the War Cabinet authorised the laying of a third rail on the track between Broken Hill and Port Pirie in South Australia which would have allowed unbroken standard gauge running between Brisbane and Kalgoorlie. But this was not implemented. As proof yet again that governments have been more sympathetic to road than rail, the decision was taken to upgrade the highway between Port Pirie and Norseman, Western Australia, for troop movements.

The military authorities found themselves up against a significant logistical problem when United States' forces and their equipment were landed in the south of Australia and had to be transported by land to North Queensland. This meant two breaks of gauge, from broad to standard in New South Wales and then to narrow gauge in Queensland. The lines were also clogged by all the empty wagons which had to be taken back south to get another load.

Clapp did not hold back when it came to recommendations delivered to the government in March 1945. The fact that, when running the Victorian system, he had ordered that all new locomotives should be built in such a way as to be convertible to standard gauge, should have been a clue to his thinking. Essentially, in 1945, he was in favour of converting almost all the rail lines to standard gauge, including those in his own former bailiwick of Victoria, along with the vast narrow gauge s systems in Queensland and Western Australia.

Perhaps the most ambitious element of Clapp's report was a new line from the railhead at Bourke, New South Wales, to the narrow gauge railhead in Queensland at Cunnamulla via the tiny settlement of Barringun, a distance of 236 km; then to convert the narrow gauge track from Cunnamulla to Charleville to standard gauge. From there, a new railway line would be laid to Blackall, then Longreach and finally on to Winton, this last section to use existing track converted to dual narrow–standard gauge.

The line from Winton to Hughenden, and the entire Townsville–Dajarra line, were to be converted to standard gauge, that alone costing more than ten million pounds. From Dajarra, a new line would be built over 1,037 km to Birdum in the Northern Territory, the southern terminus of the North Australia Railway. Another three million pounds would see the North Australia Railway to Darwin converted to standard gauge (the three largest bridges had been built wide enough to take standard gauge lines). Had this been adopted, it would not have taken another fifty-eight years to connect Darwin, and it would have been by a route that made a good deal more economic sense than the one now existing.

Again, the states bickered among themselves and

RIDING ROUGH

NEW SOUTH WALES ABOLISHED third class rail travel in July 1863. When the government bought the troubled Sydney Railway Company in 1855, it inherited twelve third class carriages. These were enclosed to only about half-way up each of the two sides, making for unpleasant travel in wet weather. Moreover, the compartment ceilings allowed standing height of just 5 ft 6 in, which meant that men could not stand up in an era of tall hats. The four-wheeler carriages had plain wooden boards for seating and could accommodate thirty-six passengers. However, Victorian Railways decided in 1869 to introduce third class travel on its trains. Initially, it attracted large numbers of people wanting to pay cheaper fares but soon there were complaints about the standard of accommodation; there were plenty of remarks about 'sheep trucks' and 'dog boxes'.

progress towards a national standard gauge network proved to be beyond the railway administrators of Australia.

The main standardisation milestones were as follows:

1930 A standard gauge line from NSW was laid into Brisbane, before which all traffic between the two states went though the break-of-gauge station at Wallangarra on the border.

1962 A standard gauge line, running in parallel to the broad gauge line, was laid from Albury to Melbourne, for the first time allowing standard gauge trains to operate between Sydney and Melbourne.

1955 The Commonwealth Railways built a new standard gauge line from Stirling North to Marree to provide for haulage of coal from the Leigh Creek mine through to Port Augusta.

1968 Standard gauge trains began running between Perth and Kalgoorlie.

1970 South Australian Railways converted the narrow gauge line from Broken Hill to Port Pirie, thus allowing through standard gauge running between Sydney and Kalgoorlie.

1980 Federal Government initiatives saw the completion of a standard gauge line from the Trans-Australian track at Tarcoola to Alice Springs, after which the narrow gauge Marree–Alice Springs line was closed and lifted.

1984 A standard gauge link was provided from Port Pirie into Adelaide, joining the South Australian capital to the interstate rail network.

1995 The Adelaide–Melbourne line was converted from broad to standard gauge.

2003 Darwin was connected by new 1,420 km standard gauge line to the Australian rail network.

By way of a footnote, while the main east–west corridor was standardised so that trains could run from Sydney to Perth, the line was still subject to several management structures. Even into the new millennium as late as 2003, a freight train running from Sydney was on rails administered by the NSW Rail Access Corporation all the way to Broken Hill. From there, it ran on track looked after by the Commonwealth's Australian Rail Track Corporation — at least until Kalgoorlie. The last stage of the journey was in Australian Railroad Group territory.

But there is still much to be done. Queensland will, for the foreseeable future, remain a bastion of the narrow gauge although it is possible to imagine that a standard gauge line could be laid along the main coastal route. Similarly, there seems no great imperative pushing Western Australia toward standardisation. Tasmania, being isolated, can be secure with its narrow gauge. However, Victoria remains the one issue of standardisation. In 2002, the state government began making plans to standardise many of the lines outside the Melbourne suburban system, but the plan seemed stalled as this was written. The will to remove large sections of the broad gauge appeared to have evaporated. The more things change on Australian railways, the more they stay the same.

Peterborough yard was still a narrow gauge redoubt when this photograph was taken from the light tower. Later, three gauges would be in use here. *John Mannion collection.*

6

TAKING STOCK

LOOKING BACK TO THE RAILWAY AGE, and then at today's scene, one does not know whether to laugh or cry. It has already been established that there was never a golden age of rail in Australia. There was a railway age mainly because there was no alternative. And when there was an alternative, most people grabbed it with both hands. After all, as this book testifies, rail travel was often miserable and long. Given the choice between that and jumping into one's own motorcar, there was no competition. Since the end of World War II, total travel in the urban areas has grown nine-fold, but almost all that went to road. The motorway between Sydney and Canberra makes it impossible for rail, which still uses a line with many curves, to compete with motorcars in terms of journey time.

That said, there has been a resurgence of rail. Private operators have been prepared to pay hundreds of millions of dollars to buy rail systems. They have invested in new rolling stock. They spent more than $1.3 billion dollars to lay track all the way to Darwin, something every federal government since 1911 has flubbed. But at least the federal government has done a good deal, albeit much later than desirable, to bring about standardisation. Its greatest achievement in railways will always be the long steel road across the Nullarbor. But since then it has undertaken a standard gauge link into Perth from Kalgoorlie, the concrete re-sleepering program initiated by Australian National and the standardisation of the Melbourne–Adelaide route.

As this was being written, thanks again to Canberra, there was at last some movement on upgrading the main Melbourne–Brisbane rail corridor. Still, in 2003, the line had a bridge over the Murrumbidgee dating from the nineteenth century with a speed limit of 20 km/h, signalling and curvature that dated from the steam era and passing loops too short to accommodate the modern, long freight trains. It will be a big job; the section between Albury and Junee needs to be entirely re-laid with new concrete sleepers and new bridges built across the Murrumbidgee and Murray rivers.

In Sydney, the suburban train system was falling apart. Victoria was back-sliding on its commitment to convert many of the grain lines from broad to standard gauge. In New South Wales, grain lines expected to carry vast numbers of trucks at harvest times. In one case, the track had spread under a wheat train sending its wagons and their loads spilling across the surrounding land. In fact, throughout Australia rural rail services are in decline and many argue that this process has occurred more quickly than it need have. Indifference in government railway head offices started the process and either the inability or unwillingness to do anything to reverse that decline did the rest of the job. Queensland, for example, has actively promoted their Qlink road transport arm at the expense of rail.

Victoria was upgrading lines for new fast passenger services but cutting costs by using new concrete sleepers that were not capable of being converted to a standard gauge track should that need arise. Some rail commentators see governments spending money on grandiose, politically driven projects — like Queensland's Tilt Train — while starving other rail services of much needed capital.

And, for all the Millennium trains, Tilt Trains and double stacking of containers, the railways have been slow to adapt. Guard's vans lasted well beyond the introduction of automatic brakes that made the guard's role of brake man at the rear of the train redundant. Firemen were around long into the era of the diesel–electric locomotive. With one exception, no one

tried running small trains and small-sized locomotives on less densely used lines to try to scale down the operation to an economic level. Between Maryborough and Monto in Queensland, the goods train service had been reduced to once a week but that train is hauled by two locomotives. New Zealand has introduced remote control shunting of locomotives, something that has yet to be accepted throughout Australia.

Figures from the Bureau of Transport and Regional Economics show that rail's share of land freight has fallen since the 1970s, and the Bureau projected that the share would continue to fall in the coming years. Trains carry only 10 per cent of freight moving between Sydney and Melbourne; it rises to only 20 per cent when the distance is extended to Melbourne–Brisbane. Only where the distances are very great can rail compete. Thus, between Adelaide and Perth, 80 per cent of the freight moves on rail

Apart from occasional bursts of enthusiasm, governments have been grudging toward railways. That is why we have all the problems today. Depressingly, one can only assume that ministers at both federal and state level will continue to believe that there are more votes in roads than in railways.

SPECIAL OCCASIONS

STARTING WORK ON, or opening, a railway line was an occasion for celebration. It signified the political importance of the railways that leading colonial dignitaries inevitably associated themselves with the projects — a practice that continues to the present day, as we have seen with the opening of the line to Darwin. But new lines also excited the local populace. Not only were there fewer things in those days to divert people away from their usually hum-drum lives, but the steel road meant a transformation of those lives. They could get to the nearest big towns quickly and orders of produce and goods now took a matter of days rather than weeks to reach them. Turning the first sod or the running of the first train brought people out in their finery. Huge banquets would be arranged to take place following the arrival of the official train. The laying of the foundation stone for the Geelong railway station was a mere preliminary to the feasting that ensued. The directors of the Geelong and Melbourne Railway Company catered not only for invited guests, but also for those who turned up just to watch. For them, there was provided a roasted bullock and barrels of beer were provided. The company was £1,000 poorer after the day's events.

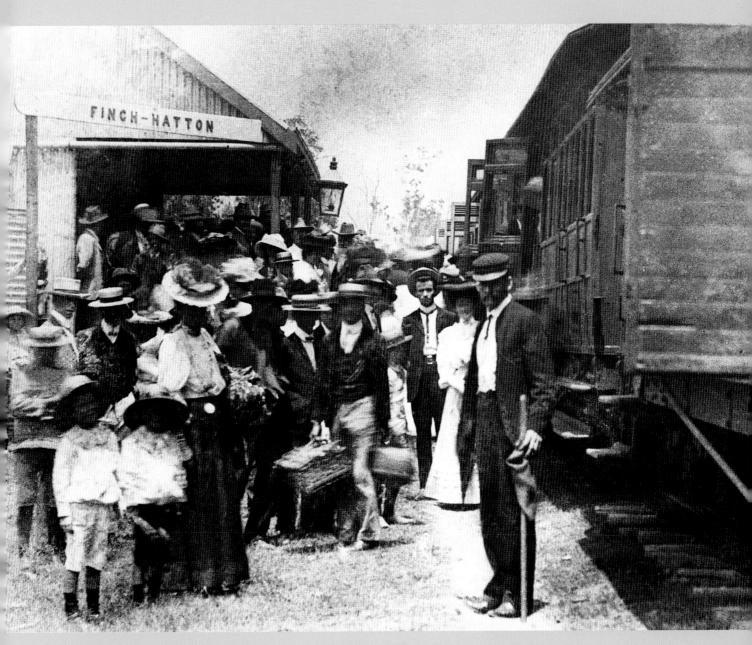

The line to Finch Hatton had been opened
in 1904 by the Pioneer Shire Council, and
then absorbed into the Queensland
government railway network on 1 July 1910.
The locals turned out for the arrival of the
first government train. *Author's collection.*

Vital statistics

The Peterborough Homing Pigeon Club (Juniors).

- The longest straight stretch of railway in Australia (and the world) is the 478 km section between Ooldea and Nurina on the transcontinental rail line. However, the idea that the transcontinental line is just one long straight section is a popular misconception, largely due to the well-known photographs that show the line disappearing into the distance without a curve. In fact, there were 443 curves between Port Pirie and Kalgoorlie. There was a 187 km straight stretch of railway in New South Wales — the section between Nyngan and Bourke — on the now closed line that terminated at the latter station. The new line from Alice Springs, although it traverses some bleak and often flat country, challenges neither of the earlier straight sections; its longest section starts 8 km north of Alice Springs (the
1,413 km peg) and takes its first curve 115 km farther on.
- The highest point on Australian railways was found at Ben Lomond, New South Wales, on the now closed section of the Main North line to Wallangarra, where the tracks reach
1,370 metres above sea level.
- The longest railway bridge in Australia crosses the Coomera River in Queensland at
858 metres in length. The line connects Brisbane with the Gold Coast.
- The highest railway bridge carries the Northern Line over the Sydney Harbour Bridge at
60 metres above the water surface.
- The longest timber rail bridge in Queensland was the trestle at Angellala on the Western line. It was 643.5 metres long, although 84.7 metres of that was rebuilt with steel. Until 1949, when signal arrangements were changed, down trains had to stop at the Charleville side of Angellala Creek where staff would walk across into the station yard to place the 'Up' home signal at 'Stop'.
- Australia's longest railway platform is the No. 1 platform at Flinders Street station, Melbourne, at 639 metres. It is followed by the 508 metre platform at Kalgoorlie, Western Australia and the 460 metre platform at Albury, New South Wales.
- The longest tunnel in Australia, excluding tunnels made for city undergrounds, is the Cox's Gap bore on the Sandy Hollow–Ulan coal line in New South Wales at 1.93 km.

RAILS IN THE ROAD

A picnic train for the smelter workers eases along Ellen Street in Port Pirie in 1964.
John Mannion collection.

RAILS RUNNING DOWN a busy street was very much a South Australian thing. The Adelaide–Glenelg railway was placed in the middle of roads at both ends, and the branch in Adelaide to Semaphore had its outward end located in a busy street. At Port Adelaide, there were rails in St Vincent and Lipson streets. In the early days, the horse-drawn road traffic battled for space with trains. But perhaps the grandest of these occurrences was at Port Pirie, partly because it also became a dual gauge line.

In 1875, the narrow gauge line from Peterborough (or Petersburg as it was then called) was laid down Ellen Street, the main thoroughfare in Port Pirie, the town not being very big or busy. When the lead smelting began in 1889, it was considered necessary that Ellen Street have a station befitting the town's new importance and an ornate structure (owing something to Brighton Pavilion in England) was constructed, including a clockless clock tower. There was no raised platform, with passengers simply walking out into the street and climbing the steps to the carriages. The ticket box window opened onto the footpath.

Then, in 1937, with the broad gauge reaching town from Adelaide, a third rail was laid down the street to allow trains of both gauges to reach Ellen Street. Ian Kauschke, who joined the South Australian Railways on 6 October 1943 and became a driver in 1950, spent most of his working life at Port Pirie. The line ran past the station and into the lead smelter. Trains were limited to 6.4 km/h on the street. Shunter engines would push wagons for the smelter down past the station, just as they would push carriages, sometimes as many as fifteen cars, down to the station with the main locomotive backing down later and on to the train ready for departure. Wagons were also pushed down to the station to be attached to the passenger working to be loaded with market garden produce for the Adelaide market. Again, the shunting engine would propel these down Port Pirie's main street and the lorries would arrive with peas, tomatoes and other vegetables, their loads being transferred to rail in the middle of that same main street. However, by the 1950s, the street was becoming congested with motor traffic. Yet it was not 22 July 1967, that Ellen Street lost its railway, replaced by a new station at Mary Elie Street.

ACKNOWLEDGEMENTS

Many people are owed gratitude for their help on this project. What was most extraordinary was the fact that so many were prepared to go to a great deal of trouble for someone they had never met or spoken to before. I hope that they feel their efforts have not been totally wasted. While many people have been asked questions or to check facts about which the author was not sure, sole responsibility for errors or omissions is accepted by that same author.

Special thanks go to John Beckhaus and Brian Webber. Both responded to several requests for help when gaps in the illustrations collection were discovered, and volunteered to do more.

A number of people have recalled their years on or in association with the railway systems of Australia.

In New South Wales: Don McGregor remembered his father's years as a stationmaster; Ron Haley in Tocumwal spent much of his working life kept busy by the break of gauge at that station between the New South Wales and Victorian systems; Chris Holley was most helpful on Werris Creek, which is still his home and where he has made considerable effort to help preserve the railway heritage; and John Currey answered a panic call for pictures of Werris Creek.

In Victoria: Allan Butt had plenty of memories of Ararat; Bruce McLean's history of the Mildura railway was a treasure trove of fascinating information; Bob Whitehead not only helped with his vast knowledge of Victorian Railways but pointed the author to other sources of help, one of whom was Des Jowett and his photograph of Tocumwal used here.

In Queensland: John Hoyle fielded many questions the answers to which he probably thought the author should already have known; Douglas MacGregor had many personal experiences of Cunnamulla to recall; George Balsillie brought to life the existence of the railway worker stuck out in some lonely part of the Queensland system and entrusted the author with family photographs; Eddie Hoch, while never having worked for the railways, spent most of his life at Alpha and had sharp memories of its days as an important railway centre; and Arthur Shale did not hesitate when asked for help with pictures at Townsville. Rob McQueen went out to take a photo on the author's behalf.

In the Northern Territory: Peter Dunham's forebears were hotel owners at Birdum, Larrimah and other spots along the North Australia Railway. He was generous with the fruits of his many years of collecting historical documents.

In South Australia: John Mannion has accumulated a great deal of information about the glorious rail history of Peterborough, both in document and oral history form, and was an enthusiastic helper on that part of the book. Mark Carter continued to be a mine of information about South Australia. Stuart Dix and Peter Mackenzie came to the rescue with Tasmanian photos.

In Western Australia: Mavis Shaw and Dolores Bone worked at Mullewa when trains still stopped there; another ex-Mullewa railwayman, Colin Browning now of Northam, also shared his experiences there; and Noel Inglis of Albany took the time to write down his recollections and dig deep into his private photographic collection. Don Copley sent a selection of pictures.

Among the many organisations and people to help with the task of tracking down information and photographs were the Mareeba Heritage Centre, the Ararat Railway Heritage Association, John Collins (who went to some lengths to help with important photographs) of the Great Cobar Heritage Centre, the Eastern Goldfields Historical Society in Kalgoorlie, Angela Heinrich at the Serviceton Railway Station Committee, Nancy Woods at the restored Ellen Street railway station at Port Pirie, the Coffs Harbour Historical Society and Museum, the Sulphide Street Railway Museum, John Strudwick at the Junee and District Historical Society, while Ross Willson provided detailed information of racecourse lines.

Just as much gratitude goes to those earlier generations of rail enthusiasts who painstakingly researched and wrote articles over many decades in the various railway publications which I have mined to come up with the many facets of life in the railway age. I have named in the text those from whom I drew heavily, and too often we know only their initials and surname, such was the normal form of by-lines in a less informal age. The entry on the Adelaide, Glenelg company was based on a superb series of articles written during 1952–53 in the ARHS Bulletin by Gifford Eardley.

Thanks also to Brian Gauci, Jennifer Norton, Daryl McLeish, Aramac Shire Council, Barry Fell and James Brook.

BIBLIOGRAPHY

Periodicals

Bulletin (Australian Railway Historical Society); Newsrail; Railway Digest; The Railway News; Railways in Australia; Tasmanian Rail News.

Books

Adam-Smith, Patsy, Romance of Australian Railways (Rigby), 1973

Australian Railway Historical Society, Centenary of the Midland Railway 1894–1994 (ARHS, WA Division), 1994

Barden, W. D., Mullewa Through the Years (Mullewa Roads Board), 1961

Bayley, William A., Border City: History of Albury NSW (Albury City Council), 1954

Bayley, William A., Railway Centenary in Tasmania (self-published), 1971

Bromby, Robin, Rails to the Top End (Cromarty Press), 1982

Bromby, Robin, The Country Railway in Australia (Cromarty Press), 1983

Cobar Historical Society, The Rattler (self-published), 1992

Carroll, Brian, Australian Railway Days: Milestones in Railway History (Macmillan), 1976

Cooley, Thomas C. T., Railroading in Tasmania (Government Printer), 1964

Ferry, John, Junee and the Great Southern Railway (Junee Shire Council), 2001

Fitch, R.J., 'The Branch Line — What is its Future?' in Robin Bromby (ed), Australian Railway Companion (Sherborne Sutherland), 1989

Fitch, R. J., Making Tracks (Kangaroo Press), 1989

Fluck, R. E., Sampson, R. & Bird, K. J., Steam Locomotives and Railcars of the South Australian Railways (Mile End Railway Museum), 1986

Gifford, Eardley, The Railways of the South Maitland Coalfields (Australian Railway Historical Society, NSW Division), 1969

Gregory, J. W., The Dead Heart of Australia (John Murray), 1906

Jennings, John & Whitehead, Bob, Seymour: A Railway Town (Seymour and District Historical Society), 2004

Kerr, John, Triumph of the Narrow Gauge (Boolarong Publications), 1990

McKillop, Robert F., Railfan's Handbook: New South Wales (Australian Railway Historical Society, NSW Division), 1998

Laird, Philip, Bachels, Mark & Kenworthy, Jeffrey, Back on Track (University of New South Wales Press), 2001

Maclean, Meta, Drummond of the Far West (Manly Daily), 1947

McLean, Bruce, Mildura Railway History (published electronically by the author), 2003

McLeish, Daryl, The Maryborough Railway Station History (self-published), 2000

Phillips, Joy (ed), Charleville Railway Centenary 1888–1988 (Charleville Railway Centenary Committee), 1988

Preston, R. G., Day of the Goods Train (Eveleigh Press), 2002

Quinlan, Howard & Newland, John R., Australian Railway Routes 1854–2000 (Australian Railway Historical Society, NSW Division), 2000

Serviceton Centenary Committee, Serviceton: A Frontier Town on No Man's Land (self-published), 1987

Smith, Keith, Tales of a Railway Odyssey (Railmac), 2001

South Australian Railways, Rules to be Observed by Officers and Employees (SAR), 1947

Thomson, James, Nor'West of West (Gordon & Gotch), 1908

Twain, Mark, Following the Equator: A Journey Around the World (American Publishing Company), 1897

Ware, Syd, A History of Werris Creek & District (Quirindi & District Historical Society), 1976

INDEX